AGAINST THE WALL

NEVA J HODGES

Russian Hill Press Book
United States • United Kingdom • Australia

R
 H
  P Russian Hill Press

ISBN: 978-1-7351763-3-8 (softcover)
ISBN: 978-1-7351763-0-7 (eBook)
Library of Congress Control Number: 2020915568

First Printing 2021

Cover designed by Christine McCall

To Jim

Acknowledgments

I want to thank the members of my critique group, Vee Byram, Paula Chinick, Lani Longshore, Violet Moore, Julie Royce and Elaine Schmitz, for their superior edits throughout the process of writing this book.

My beta readers, Rebecca Bartow and Cindy Danielson, kept me on track.

Margaret Lucke did a superb job as my developmental editor. Her suggestions improved my story.

Many thanks to Violet Moore for her excellent final edits before the book went to press.

My book cover designer, Christine McCall, captured the essence of the story.

California Writers Club Tri-Valley Branch provided monthly professional speakers, published authors, and others in the writing business. They inspired excellence.

My husband Jim Hodges encouraged me to keep writing.

AGAINST THE WALL

ONE

Elise

MUFFLED VOICES CAME TO ELISE FROM A DISTANT PLACE. PERHAPS God had allowed her to enter heaven. But why would he? *I committed suicide and that's murder. Am I in hell? I'm not screaming in flames of fire.*

"Elise." Loud, the voice moved her from a haze of thoughts to a room with white walls and muffled voices. "Elise, wake up."

"God?" she whispered.

"I'm Dr. Ed Beckwith. Open your eyes and look at me. I'm the psychiatrist in charge of you at this hospital."

She viewed him through hooded eyelids. He wore khakis and a long sleeve dress shirt. Her bed was narrow with rails raised at the side. A machine beeped like the sound of a heart and a small device was clamped over the tip of the forefinger of her left hand.

"Where am I?" Her voice trembled.

"You're in ICU. You've been in a coma from the Tylenol you took."

This can't be real. She shook her head. "No. Please. Leave me alone. I should be in hell."

"How many pills did you swallow?"

"I don't know."

"You wanted to die?"

Elise nodded her head.

His tone gentle, he said, "I'd like to hear why you think you should be in hell." He pulled a chair to the side of her bed and sat down.

"I can't." *How can I explain my agony?*

"Maybe you could start with what caused your attempt at suicide."

"It wasn't an attempt. I intended to end my life," she said, her voice lifeless.

"I'm sorry to hear that. Help me understand you."

"I ruined my life."

"How?" Dr. Beckwith leaned closer to hear Elise.

She tried to think through the fog. "Sometimes, sometimes, I lie in bed all morning. I don't care about anything. I . . . I can't think. Oh. Zed says I'm lazy, and that I don't have enough faith in God for him to heal me. I embarrassed Zed." Elise's nose dripped. "We argue a lot too."

Dr. Beckwith handed her a tissue from the table tray. "Depression plays havoc with those who have it. My staff and I hope you'll discover the root of your hopelessness. We'll work with you on it."

Why all the questions? Maybe he'll leave if I close my eyes.

"Elise. The ER doctor said your husband, Reverend Norris, called 911 and saved your life. He's here with your parents. They want to visit you."

"Leave me alone."

"Your family is worried about you."

"I won't see Zed."

"Okay. I'm going to leave now. I'll see you tomorrow morning and we'll talk about transitioning you from here to the Psychiatric Ward. The doctor and nurses here in ICU will make sure you're okay. I'm going to talk with your family."

"I don't want you to."

"They need to know what the next step is. Your conversation with me is confidential. See you tomorrow."

Dr. Beckwith waited a moment before he entered the ICU waiting room. He assumed the blond young man with the animated voice was the preacher. Zed's blue golf shirt revealed fit muscles. He gestured toward the silent older couple.

Elise's parents slumped in their chairs, clothes and graying hair disheveled.

The doctor strode forward and extended his hand to Zed and then to the Olsens. "I'm Elise's psychiatrist, Dr. Beckwith. Let's go to the conference room where we'll have privacy."

After they sat down, he said, "Elise's medical team already told you she's past the crisis and will be alright physically. However, she—

"When can Elise go home?" Zed asked.

"Like I was going to say, she's on some heavy-duty drugs to stabilize her depression. And she won't go home until she's spent seventy-two hours in the psych ward. The clock starts after she leaves ICU."

"She doesn't need psychiatric treatment. God will heal her if she has enough faith."

Dr. Beckwith opened and closed his mouth before he continued. "By California law, I can keep her here longer if she doesn't make progress. We have to make sure she won't harm herself again."

"That can't be right. How dare you."

"Check the law, Reverend Norris. Mr. and Mrs. Olsen, Elise is willing to see you. Five minutes only. One at a time—"

Zed raised his voice. "What about me? I'm her husband."

"She said she won't see you. I'm sorry."

"I know she'll see me," Zed said. "And besides, I'm a minister. I want to lay hands on her and pray."

Dr. Beckwith wanted to punch Zed in the nose. "Again, by California law, she can say who she'll see. Patients have rights."

Zed clutched his small Bible. Through clenched teeth, he said, "I want to read God's promises to Elise. I'm desperate for her to get well. She's my wife. Do you understand how traumatic it was to find Elise in bed and unable to wake up? I want to see her. She needs to believe God's word."

"I understand your distress, but you sound angry and Elise can't bear that. Go home and get some rest. It's been a long day for you and you're tired. Maybe she'll change her mind."

"You heard the doctor," Stephan Olsen said. He put his hand on Zed's shoulder. "We're all frightened and in shock. We can't change what Elise wants right now. We'll see you later at your house. Thanks for letting us stay with you."

"I'll wait here until you're finished visiting her. I demand to know the details."

Dr. Beckwith spoke to Elise's parents. "Be gentle with Elise. She's fragile mentally. Tell her how glad you are she's alive. Please don't chastise her for attempting suicide. Emphasize how much you love her."

Janet's voice quivered. "We didn't know what to say to her."

"What are her chances of recovery? Stephan Olsen asked.

"If she takes her medicine and goes to counseling, she'll recover. But it's imperative she chooses to get well mentally. I think she can with the support of both of you and hopefully you, Zed. Does she have close friends?"

Dad Olsen said, "I don't know."

"Zed?" Dr. Beckwith asked.

"Not for quite a while."

"I hope she'll reconnect with someone she trusts. I'll see her tomorrow morning. She's over the crisis, so go home and rest."

Stephan said, "Thanks."

Janet touched her husband's arm. "Honey, go and see Elise, and then I will."

She turned to Zed. Her voice trembled. "Why is Elise depressed? Why would she want to take her own life?"

"I don't know. She called in sick at work a lot, and they fired her this past week. Elise won't get up until noon. She refuses to go to church. I tried to get her to go to a Christian counselor. She wouldn't."

"That's not like her. How long has she been this way?"

"Several months."

"And you didn't call us? What's with that?"

"She didn't want anyone to know. I did my best," Zed said.

"Anyway, I preached a sermon not too long ago about the story in the Old Testament of how Joshua marched his men around the city of Jericho until the walls crumbled. Today's barriers are often invisible. Sins we can't see. For instance, jealousy or lust."

Janet stared at Zed. "Are you saying Elise has these sins in her heart?"

"She has something. The devil is after her. What if Elise had died of suicide? She'd have gone to hell. Let's pray together, Janet." He took her hands.

Janet jerked free. "You're not helping anything. And Dad and I have never quite swallowed the idea Satan is so powerful."

"You're in jeopardy of losing your faith."

Janet heard her husband sniffling as he walked into the room. She rushed to his side. "What'd she say, honey?"

"Not much. She still wants to die. I rubbed her forehead like I did when she was a little girl. I told her we want to help her and maybe Dr. Beckwith had some answers. Elise shook her head and turned away from me. Maybe she'll talk to you." He took Janet's hand. "Prepare yourself. Her vibrancy is gone. She looks as if she'd been dragged from the ocean after nearly drowning. Lifeless."

"Oh, God." She hugged her husband until her arms hurt and whispered in his ear. "We have to get through this. For her sake." Janet Olsen turned to Zed. "Stop the devil talk. You're talking about Elise, our lovely daughter. And she's your wife."

Zed lifted his shoulders and let out a long breath. "I love her with all my heart, but I don't know what to do with her. Now this. What will the people at church say?"

"How will they know?"

"Everyone suspects something is wrong with her. Elise is mean to people. And I'll have to tell my elders she's in the hospital."

Elise's dad intervened. "It seems to me you could keep this private. Tell them she went on vacation with us."

"I can't lie."

"Maybe *just* this time you could. For the sake of Elise, don't expose her to ridicule."

Janet said, "I don't know what to say to you, Zed. You're cruel. I'll go to my daughter." She shook her head and left the conference room to visit Elise.

Janet took a step back when she saw her daughter curled into a fetal position. Her face was pale. Tears oozed from her eyes.

Janet watched the squiggly lines of the heart monitor. A primal scream rose to her throat. She covered her mouth. *This is . . . I have no name.* Janet tiptoed to Elise's bedside and reached over the rail to touch her shoulder. *If only I could climb in bed with her.*

"Hi, honey. I love you." Janet wiped Elise's face with a tissue "What can Dad and I do for you?"

"I don't know."

"Is it okay if I sit by your bed for a while?"

"Not long." Elise closed her eyes.

"I'm here if you want to talk."

The nurse came into the room. "Do you need anything, Mrs. Norris?"

Elise didn't answer.

"Okay. Have a good night of rest. We're going to monitor your vitals all night to make sure you're stable. It's time to go, Mrs. Olsen. Come tomorrow."

"Thanks for taking care of her."

Janet stood and took Elise's hand and kissed it. "Bye, honey. Dad and I love you."

Silence.

TWO

"GOOD MORNING, ELISE," DR. BECKWITH SAID WHEN HE STEPPED into her room. "How do you feel today?"

Why can't he leave me alone?

"Do you still want to die?"

"Why live? There's nothing for me."

"We're going to help you with that. Your medical doctor said I can move you to the psychiatric ward this afternoon."

"I won't go."

"You're still at risk for hurting yourself." He repeated California's law about suicide attempts. "Trained staff will work with you, and I will see you every day too."

Elise stared at the wall, her eyes vacant and her voice flat. "My church believes psychiatrists are of the devil. The people think I'm plagued by him."

"Is that what you think?"

"I guess so."

"You might want to give that more thought. Let's talk about that tomorrow. One of the psych nurses will move you upstairs after lunch. Your mother can bring you some clothes. However, toiletries may not include razors, scissors, fingernail files—anything you might harm yourself with. The nurse will check your bag before she gives it to you. See you tomorrow."

Elise skipped the lunch of mashed potatoes, gravy, and canned fruit. She looked toward the door as Janet walked into the room.

"I brought the toiletries the ward permits, as well as some jeans and knit shirts. Oh, pajamas too. The nurse told me you can change into street clothes. Zed helped me pick them out."

"I'll stay in this ugly hospital gown. I won't wear what he chose."

Janet put her hand over her open mouth and regrouped. "What did you do to your hair? Did you take scissors to it? You have such beautiful auburn hair."

"I'm fat and ugly. I cut my hair because I hate myself. Now I hate my hair. I hate everything. Go home, Mom."

"I don't mean to upset you, honey. Is this like the arguments you had with Zed? He's upset and doesn't know what is happening."

"Me either."

"And, honey, you're not fat and ugly. The doctor said the nurse is coming soon to take you upstairs. Do you want me to go with you?"

"Mom, I don't want to do this. Let me be."

Janet's shoulders slumped. "All right. I'll come another time. Here's the nurse with a wheelchair to transport you. Please cooperate."

"No promises."

Elise watched as a nurse wheeled the black chair to the bed. Her brown hair, tied in a long ponytail, swung in time with her perky gait. Her casual belted dress hung below her knee. Early forties, Elise thought.

"Hi, I'm Sandy, your primary psych nurse."

"I'm not going to ride in that. I can walk."

"Likely you are a bit weak from your time in ICU. Take your time getting up and I'll hold your upper arm when you're ready to sit in the wheelchair.

Elise wobbled, and Sandy grabbed both shoulders and turned Elise so she could sit down. Sandy eased her into the chair. "Let's go upstairs."

Sandy punched in the numbers to open the secured door

to the psychiatric ward. She wheeled Elise into her private room. "There's a closet for your clothes and you can put your toiletries on the bathroom sink. Let's get you out of the wheelchair into the recliner."

"I'll do it. Let me be."

"Okay."

Once she was settled, Elise mumbled, "At least there're two pictures on the walls of this white room, and they're of the ocean." She sneered. "And yay, a TV."

"Do you like the sea?"

"My favorite."

"What about TV? You sounded sarcastic."

"Hate it."

"Let's have a chat. I have a list of questions I need to ask you." Sandy sat in a chair in front of Elise. "We do this with every new patient. Ready?"

"If you insist."

"Do you hear voices?" Sandy spoke in a clipped tone.

"No. What kind of question is that?"

"Do you take drugs, either as prescription or street?"

"Absolutely not."

"Do you drink alcohol? And how much?"

"No. I've thought about it though."

"Do you sometimes think you can do anything? If so, what?"

Elise hesitated, not liking the questions. "I thought one of our guest rooms was too small. I took a sledgehammer to one wall. Knocked a hole in it. Zed was home and stopped me. He was so angry he exploded. He hit the table. Almost broke his hand."

"Do you sleep a lot?"

"Yes."

"And if you're not?"

"Sometimes I stay up all night."

"What do you do?"

"I plan activities for myself or the church, redecorate a room in the house."

"Why are you depressed?"

"I don't know," Elise said.

"Dr. Beckwith told me you think you have nothing to live for. Why is that?"

"Nothing is left of my former life. I really don't want to talk. You're nice, but please leave me alone."

"I want to help you by getting acquainted. The whole staff wants you to get better. Can we talk another time?"

"Maybe." Elise watched Sandy walk out the door. *She's pretty. Why does she want to work with mentally ill patients?*

THE NEXT MORNING Elise refused her breakfast tray except for the coffee. The aide said, "Dr. Beckwith will be here at nine o'clock."

"I'm not dressed." Elise screwed up her face.

"You can go in the bathroom and shower. Get dressed."

"No."

"It's up to you." The aide left the room.

On time, Dr. Beckwith greeted Elise when he stepped inside her room. His gaze swept over her. "Good morning. How are you today?"

"Fine."

"Your file says you didn't eat breakfast, and I see you didn't shower or dress."

"Do you know everything?"

"The nurses have to write notes on what you do or don't do." He pulled a chair across the room to sit in front of Elise, who sat in the recliner. "Are you ready to see your husband or take calls from him?"

"No. I don't know if I want to ever see him again."

Elise turned her hands over in her lap and stared out the window. "He's a pastor of a large congregation. I quit his church. They think they know everything. They accused me of not having faith. I thought I was okay with God. It doesn't matter."

Dr. Beckwith raised his eyebrows. "Sounds like we need to explore that. Do you have a secular job?"

Elise turned her head and narrowed her eyes. "Part-time. Or, at least I did."

"What happened?"

"I missed too much work because of my depression."

"I see."

"What do you see?" *Why can't he leave me alone? He doesn't know how I feel. I don't even know him. No one understands.*

"You're quite depressed or you wouldn't have attempted suicide. The best way for me to help you is for you to volunteer information about yourself. I hope you will. By the way, how well do you sleep?"

"Good. I sleep a lot during the day too."

"I hope you'll participate in some of our activities. The first one is this morning at ten-thirty. We have group therapy with all the patients on the ward. The facilitator will help you set goals for the day. He'll help you express your frustrations."

"I have to attend?"

"No, but I recommend it if you want to leave here."

Elise rolled her eyes. "Why tell me about it?"

"You'll meet other people who, like you, need help. You won't feel so alone. Also, it gives you a chance to talk about your feelings and problems. It's up to you." Dr. Beckwith smiled. "Any questions?"

"I don't want to be here."

Dr. Beckwith stood to leave. "You said that last night. I'll see you again tomorrow." He shook Elise's hand before he left.

She considered her options. *I'll go to the damn meetings if it means getting out of here.*

Elise shuffled to the therapy session in her hospital gown and robe. The barred windows of the room kept out some of the sunlight. There were beige-cushioned chairs arranged in a circle on brown carpet. *Stale stuff. Looks depressing.* She sat down. Ten or so people looked normal to Elise, except for one. An olive-skinned woman wore sunglasses, a straw hat, and a short jersey dress. She smiled at everyone.

A man in cowboy boots, jeans, and a tight plaid shirt looked at his watch. He put his fingers in his mouth and whistled. "Attention, everyone. Quit talking. Sit up straight."

Elise spoke to the woman next to her. "Who is he?"

"Group therapist. Nice guy. He's kind of rough in his manner, but he gets us to talk."

"Does he think we're cattle?"

"No. By the way, I'm Mary."

"Elise."

"We'd better be quiet, or he'll call us out."

"Hi, everyone. I'm Robert, the leader of this group. I'm a licensed therapist and ride herd on group sessions here at the hospital five days a week. Weekends, I'm a cowboy. We have three new people. Let's go around the circle. Give your first name and why you're here. Mary, let's start with you. Oh, and name one thing you'll do today to help yourself. For instance, take your medicine, shower, get dressed, talk to your nurse, eat, and so on."

"I'm Mary. I overdosed on pain pills. My husband brought me here. My goal is to talk to my nurse about my problems." She smoothed her blond hair and crossed her legs.

Elise held her head down and mumbled, "Elise."

"What's happening with you?" Robert asked.

"Who do you think you are? Who made you God?"

"I want you to talk. What specific thing do you want to accomplish today? You'll report on your progress when you go to group therapy this afternoon."

"I don't know."

"You're still in your nightclothes. Make a goal of getting dressed."

"I'm going to take a nap after this."

"Okay. Next person."

The sunglasses lady spoke. "I'm Leslie. I'm high. Love it. I got in a fight with a police officer." She laughed. "They put me here instead of jail. This is my second time. They say I'm bipolar."

She's strange. Scary. Elise squirmed in her chair.

"It isn't funny, Leslie," Robert said. "Stay on your meds."

"I want to be manic. And by the way, my nurse told me I could go home. She's great."

"I'll check with Sandy on that."

"You're jealous of me and her. We're thick, as if we're sisters."

"I'll talk with Sandy. Since she's your nurse, she tells me and the doctor about your activities and what you say. You're like a calf that needs to be lassoed and taken to its mother."

The man next to Leslie stared at the ceiling. "See that man? He's trying to kill me."

"I don't see anyone, John." Robert shook his head.

"He's there." John pointed with his middle finger. "Did you know I got sick from breakfast? The cooks tried to poison me."

"No, they didn't. Have you had your medicine today?"

"I fooled 'em. I pretended to swallow the pill."

"If you want to get out of here, take your medicine."

Robert turned to Elise again. "Everyone talked except you. You might be here a short time. Express your feelings. There's more than one person here who attempted suicide."

"I already told Dr. Beckwith." *Robert irritates me.*

"These people don't know."

"They scare me. And it's none of their business. Yours either."

"Anyone have a comment?" Robert asked.

"I'm cool," Leslie said.

"Elise, pretend this is an outdoor campfire with your friends sittin' with you."

Does he have to talk like a cowboy? Geez, maybe he'll get off my back if I talk. In halting words, Elise repeated what she had told Dr. Beckwith.

Mary replied, "I'd be out of that church in a second. Strange husband too. Who in the hell thinks that way?"

Elise looked at Robert.

"Spit it out, Elise. Get mad as a bull."

"No."

A guy across from Elise spoke with authority. "I'm Steve. You might love him, but he has crazy ideas about the devil and God. I went to a church that preached that way. Not good for you."

"What do you think, Elise?" Robert asked.

15

"I don't know. Either way, nothing helps. Does God care?" Silence. Like the moon. Elise looked at each person. Most stared at her.

"That's a tough question for everyone in this room," Robert said. "You're the one who has to decide if God cares. You're the one who has to sort out your doubts and fears. You're the one who has to decide if you want to get better."

"I don't know if anyone can help me."

"We'll do our best."

ELISE WALKED BACK to her room after the meeting was over. Noon. Time to eat. Elise wrinkled her nose. Her lunch of chicken broth and toast was for babies.

Sandy walked into Elise's room smiling. "We can chat after you eat."

"I'm not hungry."

"How about half of it? Your stomach needs some food to balance your system. The Tylenol created havoc inside you. I'll be back in twenty minutes."

Elise ate part of her lunch. An aide came in and removed her tray. "Good. That's better than how much you ate for breakfast."

"Does everyone know my business?" Elise asked.

"Yes. Ah, here's Sandy."

Sandy sat in the empty chair. "Mind if I chat?"

"I guess not."

Sandy opened Elise's chart. "I see you're thirty-two. Anything else you want to add?"

"I'm an artist. I haven't painted for a long time."

"Why not?"

"I work, or did work, part-time as an administrative assistant for a heating and cooling company. And I helped Zed with some of his church duties. We were a close-knit team."

"Did you like your secular work?"

"Not really. I wanted money of my own to spend. It wasn't much."

"So, what did you do in the church?"

"Sometimes I went with the deacons to the hospital to visit sick people. I started a soup kitchen."

"Ambitious. Do you have children?"

"Uh, no." Elise looked across the room.

"Sore spot?"

"I don't want to talk about it."

"How do you feel about being here?" Sandy smoothed her blue dress.

"I have no rights, and I almost have to ask permission to pee. I'm in prison."

"You understand why, don't you?"

"So I won't harm myself." Elise's head rested on her hand, elbow on knee.

"Right. Let's talk about it. You didn't want to live. Did you fight with your husband before you became depressed?"

"Our marriage was okay most of the time before I hit bottom."

"How long have you been this way?"

"About nine months."

"What happened before your depression? Did someone die? Did you have a miscarriage? Anything at all?" Sandy pushed stray hair from her forehead.

"No. I've been down several times in my life, though not like this. I don't know what's wrong."

"Do you have friends?"

"Not now."

"Why?"

"I didn't answer their phone calls. No one comes to see me either. I won't let them."

"All signs of depression. What did you enjoy before you got so down?"

Elise's face brightened. "Church. And I love to decorate. One time I worked all night to paint our living room. Then I bought new furniture for it. Zed said not to do it, but I did anyway. It was quite expensive. We can afford it. He owns a Porsche and earns big bucks from the church."

"What happened next?"

"Zed took my credit card away. We argued about that. I

promised I wouldn't do it again."

"Did you?"

"Sometimes."

"He gave you the credit card again?"

"Once in a while."

"You said you painted all night. Do you experience more energy than normal very often?"

"I don't know. But when I get that surge, I get a lot done. I plan activities for church, cook new recipes—many things."

"How long does this energy last?"

"I don't keep track. It's okay, isn't it?"

"It caused problems between you and Zed. Think about that. One more question. Besides these outbursts of energy, do you get unreasonably irritated or angry?"

Elise stared at the floor. She whispered. "It gets me in trouble."

"Okay. It looks like we have some things to work on." Sandy looked at her watch. "Meditation starts in a half hour if you're interested. You'll learn how to relax your body and mind. See you tomorrow. Are you going to group therapy?"

"I went this morning. I'll read instead."

"I'd go if I were you."

Elise watched Sandy leave the room. *What is wrong with high energy?*

THREE

DR. BECKWITH ENTERED ELISE'S ROOM. "GOOD MORNING." HE SAT in front of Elise's recliner and opened her chart. "It says that you attended therapy yesterday morning, but not afternoon. What did you think of the morning session?"

"Damn scary. Some of those people are crazy."

"Think so?"

"Don't you?"

"They're ill. Did you relate to Robert?"

"Can't stand him. He irritates me."

"How so?"

"He thinks we're like cows that have no sense. And he pushes me to talk even though I don't want to."

"Our staff has different personalities. You'll relate to some. Not everyone. Do you like Sandy?"

"So far."

"Good. How do you feel today?"

"Angry."

"Do you know why?"

"It's how I am sometimes."

"What do you do when you're angry?" Dr. Beckwith asked.

"I'm rude. To everyone." She decided to be honest. "Sometimes people make my skin crawl and I hate them. Not good for a pastor's wife because then I say rude things to people in the church. I told them not to crap on me. I don't understand myself. And Zed doesn't either. He only knows

Biblical clichés. Oh, and Zed says I talk too much and too loud sometimes. Zed doesn't like me."

"Would you say you're often irritated?"

Dr. Beckwith took off his suit coat. "Warm in here. So?"

"I already told Sandy."

"I'd like to hear it."

"A minister's wife is expected to be perfect and live an exemplary life. What does it matter? I failed."

Dr. Beckwith crossed his legs. "Based on your conversations with me, Sandy, and Robert, I'm pretty sure you have bipolar disorder II. There's also bipolar I. Sometimes people call it manic/depressive."

"I'm crazy. That's what people think of bipolar."

"People misunderstand the disorder because patients sometimes refuse medication and therapy. Manic behavior is less extreme in bipolar II and is often referred to as hypomania. Depression is a big issue though. I think that's why you attempted suicide. You need specific medication for bipolar disorder. Also, therapy until you're stable. We can help you.

"And you need to understand that bipolar disorder is serious. If untreated, bipolar II hypomania can lead to full-blown mania. As you know, severe depression can lead to suicide."

Elise bowed her head. "You're scaring me."

"That's my intention. I want you to accept treatment. You'll have bipolar the rest of your life. There's no cure."

I refuse to cry. "How do you get bipolar?"

"Researchers don't know for sure. But it involves brain chemicals that go awry. It might be genetic or caused by severe environmental factors. About two and a half percent of the population has it."

"Oh, yay, I get to be a minority. And people can hate me."

"You don't have to tell anyone. Some people have the capacity to understand. Some don't."

Sandy entered the room. "I didn't realize you were still here, Dr. Beckwith."

"I'm just finishing. See you tomorrow morning, Elise."

Sandy sat across from Elise in a straight-backed chair. "So, you don't want to see or talk to your husband after you leave here. Do you have a plan?"

"No."

"What do you want to do?"

"I don't know. What am I going to do with my life? I'm lost, tormented by demons. My mind turns in circles and asks the same questions. I don't have answers."

"I think you can find them. People make changes in their lives all the time. You have choices."

"Really?"

"Don't you? Where do you want to live?"

Elise wiped perspiration from her forehead. "I could get an apartment."

"By yourself?"

"Yes."

"What about a roommate?"

"I don't want any of my friends, and I won't live with a stranger."

"So, who can you live with until you feel better?"

Elise rubbed an imaginary spot on her jeans. "Maybe my parents."

"Where do they live?"

"Ferndale, up in Humboldt County."

"You could have therapy there."

"Impossible. It's a historical Victorian Village of around fifteen-hundred people. They have to go to Eureka to see a doctor."

"Did you grow up in Ferndale?"

"My grandparents settled there, and my folks stayed. I wish I could afford to buy one of the beautiful craftsman homes. And Main Street has stores with Victorian facades. Tourism is big business in the summer."

"Sounds like you're attached to it."

"I am."

"I'll tell Dr. Beckwith living with your parents is an option."

Elise hit the arm of the chair. "I'm not a child. Why should I live with my parents? I want a normal life."

"Of course. I've been to Eureka. It's big enough for mental health care. Dr. Beckwith can find a psychiatrist for you there. It's close enough for you to travel a few miles."

"I'll be okay soon, right?"

"Time. You need time to learn about bipolar and for your medicine to take effect. If it must be changed or the dosage increased, you'll need to see a psychiatrist for a while."

Elise slumped in her chair. "I made a mess of my life. Does it have to be this way? I had everything—money, large home, position, friends."

"Until you had severe depression. What kind of life is that?"

"That's why I wanted to die."

"Do you want to change your life?"

"Does it matter?"

"That's up to you. I think it would be helpful to you for Zed to attend the team meeting."

"What team meeting?"

"Dr. Beckwith scheduled a time day after tomorrow with him, Robert, me, a spiritual advisor, Zed, and your parents."

"What the heck? What's it about? I won't do it. Not with Zed there."

"Okay. I still think Zed should be there. He needs to understand you better. Anyway, your team of professionals will help your family understand bipolar and how to help you. You'll need their support until you're back to normal."

"Do I have a choice about attending?"

"You can stay here longer."

"Then I'll go."

"Good. Have you thought of marriage counseling for you and Zed?"

"Stop," Elise screeched. "I won't take more crap from Zed. He preached enough to me."

"What do you want to do?"

"Leave Zed?"

"You don't sound confident."

"I have to think about it some more." *I'm ninety-nine percent sure.*

THE NEXT DAY, Elise walked into the afternoon group therapy late. Embarrassed her jeans were too tight, a long sweater hung past her hips. She had gained ten pounds in the past months due to her depression. She had eaten too much and drank copious amounts of coffee. And no more makeup. Church people wouldn't recognize her. She sat in the only available chair.

Robert spoke to Elise. "You're late. Be on time from now on."

"Sorry."

"We're in the middle of a conversation with Leslie." Then Robert looked around the circle and said, "She isn't wearing her sunglasses today. Any comments from the group?"

Mary said, "You have pretty brown eyes. Wear your sunglasses only in the sun. And I hope you stay in therapy and take your medicine."

"Maybe." Again, Leslie hung a leg over the arm of the chair. "I guess I'm tired of being here so often. My moods cycle fast— every two weeks. My family is tired of my condition and that I don't take care of myself." Leslie's eyes were half-closed, and her smile was gone.

"Do you have something to say to her, Elise?" Robert asked.

"You're the expert. I don't even know what's wrong with her."

"You don't have to. Does her behavior affect you?"

"She makes me nervous."

"Do you hear that, Leslie?"

"Yeah. Doesn't mean I'll take my meds."

"Okay. Elise, tell us how you are."

"I don't want to discuss me."

"Why?"

"It won't help."

"Dr. Beckwith said you're bipolar II. That's something to talk about. There's a book I recommend. I'll write the name down and give you some websites to visit. Your family needs to see these too."

"If I can't get rid of it, why read a book?" Elise crossed her

23

legs and folded her arms against her chest.

"Look. A cowboy has to know his horse and cattle. You need to learn about your disorder. It's the only way to live with it. Why the scowl?"

"Because I damn well don't want to be this way. Look what it did to me."

"No one deserves bipolar or any other vile disease or disorder. If you take the medicine Dr. Beckwith prescribes, you can control it. If one drug doesn't work, there are others you can try until you find something that does. It's like roping a calf. You throw the lasso until you get it. For the present, that also includes therapy. Will your husband be supportive?"

"Damn if you don't think we're like your cows. Stop it."

"I don't intend to offend. It's just an analogy. Back to your husband. Will he help you?"

"Hell no. I want to leave him. The Bible says it's a sin, though."

Mary questioned Elise. "Do you think God wants you to suffer? If you do, maybe you need a different god."

"Who are you to talk? You tried to take your own life. What makes you different from me?"

Robert intervened. "Mary, Elise is angry. Do you wish to answer her?"

"Listen to me, Elise. My husband had an affair. I learned in therapy with the nurses that depression is normal. Suicide is not an answer. They think I can make a new life. I want to try. Don't you?"

"All of a sudden, you have all the answers. Crap. Crap on all of you. I'm leaving."

"Are you sure?" Robert asked. "I think it's important you stay. You're angry. Go with that and talk some more. Or, at least set a goal of what you'll do in your room. How about that?"

"I'm scared." Tears flowed down her cheeks. She jerked herself up to stand. Elise ran from the room.

She entered her room and shut the door. Elise half fell into her recliner and sobbed until someone knocked on her door.

Sandy said, "May I come in?"

"I want to be alone."

"Okay. Once you've settled down, write about what you're feeling."

"I'll think about it." *Let me be.*

SANDY STEPPED INTO Elise's room the next morning. "I hear you watched the DVD on bipolar yesterday evening. What did you think about it?"

"It reiterated what you and Dr. Beckwith discussed about depression and the highs and lows of both bipolar one and two."

"Good. Robert told me about the group therapy meeting yesterday afternoon. I'm glad you got rid of some anger."

Elise looked down *I hate myself.*

Sandy escorted Elise to the team meeting. Janet and Stephan rose from their chairs to hug her.

"So good to see you, honey. How are you?" Janet asked.

Elise kept silent and sat down beside them. She glanced at the group and saw Zed wasn't there. *Thank God.*

Dr. Beckwith started the meeting. "Elise, except for your mom and dad, these are the professionals who've been treating you. I've also brought a different kind of expert. This is Dr. Singh. She's a spiritual counselor and has extensive training with people of faith. The reason I invited her is that you've been active with your husband in the ministry for a few years, and I assume you had religious affiliation before that. I remember you said you gave up on any kind of church involvement."

"I don't want Christian counseling."

"She's a therapist for many religions."

Elise shook her head at the woman. She appeared to be of Indian descent. "No."

Beckwith sighed. "What do you want to do?"

Elise looked at her parents. "May I live with you awhile? I know I'm too old. However, you can't preach to me."

"Of course," her dad said. "Anything to help."

Dr. Beckwith handed Mr. and Mrs. Olsen a few pages of paper. "Here's some information about bipolar disorder. It will help you monitor Elise's moods. And I'm giving you the name and phone number of a reputable psychiatrist in Eureka. He can answer any questions you have once you see him. Make the appointment immediately. Do you have questions?"

"No," Elise's dad said. "Thanks, doctor. We'll follow your orders."

"Good. "I'll release her late tomorrow morning."

"Geez, you don't give me much of a choice," Elise said.

Dr. Beckwith said, "By law, I can keep you here longer if you don't go with your parents."

Elise nodded. *He's like a raging waterfall. I can't stop him from threatening me.*

"While you wait for the medicine to even out your moods, I want you to start and end every day by journaling your thoughts and feelings. They're private, for your eyes only. So be honest about what you write."

Elise twisted in her chair. "I'll try to remember what we talked about and hope it works." *If not, I'll make sure I commit suicide next time.*

FOUR

AT NOON THE NEXT DAY, ELISE'S PARENTS ARRIVED. JANET ASKED, "You ready, honey?"

"I've been up for hours. I want to get more clothes. Is Zed at home or the church? I don't want him near me."

"He went to his church office," her dad said. "He doesn't understand you and is quite angry right now. He thinks you ought to be with him."

"Please, Dad, I don't want to know what Zed thinks or what he does. Not right now."

"Okay. Let's go to your house and get what you need."

Once they were outside the hospital, Elise slid into the backseat of the car. "Let's go, Dad. I might see someone I know. They'll ask questions."

"You've got it, honey."

On the drive to her home, Elise twisted and turned as much as the seatbelt allowed. She bit a nail and ran her hands through her shaggy hair. *What if Zed has decided to stay home?*

"Dad, Mom, could we go straight to Ferndale now? Maybe you can ask Zed to mail my clothes later."

"Why, honey?" her dad asked.

"I can't face going home. I want out of here." She sniffled.

Her dad turned left at the next corner, heading in the

direction of the freeway. "All right. We're on our way north."

"Thanks."

Elise was quiet on the drive to her childhood home. Her parents tried to start a conversation, but she didn't answer. Soon they gave up. Elise watched the scenery change after they left Santa Rosa. Highway 101 became less crowded. A few wineries beckoned travelers to stop and taste the fruit of the vines.

"Let's fill the car with gas and stretch our legs," her dad said. They stopped at the Chevron station in the small town of Laytonville. "My behind is tired after two hours in the car. I could use a cold drink and a chance to use the restroom too."

Janet turned to Elise. "What about you?"

"Yeah, I'll use the facilities. I hate to ask, but would you buy me a Coke? And a small bag of peanuts too. I don't have any money with me."

"You bet," her dad said.

After they were back in the car, Elise tried to sleep despite the curves of the road and the mountainous climb, but she couldn't. Her attention turned to the redwoods after they passed the sign pointing the way to Leggett, the site of the drive-through redwood tree. She remembered the trees' beauty and let it sink into her troubled mind. *If only I could stand as tall as these majestic trees and let nature heal me.* Her mind went in circles about all that had transpired in the hospital. *How can I face the future?*

ELISE CLOSED THE door to her childhood bedroom after her folks left her to unpack her small bag. They had told her to rest before dinner. She glanced at the white girlie furniture. The pink flowered wallpaper smelled of her old perfume. Ten years had passed since she left home. The double bed brought memories of the times she and Zed had stayed here during the Christmas celebrations. Her parents liked Zed. He fit into the family except for his type-A personality. Her sister Dana and her family had also joined in the festivities. Good times gone forever.

She sat in the overstuffed white chair by the window and screamed from the lowest level of her gut. The sound vanished into the pillow she held over her mouth. *This isn't fair. I didn't do anything wrong.*

She shifted her attention toward the window and tried to take in the beauty of her parents' small yard. Daffodils and hyacinths bloomed in one corner and the roses along the fence sprouted new leaves. March was a pretty month. Nature usually calmed her. Not this time. She slipped off the chair and knelt by her bed with her head on the cool, smooth spread until she could think coherent thoughts. Prayer and God eluded her.

Elise muttered, "If I divorce Zed, he can't remarry and remain a minister in his church." She broke out in a sweat. *Do God and the church really care about me? Did Zed? Or was it all for show, putting on a religious facade at church and pretending to have all the answers?*

ELISE AND JANET sat in the waiting room of the new psychiatrist in Eureka. The waiting room, though small, had two brown leather wingback chairs. A table stood between them. Magazines such as *National Geographic, Smithsonian,* and other magazines were on it. On the wall, across from the chairs, a painting of wide red and brown stripes caught her attention. *A seventh-grader could do that. Yet people pay large sums of money to collect modern art.* She wondered if Dr. Mueller resembled the hanging. It seemed stark to her. No life.

He opened the door and greeted her. His suit, vest, and tie made her blink with their formality. His gray hair belied his youthful face. "You're Elise Norris? And this is?"

"My mother, Janet Olsen. She drove me here."

"Come in." He held the door open for the women to follow him into his office. A stiff leather brown sofa matched Dr. Mueller's posture. His wooden desk dominated the other side of the room. Modern art adorned his walls. Everything in the room lacked warmth.

"Sit on the sofa. I'll get my notepad."

Elise dreaded the upcoming conversation with Dr. Mueller and squirmed on the couch next to her mother.

"Dr. Beckwith thought it imperative that I see you as soon as possible. What is happening?" Dr. Mueller balanced the pad of paper on his lap.

Elise explained her short hospital stay, and what she had learned. "I'm sure Dr. Beckwith told you about my attempt, my . . ."

"How strong is the urge now?"

Elise's voice grew louder, and she looked across the room at Mueller's desk. "At the very least, I want to run away. I'm sure most of your patients do."

"Some." Dr. Mueller scribbled a few notes on his notepad and then stared into her eyes. "You are only a few days away from your attempted suicide. Consider another hospitalization."

"I'll go to hell first."

"We don't want that. Then I expect you to have intense counseling for three weeks—with me. I'm prescribing a medication specifically for bipolar. I want the drug to build in your body to a level that keeps you stable. After that, I'll refer you to a licensed marriage and family therapist."

Dr. Mueller directed his attention to Janet. "Mrs. Olsen, I want you to keep a close eye on your daughter and then bring her back in a couple of days."

On the drive home, Janet asked, "Honey, how do you feel about having therapy so often?"

Elise looked out the car window and took in the green grass and the wildflowers in the valley. Spring offered new hope—at least she wanted it that way. Dr. Mueller irritated her. His manner was like a straight stick. She took a deep breath. "He did something besides quote scripture to me. I want to try it."

"I don't know, honey. It's so at odds with what Zed Norris Ministries believes and our church too. You know that."

"I need help, Mom. What do you want me to do? Commit suicide?"

FIVE

Zed

IN HIS CHURCH OFFICE, ZED PACED BETWEEN HIS OVERSIZED mahogany desk and the conference table. The cost of the furniture could have fed a family of four for many months. The designer-curtained windows looked out over the expansive green lawn, but the view did little to warm his mood. Darkness invaded his soul.

Elise's parents had called him out of courtesy to let him know she was with them. Zed had called her several times, but she had refused to talk to him. *Why? What could he do to help her?*

His secretary reminded him at the end of each day what the agenda would be the following day. He depended on her to keep him on track. Elise used to help with that. He tended to procrastinate.

Zed enjoyed being the pastor of a fifteen hundred-member church—even though there were endless meetings. Excitement about the various programs made it easier for his associates to find volunteers for them. Deep satisfaction filled him every Sunday when he preached, and counseling parishioners about their various problems bonded their relationship.

His busy schedule only allowed him to meet with the most critical. The others, he referred to the ministers he employed.

His thoughts turned to Elise again. With God's help, he would win her back. He loved her and believed they were meant to be together. When they first met, he had been attracted by her beauty. Six months into their courtship, he realized her devotion to God was sincere. That sealed his desire to marry her.

It seemed like a happily ever after relationship except for their disagreement about whether he was sterile or she was. Her tests showed she was fertile. He had refused examination. A mostly idyllic life until her depression.

Sunday morning's sermon loomed ahead of him. Three days to figure out what to preach. Should he include a statement about Elise's problem? He had told his governing elders about her, and he knew word had leaked to others in the congregation. He put his head in his hands. *Why, God, did Elise try to commit suicide? We have everything.* He thought about their seventy-five hundred square foot Tudor-style home, their luxury cars, and the income that was large enough to accommodate upscale vacations. The gated community helped secure their privacy. The church people, for the most part, loved him and Elise. *Where had she gone wrong?*

He had found her white-faced and unconscious on their king-size bed when he returned from meeting with his church elders. He shook her and yelled at her to wake up. No response. His desperate call to 911 resulted in the immediate arrival of paramedics and an ambulance. They gave her oxygen and loaded her onto a gurney. Zed had begged to ride with Elise to the hospital, but to no avail. He followed in his car. In a daze, he arrived and went to the waiting room. Elise's parents arrived a few hours later, and for interminable hours they prayed she would live. He didn't want to dwell on it.

Zed opened his Bible and turned to the book of Deuteronomy, chapter twenty-nine, verse nine. "Keep . . . this covenant . . . that you may prosper in all that you do."

SUNDAY MORNING ZED paced the platform inside the church sanctuary. Its stained glass windows showed the life of Jesus. His favorite was the one of Jesus surrounded by children because it showed that everyone was a child of God if they believed. The red cushions on the solid oak pews matched the carpet. Behind him, the worship team had just finished singing "Our God Is an Awesome God." He was pumped. The sermon would inspire the congregation to pray for Elise. He also wanted them to live according to God's will. He read the scripture to the people and then spoke.

"God is like our CPA. He *Covenants* with us, *Prospers* us, and it is for *All* areas of our lives. He does not come around handing out presents to us. God enters into agreements with us and if we are faithful to him in doing our part, he will fulfill the covenant or promises he makes to us. If we invest in God's work with our money, time, and talents, he will provide a return on our investment that is beyond what we ask or think. Praise God. And everyone say, amen."

The sanctuary echoed with amens.

"What is God's Covenant with the Children of Israel here? In this scripture, God reminds them how he miraculously brought them out of slavery in Egypt. He miraculously delivered them and provided all their needs during their forty years in the wilderness."

Zed waved his Bible toward the congregation.

"They stood on the verge of entering the Promised Land and God told them they must serve him as their only God or be cursed with evil." Zed raised his voice. "We must obey his words in order to receive the blessing." Stand up if you believe God's word. Praise him."

The congregation surged to their feet, as if at a football game after a touchdown, and clapped.

"You may be seated."

"So. What does it mean to *Prosper*? For the Children of Israel, it meant they would be able to subdue all the inhabitants of the land and live there in peace and abundance. For us, it means we have conquered all the enemies in our lives and have victory, success, growth, and goodness."

The crowd shouted, "Praise God!"

"Does God promise to prosper us in just one area of our lives? No! He promises to prosper us in *All* aspects of our lives—with rewarding jobs, good health, nice homes, and great relationships with our families and friends.

"Listen to me. God is the God of the *Covenant,* which means *Prosperity* for *All* areas of our lives. I repeat. God is our CPA. Hallelujah. Praise God."

"If what I have said is not true in your life, you need to examine your heart and ask yourself why. Let's bow our heads before Almighty God. God, please help us as we sit here in prayer."

Zed paused. The silence indicated the presence of the Holy Spirit among the people.

"Jesus, your Spirit is leading me to say there are at least three people here today who have been holding back on their commitment to God.

"Children of God, I want you to come to the front so that I and my associates can pray for you. You won't regret it. Hallelujah. Listen to the words of this song, 'Open the Eyes of My Heart,' as the worship team sings. The words remind us to stop seeing things through our natural eyes and open our hearts to God's blessings.

"Praise God for this brave soul who is coming forward. Are there others? Yes. Here comes another one, and another. Thank you, God. And folks, let's believe God to speak to those who aren't here today to listen to God's word."

Some will know I mean Elise.

He heard a "Praise God" from James Prescott, his lead elder, who sat in the front row. Bowing his head, Zed prayed.

"Father, thank you for those who have come forward. Give them courage and wisdom to follow you with their whole hearts. Amen."

He spoke to them. "Now, I want you to repeat this prayer after me. Father God, I've failed in keeping your covenants. I'm sorry. Forgive my sins. I want a life blessed by you. Keep the devil away. In Jesus name I pray. Amen."

Zed's chest expanded.

"Okay, those of you who came forward may return to your seats. You'll be different after this consecration. Worship team, lead us in the song, 'There's Something About That Name.'"

Zed walked to the middle door at the back of the sanctuary while the congregation sang. He wanted to greet some of the people as they left the service. James Prescott was the first one to reach him. His thick white hair and tall stature caused him to stand out from the surrounding crowd.

"Pastor, exceptional sermon. Couldn't be better. You preached the truth. Praise God. Praise God."

A long line of people waited to greet him. Many thanked him for his sincerity and God-anointed sermon.

"You sure know how to tell the truth, Pastor," one congregant said.

Nancy, one of his deacons and a pretty, bleached blond, was next. "Pastor, I think you're a wonderful person. You're always kind and thoughtful."

"Thank you."

"But I have a question. I have diabetes and God has not healed me. I do everything God tells me to do. What's wrong with me?"

Zed gave Nancy a hug. "I know you're faithful. It has to be the devil after you. Let's say a quick prayer. Jesus, in your name I say to Satan, be gone with your affliction from Nancy's body. Amen. You're free, Nancy. Rejoice in God."

He shook hands with the rest of the people in line as fast as he could and still be courteous. He was exhausted and anxious to go home.

At home, Zed leaned back in his leather chair in his office. Elise had painted the room herself instead of using a professional. And she had shopped for the accent sofa pillows of sage green and brown. Her friends thought she should have hired a decorator to show God's blessings. *What was wrong with her? I have plenty of money.* A pang of conscience hit him. *My parents had to scrimp and save on a teacher's salary when I was a kid at home. They have plenty of money now through careful buying of rental property.*

He decided to call Elise again. Janet had hung up on him

the last two times. It wasn't fair. It was his marriage. He tapped his fingers on his desk. Maybe Elise would talk to him now. He punched in the Olsen's number on his cell. "This is Zed, Janet. I want to speak to Elise. Don't say no."

"I can't make her talk to you. I'll ask."

He heard a scream of *no* resound in the background.

"I think you heard that."

"Tell her it's imperative we talk. And I want to see her. Have her call me. I'm tired of this rejection." He hung up. He wanted to play golf to ease his mind. It was raining though.

He phoned his friend Joe and invited him to meet at the coffee shop for lunch. Joe had been Zed's best friend in seminary and was also the pastor of a large church in Santa Rosa. "It's urgent, Joe."

THE CAFE WAS crowded. Zed ordered his sandwich and cappuccino. He snagged a table just as Joe got there. "Hey, Joe. How's my best bud, carrottop that you are? God's blessing you, I hope."

"You bet, Zed. And here's the thing. King David had red hair. I'm like him. A warrior too."

"Always a comeback."

"Wanna see my new wheels after lunch? I bought a Lexus. Love it. I saw your Porsche parked in the lot. That's how I knew you were here. Let me get my food. Be right back."

What should I tell Joe about Elise? The truth? We have always been honest with each other.

Joe returned to the table with his food and sat down. "How are you and Elise? Haven't heard from you for a long time."

"I've been avoiding you. I wanted to hide my problems."

"What's going on?"

Zed explained the whole situation and sat back in his chair to wait for Joe's reaction. He bit his cheek and tried to look calm.

"Wow. What a load. I have to say, she's not a Christian if she behaves that way. She's a hindrance to your ministry. If she wants a divorce, give it to her. No one would blame you.

They might even let you remarry considering the circumstances."

"She was great before she got depressed. Most of the time she was happy and interested in our life together. I'm confused." Zed sipped his coffee and munched on his stale turkey sandwich.

"That's Satan talking to you. I'll pray for you and her too."

"Thanks."

Joe finished his sandwich. "Sorry, but I need to go. Worship committee is meeting soon. And stay in touch."

"You do the same. Oh, I want to see your Lexus."

"Let's go. Still raining, but we're tough."

Outside, Joe opened the car door for Zed. "It's the top of the line SUV with 383-horsepower, 5.7-liter V8 engine. It'll pull 7,000 lbs. And it's all-wheel drive. It also has a rear-seat entertainment system. What do you think?"

"God is good! It should be great to drive to your cabin at Tahoe for skiing. Well, have a good afternoon. I have to get back home and do some paperwork."

As Zed drove home, thoughts of Elise troubled him. Joe was right. She hindered his way to effectively govern the church. Should he start divorce proceedings? No. He wanted her to come back. It was her duty. And he loved her.

The spacious entrance to Zed's home seemed ostentatious and cold after returning from the coffee shop. Marble floors, exotic ferns, and a flowing fountain enhanced the look. But no Elise. He missed her warm hugs. The house, his life, was empty without her.

SIX

Elise

ELISE PHONED HER SISTER AND BIT A FINGERNAIL. SHE HAD BEEN home four weeks and it was the first time she had talked to Dana. "Hi, it's me. I . . . I'm sorry I haven't called you sooner. I hope you're not upset."

"I'm hurt. We're sisters. I didn't even know you and Zed were having problems. You should have called me, or at least Mom and Dad, when you were depressed. It wasn't fair to them or me."

Elise's eyes narrowed. "I did the best I could." Her voice had an edge.

"Don't be angry with me. I think I grew ten new gray hairs after I learned about your, you know, your attempt. I've been worried sick."

"Sorry. I've struggled with depression since I was a teenager. Most of the time it went away after a short time. Nine months ago, my depression plummeted to depths I had never experienced before."

"That's hard to understand, Elise."

"It is for most people. Could we meet for lunch? I'm ready to see you."

"Come for dinner tonight instead. I have lasagna in the oven and I made a salad. Join Cliff, me, and the kids."

"Thanks. I've missed you."

"Mom kept telling me you were too depressed to see me. Is that true?"

"Yes, and I was ashamed of what I did and afraid you'd reject me. Give me fifteen minutes."

She walked two blocks to Dana's house, which was built in the 1940s craftsman style. She answered the door. "Elise, I'm glad to see you."

Elise stretched out her arms to embrace Dana, who hugged her tight.

"Why the pastel pink Sunday best dress and stilettos?"

"I always wore nice clothes in the ministry. It's a hard habit to break. But you look fine in your jeans. Hmm. I smell garlic and oregano. You know how much I like lasagna."

"Make yourself at home. Hang your jacket in the closet."

"Come to the dining room. I have to check on the food."

"Hey, Elise," Cliff said, as he entered the room. "How's it goin'?"

"Better."

"How's my favorite sister-in-law?"

"Nice of you to say that since I'm your only one. Hey, looks like Dana is feeding you well." Elise patted his paunch.

"Thanks a lot. You know how to—"

"I'm teasing." She messed up his dark brown hair. "I've missed your steady, patient personality. How's your job? Are you still a building inspector?"

"I am. Wish the salary was more. Dana needs to go back to work. The kids' school expenses create havoc with our budget."

"I hope she will. She's a good music teacher. Where are the boys?"

"In their room engrossed in Play Station. They'll be down. We've really been concerned about you. Don't know what to say."

She pressed her lips together. "I was afraid you would judge me."

"You had everything with Zed. I hope you two work it out. Anyway, we're glad you're here."

"Thanks," Elise said as a tear escaped. *No one understands me.*

Cliff patted her on the back. "Let's eat. Here're the kids. Say hello to your Aunt Elise."

Elise's face brightened. "Mark and Sammy, come here."

"Aunt Lisi." Sammy ran to Elise. "I thought you'd never come." He grabbed her as if he'd never let her go.

"It's been almost a year. Far too long, Sammy. And look how tall you are."

"I'm six."

"I know. Did you get the birthday card I sent you?"

"Yep. I bought a Batman T-shirt with the money."

"Cool. So, Mark, how about a hug?"

"Ah, do I have to?" Mark shrugged. "I'm too old."

"So how about a fist bump?"

"Okay."

Elise said, "I've missed you boys. Mark, you look more like your dad every time I see you. Your big brown eyes and thick head of hair are beautiful."

"Who do I look like Aunt Lisi?" Sammy asked.

"Oh, let's see. How about the man in the moon?"

Sammy giggled. "No. Tell me."

"Like your mom. You have blond hair and blue eyes. How about that?"

"I love her."

"Good."

Dana called out, "Come to the table." Once seated, Cliff prayed, "Thank you for this bounty of food and bringing Elise to us. Help her find the way to you. Amen."

Elise tightened her fists as if ready for a boxing match.

"Dig in, Elise. Not much though. Looks like you need to lose weight," Dana said.

Elise wanted to kick her sister. She took a bite of food instead. "Delicious as usual."

The sounds at the table made Elise wish for a home of her own. *Oh, Zed, why did I leave you? And I gave up a beautiful house. How dumb am I?*

After dinner, Cliff went upstairs with the boys to the

computer room to resume their games. Dana and Elise took their chocolate cake and coffee into the living room to chat and sat near a low burning fire.

"I love how you decorated, Dana," Elise said. "Your mix of country and modern go well together. My favorite is this comfy settee with the dog and cat scenes on the fabric." Elise took a bite of her cake. "Yum. My favorite. I love anything chocolate. I think you gave me my first candy bar when I was five and you were seven. Mom wasn't happy.

"Dana, could I ask you a question? Different subject."

"Sure."

"Do you think it's strange that I miss Zed?"

"Of course not. He's a great guy, Elise. And I think you're a perfect couple." Dana leaned forward in her chair. "I believe you need to trust God to work this out. You know what the Bible says in Romans 8:28. 'And we know that for those who love God all things work together for good, for those who are called according to his purpose.'"

"Stop quoting the Bible to me. It doesn't help. Zed gave me the same advice he gives everyone. You know what the standard is. It didn't work for me. And that busybody Mrs. Wilson said the devil chased me because depression engulfed me. I told her she was full of crap."

Through clenched teeth, Dana said, "I can't believe you said that. You're a minister's wife."

"Bipolar made me extremely irritable at times. I left Zed because we argued all the time. He didn't understand me, and I didn't know why I was depressed."

"Do you intend to divorce him?"

"I don't know. I'm far from ready to reconcile with him or the church. The truth is I miss the good I had in my life before I became ill." Elise looked at her feet. "I feel guilty as hell. Dr. Mueller, my psychiatrist, said to go easy on myself until I learn how to manage my problems."

"Mom explained the chemical imbalance. To be truthful I don't understand."

"Not sure I do either. At least they have medicine for it. Please don't fight me about being separated from Zed or the church." *Dana's so stuck in her beliefs.*

Dana pinched the bridge of her nose. "You need to look at the bright side. You had a good life. You're not saddled with kids like I am. I have no free time. And we're strapped for money."

Calm, stay calm, Elise. "You have two of the greatest boys anyone could ask for. Isn't that enough?"

"I can't express how much I love them. At their age though, I need more to do that satisfies me."

"Cliff said your finances are tight. What about giving piano lessons part-time? The boys don't need you as much."

"That doesn't work. The boys would be home from school, and that's when kids are available."

"I don't know. Give it some thought." Elise kept herself sitting in her chair. She wanted to walk out and go home. *I'm trapped as if I'm a tiger. Everyone wants to tame me.*

"You and Zed are wealthy. You could hire a nanny, do anything you want. Don't you want children?"

"I did. It's impossible now."

"Go back to Zed. Have children with him."

"It's complicated."

"By the way, I'm like you. I need a job. I'm not taking money from Zed."

"What? That's crazy. Why not? You're entitled to some money from him."

"I don't want anything from him right now. As to a job, I hope to work in an office. Something to match the skills I used in my part-time job in Santa Rosa."

"That's okay, but you're doing something I don't agree with. Mom said you won't see a Christian counselor. That's wrong."

"I've heard that many times. I plan to try a different approach."

"Reconsider it."

Elise stiffened her back and put her unfinished cake on the coffee table. She bit her tongue to stop an angry retort. "It's late. I'd better get back. Give my love to Cliff and the boys."

The walk home seemed interminable. She struggled to put

one foot in front of the other. *I need someone to understand me. Not only professional people.*

Elise gripped the railing and dragged her feet up the steps to her bedroom. She looked around. The blue walls seemed gray. *Even Dana can't support my new life. Why does she think her life is hard?*

Elise closed the door and lay on the bed face down. She heard a knock. Her voice quivered. "Come in."

"I heard you climb the stairs," her mother said. "Did something happen at Dana's?" She sat on the bed beside Elise and put her hand on her daughter's shoulder.

Elise rolled over and grabbed another pillow to prop up her head. "I can't live up to her expectations. And as usual, she thinks she knows more than me."

"Give Dana time. Even though we don't understand everything, we love you. How do you feel, Elise? I wake up in the middle of the night and worry about you. I'd be crushed if anything happened to you."

"I'm so sorry, Mom. Bipolar caused my severe depression. I didn't have control of myself. I'm better now. And you and dad are important to me. Dr. Mueller wants me to begin therapy with a lady named Karen Johnson next week. He said she's excellent." *I hope he's right.*

MONDAY AFTERNOON ELISE stepped on her parents' bathroom scale and berated herself for her weight gain. She looked like a chubby baby. At least her hair looked good. Janet had taken her to the beauty salon for a chic haircut. The hairdresser had transformed the shaggy mess to a layered shoulder-length style.

Today was her first appointment with Karen Johnson. Elise had delayed leaving because she wasn't sure she wanted to go. Now she had about thirty minutes to get there. She accelerated Janet's Honda to seventy-five and held the speed all the way to Eureka, cops be damned. She arrived with ten minutes to spare. Elise realized she had put herself at risk.

The therapist's office was in a neighborhood of Victorian

homes, which meant she had to parallel park. She maneu-
vered several times before she succeeded. Professional signs
in front of the buildings listed offices of lawyers, doctors, and
tax accountants.

She found the house she was looking for and walked up
the steps in slow motion, clutching her handbag until her
hands hurt. She tried deep breaths without success. Once
inside, she saw Karen's name on a door that opened into a
waiting room. Impressionistic art hung on the walls. One
picture showed people boating and eating at picnic tables. The
art soothed her. Zed had nixed her appeals to him for it. He
preferred religious art. Elise looked at her watch. Almost time.

The office door opened. "You're Elise Norris? I'm Karen."
The therapist's smile said welcome. Her casual brown skirt
and floral blouse gave her an earthy, warm quality. Her short,
blond hair was feathered around her face.

Elise followed Karen into her office. A loveseat covered in
soft blue cloth sat opposite a rocker padded with navy
cushions. The desk was a light honey oak, as was the office
chair. *This is better than Dr. Mueller's stiff office style.*

"Make yourself comfortable." Karen waved toward the
loveseat. "There's tissues and water on the table."

Elise sat down. "I wish I didn't have to be here."

"Many people feel that way the first time or two. Before we
start, please fill out this questionnaire. I don't have a
receptionist. I like to guard the privacy of my clients. An
accounting firm keeps books for me." She gave a clipboard and
pen to Elise and sat down in the oversized rocker.

Elise sighed. Another form. She signed her name that she
would pay at every session. Her mom and dad had promised
they would finance her therapy if insurance didn't pay. She
felt childish. Mommy and daddy had to take care of her. She
handed the completed information to Karen.

"Did your sessions with Dr. Mueller help?"

"I don't feel suicidal now. He encouraged me to research
bipolar online. I joined a chat room. I'm lucky my manic is
milder than what some people deal with."

"All that sounds positive. Tell me more about yourself."

Elise blurted, "I left my husband."

"What is your history with him?"

"We grew up in the same type of church. He was in his second year at Fuller Theological Seminary, and I was a junior at Art Center College of Design. We met at a café in Pasadena where I worked."

"Interesting. What attracted you to him?"

"Your questions are too direct. I want answers to get me out of the mess I created."

"I need to know your history and what brought you to this point. I can help you better."

Elise sat up straighter and pulled her blouse over her tight designer jeans. Then she stood and looked out the window at a couple of dilapidated houses with straw-like grass. They looked like she felt. "In college, we believed in the same spiritual values, and he treated people with kindness. He respected me and appreciated my art. I had occasional episodes of depression and he encouraged me each time. That was different than anyone else I dated. Oh, and he was handsome too—blond hair and blue eyes. Our chemistry was great. People are drawn to him. Zed's friendly and interested in everyone. His energy never stops."

"Sounds wonderful."

"He was."

"Not now?" Karen asked.

Elise's words dragged like a slug. "I'm tired. Can't we stop?"

"We could. First, tell me why you left him."

"He changed. He belittled my depression. Told me to pull myself up and believe God would heal me. I couldn't, and Zed didn't understand why." Elise sat back in the chair.

"How did you feel about that?"

"Angry as hell."

"Do you have issues with your church too?"

"Are you familiar with the prosperity gospel?"

"I've watched a couple of television evangelists, I think two times.

"And?" Elise asked.

"I'm not a Christian counselor. I don't give my opinion on spiritual matters. But I'm interested in how your religious background affects you."

"It doesn't work for me anymore."

"Why not, Elise?"

"It didn't cure my depression. My former church believes in the devil too. I don't know if I do." Elise made a growling sound in her throat.

"You can be a survivor. One who finds herself again. How long has this been going on?"

"Months. I didn't know what to do." Elise slumped in the chair. "The church says if we need help, we have to see a Christian counselor, one that quotes scripture."

"Did you seek help during this time of depression?"

"No."

"And it led to your attempted suicide."

"Right."

"What else is on your mind?" Karen jotted notes and then looked at Elise.

"I ruined Zed's life, maybe mine. And I hate how angry I am." Elise's face reddened from her neck to her face.

"Is it based on truth? Tell me how you'd change what happened." Karen jotted down more notes.

"I did the best I could. It wasn't enough."

"What is your anger about?"

"Everyone abandoned me because I couldn't believe like them. So did Zed."

"Did you understand yourself?"

"No."

"Does guilt figure in this?"

"Somewhat. If I divorce Zed, he can't marry again and remain a minister in his church."

"Why is that, Elise?"

"It's a rule of Zed Norris Ministries."

"Is he the pastor?"

"Yes. But he can't change the rules because Zed Norris Ministries is associated with a governing association. It determines how a pastor must live."

"You drag this shame and anger behind you as if you're a horse pulling a heavy load."

"What am I supposed to do?"

"Forgive yourself."

"Does that work?"

"If you let it. What do you tell yourself when your mind dwells on the negative?"

"I tell myself I'm an idiot. That I failed. That I deserve punishment."

"Write down the negative messages over and over to get them out of your system. Reread them to determine if they're true. I also want you to keep a separate journal of things you're thankful for. Write in it every day. Replace some of the pessimism."

"I'll try it."

"Good. Old teachings are playing in your head. We'll talk about that more as we go along. Call me right away if you have thoughts of suicide. Is that a deal?"

"I guess."

"I believe Dr. Mueller wants us to meet weekly. Are you willing to do that?"

"I'm tired of therapy. Sometimes I felt worse after I saw Dr. Mueller."

"Why?"

Elise crossed her arms. "It hurts. I'm weary of it all. What am I to do with my life? I walked away from everything I knew and believed."

"Do you want to attend a different kind of church?"

"No."

"Why."

"It might stab me in the back again."

"Did you have activities outside of church?" Karen asked.

Elise explained her job in Santa Rosa.

"Do you think you're ready to work again?"

"I don't know. It might take my mind off my troubles. My family is all I have right now."

"That will change. Give it time. If you don't want a job yet, what about a hobby?"

"I used to paint landscapes and a portrait now and then when I was in college. I won a few awards. The shades of various colors and shadows expressed the meaning of the picture. The whole experience fulfilled me."

"What about doing more of that?"

Elise moved her foot in circles on the floor. The corners of her lips turned up and warmth filled her. *What if painting gave meaning to my life again?* "I'll give it some thought."

"Good." Karen looked at her watch. "This hour has gone by in a flash. What about next week? Will you come?"

Elise hesitated. An image of her lying in bed most of the time flitted through her mind. "I'll try."

Karen extended her hand to Elise. "Take care and call me if you need to talk before then."

On the way home, Elise reflected on her session. *If only Zed could understand me.*

ELISE STROLLED FROM her parents' home to the Arts and Crafts store in downtown Ferndale to buy supplies. She paused at the windows of art galleries to view paintings and sculptures. Many of the artists were local. Nick's Jewelry displayed handcrafted silver jewelry. Her heart beat faster when the Golden Gait Mercantile caught her attention. She chuckled. Tourists thought Gait was misspelled. It wasn't. This had been her favorite place when she was a kid. Their imported licorice drew her inside every time she had a little money to spend. A Help Wanted sign hung in the window. *Maybe I could work here.*

She marveled at the Victorian facades of the buildings, which stretched along a few short blocks. Some were built more than a hundred years ago. Her grandparents had settled here and her sense of connection to the community made her feel at home.

Inside Arts and Crafts, Elise turned her attention to the tubes of oil paints. She rubbed her fingers on them and remembered college days. A sense of tranquility filled her. Why had she let her love of art fall by the wayside? Church and her part-time job had consumed her life. She could have painted instead of working. *I could have had the best of two different worlds.*

"Elise, is that really you?" The petite young woman dressed in Ferndale's casual style looked familiar.

"Katherine? Wow, it's years since I've seen you. Do you work here?"

"For five years now. I love art, but I wasn't as good as you were when we were in high school. I've improved some . . . I think. Do you paint a lot?"

"I haven't since college. I'm getting back into it now. That's why I'm here."

"Are you in town for long?"

Oops. A question I don't want to answer. "I'm visiting my folks. Show me the canvases and tubes of oils you have."

"Sure. Choose what you want. I'll be at the cash register."

"Thanks." *I need to get out of here before she asks more questions.*

JUNE CAME QUICKLY. Three months of therapy and medication gave Elise more confidence. She walked downtown to see if the help wanted sign still hung in the window of the Golden Gait Mercantile. Anticipation of the possibility of a job there, in a place she had loved since childhood, made her want to dance. The wood floors and cabinets with glass cases showed their scars. The worn varnish and scratches reminded her that even though most people had inner wounds, they managed to live productive lives. The candy barrels near the cash register boasted of old-time sweets. Tourists loved viewing the antiques. Pale pink Depression glass, popular with tourists, was locked in cabinets. Small tools and implements used by farmers of earlier times caught the eyes of all who entered the store.

The bell jingled when she opened the door. Elise asked the person at the cash register for an application. "Is there a table for me to fill out the application?" she asked.

"I'm sorry, but no. Bring it back tomorrow. Ed, the owner, will be here."

"Great. I'm Elise Norris. I'm originally from Ferndale, but I don't recognize you."

"Oh, I've only been here four months. My name is Jodi. I work part-time at the cash register."

"That's great. I'll see you tomorrow."

ELISE THOUGHT ABOUT her interview with Ed. Even though he had come to Ferndale only five years ago, he had the helpful village spirit. They had trudged up the stairs to his office. He explained the details of the job and said he depended on the secretary to order supplies for the store, fill in at the cash register, if necessary, and help dust the merchandise. "I want someone willing and capable of doing anything I need," he had said. Ed reviewed her application and asked a few questions. He said he would call her in a few days.

ELISE ANSWERED HER cell phone.

"This is Ed from Golden Gait Mercantile. Your experience fits what I require in the store. And you know Ferndale even though you've been gone a while. I think we'll benefit from your skills. You love the store and that's a big plus. The secretarial position is yours if you want it."

"That's exciting. When do you want me to start?"

"Next Monday morning at eight. You'll receive training the first week from our current employee. How does that sound?"

"Great. I'll see you then."

Elise danced a jig and raced down the stairs to tell her parents.

"This calls for a celebration. We're proud of you," her dad said. "How about dinner at the Victorian Hotel?"

"Yum. I'm on my way to independence."

NEW-JOB NERVES gripped Elise on Monday morning. The walk to the Mercantile did little to quell the butterflies in her stomach. *Confidence, Elise. You can do this.*

When Elise opened the door, Ed greeted her in his jeans and long sleeve western shirt. "Welcome. Come upstairs with me. Alexi is ready for you."

"Am I late?" Elise asked as she looked at her watch. Eight o'clock.

"Oh, no. We came a little early to get set up for your training."

Elise followed Ed upstairs into the large room. This time she focused on what was in the office. She had been too nervous during the interview. There were two desks. A computer sat on each. The black-and-white photos on the wall were of Ferndale during the late nineteenth century when settlers bought land to raise dairy cows. The lush valley, fed by the Eel and Salt Rivers, provided the perfect spot.

Ed said, "Let me introduce you to my assistant. Alexi, this is Elise."

Alexi extended her hand to Elise. "I understand you have business experience. I hope you enjoy this job as much as I have. Ed's a great boss."

Elise noted that Alexi's dark hair hung to her waist and she wore jeans. *The dress code must be casual.* She had dressed for church—a dress and high heels. *How stupid.* "Glad to hear it. Let's get started," Elise said. She smiled.

"I'll leave you two. If there are questions—"

Alexi laughed. "Don't worry, Ed. We'll let you know. I thought I'd start her on the ordering software first since you need stock often."

Ed said, "You know this job well. Elise, you will too."

"I hope so."

"Your former boss said you'd done a good job until you got sick. I have no worries. And you're well now?"

"That's right."

"See you later."

Ed left, and Elise dug in her bag for the pad and pen she had brought to take notes. *This is a new beginning.*

SEVEN

Zed

ZED TOOK THE MAIL FROM THE CURBSIDE BOX AND GLANCED AT IT. Still no letter from Elise. It had been four months. Maybe he should call her again.

His shoulders drooped, and his pace slowed as he returned into the house. He no longer found comfort in the home he and Elise once shared. Arguments had filled the air. So many times he had told her he couldn't live that way. She had embarrassed him by not attending church. He was the minister, and she went against his teaching. She had threatened divorce back then. A few people in his congregation asked when she would be back. He had shrugged his shoulders. A voice in his head asked if he shared in the blame for her departure.

Angry with himself for procrastinating, he threw the bills on his desk and the junk mail in his recycle basket.

Elise used to keep him organized, or he would have let too many programs languish in the church. He couldn't let that happen. Now he relied on his secretary.

He thrived on the activities and took pride in what they accomplished. New members were common, and many people were saved from their sins. It was a good life. The money didn't hurt either. God had blessed him.

He decided to phone Elise. Maybe she would see reason

and come back to him. He punched in the number of his in-laws. He heard the first ring and hung up. He pushed a lock of blond hair away from his forehead and attacked the keypad.

Janet answered. "Olsen's."

He didn't know what to call her. "Uh, this is Zed."

"Oh. It's been a while."

She was honest at least, Zed thought. Her voice had a tinge of anger in it.

"May I speak to Elise?" There. He said it even though he heard his voice tremble.

"She's at work. I don't know if she'll return your call. However, I'll tell her."

"Before you hang up, would you tell me how she is?" Zed asked.

"I think that's up to her. It's better if the two of you speak."

A curse almost erupted from Zed. A good case of profanity might help him. However, a minister kept his language clean. "You're right. What time will she be home?"

"After five."

"I'll call back. Thanks."

He looked at his watch. Four in the afternoon. Ready for a snack, he raided the pantry and went into the living room with his Pepsi, chips, and salsa. He slumped in his burgundy recliner and ate. The food was tasteless. Janet's reluctance to tell him about Elise interfered with his desire to eat. His loose khakis showed his dietary habits. The striped burgundy and green pillows on the sofa reminded him of Elise. She had decorated in style. He decided to call her again around seven that evening. Maybe she would talk.

Zed grabbed his cell from the end table and clicked on the number of the Olsen's phone. He hung up and wiped the sweat from his forehead. *Come on, you can do it.* He tried again and failed. He berated himself for his hesitation to call Elise. Gosh darn, she was his wife who belonged with him. He completed the call.

His mouth dropped open when she answered. "Elise, this is Zed. I, I . . . can you spare a moment?" He paced the floor in his home office.

"Do you have something different to say to me than you did when I lived with you?"

"Honey, I miss you and want you to come home. I think we can work this out. God will help us. I'm sorry I hurt you, but I don't understand what happened. The Bible says to not let our anger get the best of us."

"It doesn't make a difference. I'm sure your sermons are the same. Have you changed your beliefs?"

"No."

"I want to come and pick up my car and a few things from the house. I'll rent an apartment soon."

"Sweetheart, could we talk more then? Tell me what else I need to do. I want to make things right between us. We need to pray together and claim God's promise of a good life." Zed almost wished he hadn't called. She refused to listen to him.

"We've harangued each other enough," Elise said. "Let it be. I won't be back."

Zed opened and closed his left fist. He wanted to lash out at her. "Even though I said I'm sorry?"

"I'll talk to my therapist about it."

"Do you have a Christian counselor?"

"Karen never mentions her faith or quotes Scripture to me. I'd quit if she did."

Zed scratched his head. "Some of the church people ask when you're coming back. What should I tell them?"

"The truth."

"Are you bitter? Is that the reason? I thought our marriage vows were sacred. What happened?"

"God didn't heal me. I tried everything the church believes. Don't start in on all of that again. Dana already did."

"You can't do this. We've been married too long to give up. Come home."

"Will you go to a non-Christian counselor with me?"

"How can I?"

"Then we've nothing to talk about."

"Let me know when you want to come for your car."

"Of course. And I'm pretty sure I want a divorce."

"It's against the rules of the church."

"Believe me, I never thought divorce was an option until I got depressed. Think about what you teach. Does it apply to me?"

Zed hung up and covered his eyes. What would people in the church think of him? He had failed to keep his marriage together.

THE BOARD OF fifteen ruling elders to whom Zed was accountable gathered around the conference table in Zed's church office for their monthly meeting. He cleared his throat and called the men to order. The lead elder, James Prescott, opened in prayer. "God, you see our hearts. We desire to follow your word in actions and thoughts. Give us compassion for a world going to hell. Guide us in all that we discuss tonight. Help us glorify you. In Christ's name I pray. Amen."

"Thanks, James," Zed said. "The first item on the agenda is about correspondence we've received. I have a letter from Mrs. Wilson. She wants to know when we'll reopen the soup kitchen for the homeless. You know we need someone to lead that endeavor since we have a vacancy. Any ideas?"

"What if we ask Mrs. Brown? She's the head of the school lunch programs in Santa Rosa," Tom White, the associate youth pastor said. His slanted eyes sparkled.

James Prescott didn't wait to be called on. "When's Elise coming back? She started the soup kitchen and it's her responsibility."

The elders looked at Zed in expectation. He hung his head. "She says she won't return." There. He had said it. It wasn't his fault she reneged on her responsibilities.

"That's too bad," Amos Ratliff said. "She learned the hard way about how to manage it. She used that program online so people could sign up to bring food. Real talented, she was. Don't know if another person wants that job. I sure don't." A murmur of agreement went up.

"We can't cry over what we don't have," James said. "Elise won't come back, and she proved she didn't have enough faith to be healed. I'd say the devil is still after her. She left Zed.

Let's follow Tom's suggestion." Everyone nodded their heads.

Zed ground his teeth. Why did he feel angry about what Prescott said? He felt protective of Elise for the first time in months even though she didn't want anything to do with him. "Let's table that for next month. In the meantime, Amos, ask Mrs. Brown. We need to get the homeless people saved so they'll have financial wealth to fix their problems. Next item is missions overseas. James, where do we stand with funds?"

"We're five hundred dollars short for the month. We can get that easy on Sunday. I'll give a little spiel about the Africans needing food and water. People go for it every time. You know, lay it on a little about how blessed we are with money and abundance of everything because of our faith. It works. Another sermon from you on giving would help too. Can you do that?"

Zed hesitated. He wished James would drop his patronizing attitude. "Okay, I'll give you five or ten minutes before the offering. How do our finances look otherwise?"

"Excellent. We met the payment for the mortgage on the new educational wing easy this month and there's enough for the next one. It's a source of real pride for the congregation. It added a bigger space for our Sunday school to grow thanks to how you preach that God blesses us when we live for his purpose. Keep that up. By the way, do you think we should televise our Sunday morning service? We could offer a free book or DVD of your sermons for every donation of five hundred or more. What do you think, Pastor?"

Zed looked beyond Prescott at the wall. He always had one more idea. Zed's schedule was full. Another project he would have to track. Zed returned his attention to James. "I'll make a note of it and put it on the agenda for the next meeting," Zed said. "Tom, we're ready for your report on the youth ministry. What's up?"

"The kids are revved. Praise God." Tom clapped his hands and smiled. His exuberance more than made up for his small stature. "We have enough sponsors for our mission trip to Mexico this summer. We're going to help build a church in a small village."

"Great. Let us know how your plans proceed. You've been a good choice for youth minister." Zed heard the collective amen from the group.

The meeting went on another hour by the time they looked at the church calendar for upcoming events and went over the jobs that needed to be done for building maintenance. Zed adjourned in prayer.

"Thanks for coming tonight. Keep up the good work." Now he had to go home to the empty house he hated. He thought of Prescott and his constant suggestions. No, they were more than that. He tried to lead the meetings at times. Zed wondered how he could get James to tone down. *Did God only bless people when they gave money? Where did that thought come from?*

THE NEXT DAY Zed's mind whirled. Elise had phoned and said she and her parents would be down this afternoon to get her things. What if Janet and Stephan wouldn't talk to him? What stories had Elise told about him? His last conversation with her reminded him of the terse words that she wouldn't come back, wouldn't come back to him or the church. *What of her soul? How could she forsake what she had believed was right?*

Zed watched the white extended-cab pickup truck pull into the driveway and up near the house. Elise sat in the back seat. Zed waited until they climbed out of the vehicle. He tried to quell the queasiness in his stomach by relaxing his abdominal muscles. Then he opened his front door and walked outside to greet them. "He . . . hello everyone." He nodded his head at Elise. "I'll help you unload the boxes. Looks like we'll have to remove the tarp first."

"We don't need you," Elise said. "Dad and Mom, let's each take a couple of containers inside and start packing once Dad removes the cover."

"Hello, Zed," Stephan said. "We don't want to trouble you. Sorry for the intrusion."

"I said I'll do my part." Zed went to the tailgate, opened it and removed the tarp, which he laid on the ground. Then he grabbed a couple of boxes and carried them into the house. *Heck, if Elise couldn't be stubborn.*

She came in next. "Geez, Zed. Where's the housekeeper? It looks as if she hasn't dusted or vacuumed since I left. Why not? Never mind. Back to what we came for. I'll start with the bedroom and take my personal stuff. Maybe you'd let me take at least a place setting of dishes, odds and ends of pots, pans, and mixing bowls. We had an extra set of flatware. I'll take that. I want the loveseat. There isn't room in the pickup for a sofa. You and Dad can take that to the truck. Any objections?"

"Does it matter? You seem determined to end everything we had together. Take it all. At least give me the blowup mattress for a bed."

Elise put her hands on her hips. "Don't play the martyr. I'll take the bed in the ochre and blue guest room. It's more feminine and to my taste."

"Why can't we at least talk? You've been gone a long time, and I didn't hear a word from you. I know we can settle this. Your folks could go out for coffee after we finish packing and loading. We'll have some privacy."

"I'm not ready and don't think I will be—ever. It's not that I don't care, I do. It's over though. Leave me alone." Elise ran out the door and ducked on the other side of the pickup. No one could see. She doubled over in pain as if she had a migraine headache. "Oh."

Janet followed Elise. "What's wrong, honey?"

"Moving out is harder than I thought it would be."

"Let's go inside. I'll ask Dad to make you a cup of tea."

Janet wrapped her arm around Elise and moved her to the sofa near an end table.

"What's wrong?" Zed asked.

"She's not well. Ask Stephan to bring tea and crackers."

"Did you say something to upset her, Zed?" Stephan asked.

"I asked her to have coffee with me. She said no. I didn't say more."

"Good." He brought the refreshments to Elise.

The tea settled Elise and she ate a bite of the saltine.

"Don't worry. Is everything packed?" Janet asked.

"Yes, Mom."

Within an hour Zed and Stephan had filled the truck and Elise and her folks were ready to leave.

Janet asked, "Zed do you have her fobs for the car?"

"I'll get them."

Zed handed Janet the devices.

"Thanks. Elise, I'll drive your car. You can ride with me or your dad."

"I'll go with you first."

Stephan spoke to Zed. "I'm sorry things didn't work out for you and Elise, son." He waved and got in his truck.

The house seemed deserted. Zed wanted to talk to someone. Many people in his church and his friends in the ministry would tell him to divorce Elise—and fast. Maybe he should take the initiative. He didn't want to do that. Call him coward, anything, but he didn't want to lose Elise. He couldn't make her understand his love for her. *I want a second chance even if she doesn't.*

EIGHT

Elise

ELISE PICKED HER TISSUE APART WHILE SHE TALKED TO KAREN. "I get depressed if I think about my future. I feel empty. I know that's related to the loss of Zed and church."

Karen leaned forward. "That's two major life changes. How do you feel about those?"

Elise closed her eyes a moment. "I'm so sad. I hide it from my folks if I can. They worry about me. And ask how I feel all the time."

"Do you think they're concerned you'll attempt suicide again?"

"Maybe."

"Perhaps you should be honest about how you feel. It would ease their minds. Most people identify with sadness."

"You think so?" Elise grabbed another tissue and wiped her eyes.

"It's normal. Everyone experiences loss in their life at some point. Parents die, jobs end. Many things. You know that. In time, your sadness will lessen. Do you journal about it?"

"Sometimes. Then I cry and I'm tired of that. It's dumb."

"In what way?"

"I made the choices. So why snivel?"

"You gave up what you treasured the most in your life."

"How do I get it back?"

"You mean your old life?"

"Yes. I mean no. I know I can't go back. I know that. I know that from deep inside me. So, what should I do?"

"How's the painting going?" Karen asked.

"Slowly."

"Can you do more of it?"

"I suppose."

"What about friends?"

"I'm not ready."

"Try painting more. If you need to see me again this week, call me. I'll work you in. How often do you see Dr. Mueller now that you're stable?"

"Every two months. He asks questions about my moods, and he's concerned about my separation from Zed and the way it affects my life. He remains adamant that I stay in therapy with you every week."

"That's good. Monitor your sadness and anger. If you get too low, you might need a medication adjustment.

"How do I track it?"

"At the end of each day write down what your mood was. If it fluctuated, say why. Bring it next week. What's your progress in achieving independence?"

"I rented an upstairs room. There's a window bump-out that gives me more light to paint. It's near downtown Ferndale."

"Sounds perfect. Will you try to sell your art?"

"I doubt it. Competition is stiff. I forgot—I entered a couple of my landscape paintings in a contest when I was in college. I won third place for both of them."

"Great," Karen said. "What about submitting a painting in the Fine Arts division at the Humboldt County Fair? It's so convenient for you since the fairgrounds are on the edge of Ferndale. You could find out what the requirements are and see if you have time to submit before the deadline."

"I'll start tonight." Elise's lips turned upward for the first time in the session.

"Okay." Karen looked at her watch. "We need to close for

today. I look forward to hearing what you find out when I see you next week."

Elise stood. "See you next time." She hurried outside to her parked car.

Butterflies filled her stomach as she drove Highway 101 south twenty miles to Ferndale. Back to art. *Could she paint well enough for a competition?*

ELISE NUKED THE plate of lasagna Janet had left in the fridge, took her dinner upstairs to her room, and sat down at her computer. A Google search brought up the website for the fair. She clicked on exhibit entry forms and found the one for fine art. The deadline was July 31. It was only June 1. If she started now, she could sketch a scene, paint it, and let it dry in time.

Elise phoned Dana. "I'm painting again and wondered if you and your family want to go with me to Shelter Cove. I'd love to paint the Cape Mendocino Lighthouse. I also want to take some pictures to refresh my memory when I work on the painting at home. There's a nice park by the ocean and we could take a picnic. What do you say?"

"Let me get back to you. I'll check with Cliff."

"Mom and Dad used to take us there. Remember?"

"Right. It's been a while though. I hate the road to the Cove. It's dangerous. Hey, instead of a picnic, how about the Marina Deli for fish 'n' chips?"

"Sounds good. Get back to me soon. Okay? Oops, sorry, that sounded bossy. Zed reminded me that I am."

"You talked to him?"

"The folks and I drove to Santa Rosa. We packed a few things and brought my BMW back here. I'll fill you in later."

"Gotcha," Dana said.

She would start the lighthouse from memory before it had been transported to Shelter Cove and restored. It was almost in ruin the last time she saw it at Cape Mendocino.

Maybe she would try something else for practice. The race track and grandstands at the fairgrounds came to mind.

She sat in the old high-backed oak chair in her room and drew. The pencil felt comfortable in her hand. The bleachers took shape. Good start. When she looked at the clock, she was surprised to see that it was already eleven. Past her bedtime and she had to work tomorrow.

"GEEZ, I FORGOT how steep this road is. The last five miles into Shelter Cove is a killer," Elise said. "I'm white-knuckled back here."

Cliff shifted the minivan into the lowest gear. "Aw, relax. You and Dana react the same way. Mark and Sammy, you're all right. Correct?"

"Yeah, Dad. We like it," the boys said in unison.

"They had to say that," Cliff said. "Otherwise, I'd beat them."

Elise laughed. "Always the tease. You wouldn't hurt your kids. And, Dana, the great protective mother, wouldn't allow it."

"I'd better watch the road. Oops, some local wants to go around us. No place to pull off though."

"They can wait," Dana said. "We're almost there. What a harrowing drive with all those switchbacks and drop-offs down the mountainside."

"I love the forested mountains and meadows we go through to get here," Elise said. "I can't wait to see the ocean. Hope there's no fog."

"You got your wish," Cliff said, as they descended into Shelter Cove. "Not a cloud in the sky. Glad you wanted us to come."

It was almost noon and Elise's stomach was growling. "Shall we grab our food first?" she asked.

Cliff pulled into a parking space and the group got out of the van. They trudged up the wood stairs to the deck. Elise noticed the people sitting at the picnic tables. Most of them were eating fish n' chips and talking and laughing. She caught a whiff of the deep-fat fried food, which brought back memories of when her parents brought her and Dana here.

She looked past the white and red lighthouse to the blue ocean, out to the fishing boats. Elise took a deep cleansing breath to smell the saltwater. *Such a lovely scene to paint.*

"I heard that the people of Shelter Cove take great pride in the lighthouse," Dana said.

"They raised money to move it piece by piece and then restore it. What a fantastic day. I feel relaxed for the first time in a month," Elise said.

They went into the deli and ordered. Once they received their food, they went outside and ate at a picnic table provided for the use of patrons. "As delicious as I remember," Elise said.

Cliff said, "Let's walk down to the tide pools. How about it, Mark and Sammy?"

"You all go," Elise said. "I want to sketch."

"Gotcha."

While the others followed the path down to the tide pools, Elise made her way to a picnic table in Mal Coombs Park where the lighthouse stood. She sketched it and captured the rays of the sun as it shone upon the beloved structure.

I'm happy.

ELISE CARRIED THE last box up the inside stairs to the room she had rented. She set it on the floor next to her closet. "I'm glad you marked the boxes when we packed, Mom."

"Me too, honey. But I told you that you didn't need to leave so soon. We're happy you're at home with us. I know how independent you are. Wouldn't want it any other way."

"You're sweet. Thanks for helping, Dad. And you too, Cliff and Dana. I couldn't have done it without you."

Elise watched her dad and Cliff lift her bedroom furniture into the cream-colored room. Tight squeeze, she thought. "I hope the loveseat fits."

Her dad said, "I think it will. What will you do for a kitchen?"

"I can use the landlord's. It's part of the agreement. I was assigned a small area of the fridge to store my food. And I can cook every evening at six-thirty. This will be a huge adjustment. But since I refuse to take Zed's money, I'll have to adjust."

"I can't believe you gave it up. This stuff about Zed and the church is ridiculous," Dana said.

"I know you don't understand, but don't tell me to reconcile."

Janet said, "Girls, I think we're all tired. Everything's been unloaded. Let's go eat."

Mom should have been a diplomat instead of a school teacher. "I appreciate what you've done today," Elise said. "Let's walk downtown to Millie's café. I want to buy dinner for all of you."

NINE

ELISE COMPLETED THE PAINTING OF THE CAPE MENDOCINO Lighthouse in Shelter Cove. Both the bottom and second level were white, the top red. The glass top used to hold the Fresnel lens, no longer in use had lit the ocean for boats. She stood back from the easel to analyze her work. It was passable considering it was her first in a long time.

She found the website of the fair again and filled out the application. She also volunteered to monitor a section of the Fine Arts building on the weekend. Some fun, she thought, in the middle of the angst of her life.

What would Zed think if he knew her course of action? She shook her head. Why think of him? Her attorney had mailed the settlement details and asked for a signature. Zed had to give her half their assets as required by California law. She was in quicksand, reaching for help.

ELISE, DANA, MARK, and Sammy entered the gates of the Humboldt County Fair in mid-August. The carnival's loud music and the squeal of the roller coaster annoyed Elise. *I'm used to silence.* A headache ensued. People stood in line to buy hotdogs, nachos, and other fair food. The cotton candy machine whirred, and the worker made large cones to sell. The smell of sugar made her want to buy one.

"It's only eleven and I can already taste a chili hot dog," Elise said.

Mark ran from the food stands to the ticket booth and back to Elise while Sammy held his aunt's hand.

"Hey boys, are you ready to ride the roller coaster?" Elise said.

"If you go with us, Aunt Lisi," Sammy said. "It's scary."

"I'll go by myself. You're such a sissy," Mark said.

"Boys, that's enough," Dana said. "Do you want to ride the merry-go-round, Sammy?"

"Yep."

"You want to take him, Elise?" Dana asked. "I'll go with Mark."

"Sure. Let's get our tickets and then we'll eat after the rides."

"Wonderful," Dana said.

Elise and Sammy looked for the horses they wanted to ride on the merry-go-round. He chose a brown horse with a white mane, head held high, and nostrils flared. Elise helped him onto the saddle. She chose the ocean blue horse next to it. When the carousel started going round and round, her young nephew said, "Giddy-up."

Elise heard Mark and Dana squeal as they crested the top of the roller coaster. They came flying down the steep slope. Up down. Up down. She laughed.

Dana returned and the four made their way to the concession stands for drinks and food.

"By the way," Dana said to Elise, "You've never said whether you placed in the fine art competition."

"They don't tell anyone beforehand. Let's eat our hotdogs, and then we'll go to the arts building and find out."

Sammy said, "Yum. Mom doesn't let us have hotdogs very often."

"Well," Elise said, "they aren't good for you. Too much fat."

"Aw. That doesn't matter."

Afterwards, they meandered through the building until they came to the oil paintings. "Here it is," Elise said. She glanced at her painting. *The hours I spent were worth it.*

"You entered the Cape Mendocino Lighthouse," Dana said. "You said you would. Oh, only third place. Better luck next time."

"Competition is stiff, and this is my first time since college. I'm delighted. I thought you'd be enthusiastic about it."

"God and church are more important than painting. You don't want to go to hell. I'm worried about you."

Elise's lips tightened. *She can't let it go.* "We've discussed this before. I'd like us to be friends without criticizing each other. Instead of focusing on me, find a job in music. Cliff said you need extra money."

"I applied to the school district, but they don't need anyone right now."

"So, be a sub," Elise said. "And you have your husband and children. They'll fill the rest of your time."

"Mom, could we go home? This is boring," Mark said.

"Yeah. I want to play computer games." Sammy pulled on Elise's blouse.

"You can wait, boys. I want Aunt Elise to see the handcrafted jewelry," Dana said.

As they wandered over to the jewelry division Dana said, "I want to see if Nick entered a piece of his jewelry." They walked a few steps down the aisle. "Here it is. He won the grand prize for this Celtic necklace. Oh, Nick, I didn't see you sitting here. Are you watching over this magnificent piece of art?"

"Have to. I don't want someone to rip it off."

"This is my sister, Elise," Dana said.

"Hey, how's it goin'?"

Elise thought Nick's stocky build and long curly hair gave him an artist's look. She eyed the necklace to judge the quality. *It looks like excellent silver. I like how the simple oval shape is looped into a semicircle.*

"It's beautiful, Nick," Elise said. "Impressive, in fact."

"Thanks. It's called a trinity knot and predates Christianity. Do you know jewelry?"

"No, but I'm an artist and pay attention to detail and quality."

Dana said, "She received third place for an oil of the Cape Mendocino Light House."

"Oh, I saw it," Nick said. "It looks like the real thing. Wait a minute. I used to know you. We had world history class together. I couldn't get you to notice me. Your name is Olsen, right? I couldn't forget your auburn hair."

"My last name is Norris now. And you have a great memory. I had forgotten that. How are you?"

"Great. I opened my jewelry store here seven years ago. I was in Los Angeles and got tired of horrific traffic and multitudes of people."

"I'm sure Ferndale is happy to have you. Your necklace stands out among the other jewelry. And the black velvet under the silver sets it off."

"Are you interested in purchasing it?"

Kind of forward. "When I make my first million, I'll let you know. I'm sorry, we need to leave. The horse races start soon, and I want a good seat."

"So, you bet on them?"

"No. But I always hope a horse not favored to win comes from behind and places first," Elise said. Even the mule races are fun to watch. Ready gang?"

"Yep," the boys said. "Come on, Mom."

"Come to my store, Nick's Silver, soon. I have a variety of jewelry suitable for any taste."

"Thanks. Nice to see you again." The kids pulled on Elise's arms, ready to see the horses. "Ready, Dana?"

"Yes. Bye, Nick."

They walked the short distance to the entrance of the race grounds and paid the small fee. Elise led the way and found the seats she wanted close to the fence and near the finish line. "Thanks for indulging me, Dana. I know this isn't your favorite part of the fair."

"Why is it important to you?"

"If the trailing horse surges ahead of the front runner and wins, it reminds me to live akin to that. And I imagine I see the will of the horse in the toss of his head and the determined look in his eyes. I want to win my personal race too."

TEN

TWO HOURS HAD PASSED, AND ELISE STOOD TO RELIEVE HER SORE butt. The folding chair was hard as a rock. Someone was supposed to relieve her from her observation point in the fine arts room at the county fair. She watched a man approach from the door and come toward her.

Zed. Her throat constricted, and her heart pounded against her chest.

His tan marked a strong contrast to his blond hair and blue eyes. From experience, she knew he took time to golf even though his schedule was hectic. His well-muscled physique showed under his polo shirt. The smell of his cologne added to his appeal. For the first time in many months, her body responded to his sexy appearance. She squelched her feelings. Simultaneously anger clutched her heart. The word *shit* rose in her throat.

He hesitated and searched her face.

"Hi." He beamed.

"He . . . hello." *Why the grin and why the hell has he come to the exhibit?*

He cleared his throat, which meant he was nervous despite his demeanor. "I, uh, I talked to Janet the other day, and she said you'd be here. I wanted to see your painting and you."

"What gives you the right to call my mom? You've got nothing to do with my family anymore."

"They were part of my life for almost ten years. I care about them and you."

"Why are you here on a Saturday? You need to be in church tomorrow, and it's a long drive from here."

"One of my associates is in charge while I'm gone. I'd love to take you to dinner and find out how you're doing. When can you leave?"

"My replacement is due anytime." Elise let out a breath she didn't know she had held. "Haven't we covered everything there is to say? We did it for months before I left."

"I've been doing a lot of thinking and want to share some thoughts with you and also apologize for how I hurt you."

"Repeat what you said. My hearing is bad."

"You heard me. Can we call a truce? I didn't come to fight with you."

Elise's heart thumped. *He must have really wanted to see me since he drove all the way from Santa Rosa.* "Okay. But don't expect anything. I still want a divorce."

"Let's put that aside for the moment."

A young man walked toward Elise. "Hi. I've got the next shift."

Elise thanked him and started toward the open door.

Zed followed. "Will you eat dinner with me?"

"Against my better judgment."

"Thanks. Is your car parked here?"

"I walked from my room."

"Ride with me," Zed said.

Elise's stomach churned. The intimacy of riding in the car with him made her hesitate. *How would I feel if he touched me after all this time?*

Zed put his hand on Elise's shoulder.

She jumped. "Don't do that. Agreed?"

"Are you afraid of me?"

Elise almost lied and then said, "Maybe. Let's go to the hotel restaurant to eat."

"If that's what you want."

Once they were at Zed's black Porsche, Elise opened the passenger side door and slid in on the beige leather seat. Luxury. Sometimes she missed her old life. It came with a price though. One she wouldn't pay again.

Elise pulled the door of the restaurant open before Zed could do it and said to the hostess, "Two for dinner."

"This way, please."

Once seated, Elise said, "I admire the handiwork of the decorative tin ceiling, but I'm not fond of the floral motif in the carpet."

"You've always liked Victorian-era furnishings. Why?" Zed asked.

"I enjoy elegance."

"Classiness would have let me open the door for you."

"We're not a couple anymore."

"I wish you'd give a little bit. I want a civil conversation about us."

"There is no *us*."

Zed studied the menu.

The server appeared. "What can I get you to drink?"

"I'd like a glass of your red house wine and a glass of water with lemon," Elise said.

"And you, sir?"

"Iced tea, please."

After the server left, Zed said, "Why the wine, Elise? We never drank when we were together. You know what the Bible says about it."

"The Bible says drunkenness is wrong, but the apostle Paul told Timothy to take a little wine for his stomach's sake. Jesus turned water into wine at the wedding in Cana. All wine is fermented." Elise leaned back in her chair and folded her arms. "I've changed, Zed. My life is my own. Not tied to a church or a denomination or their beliefs."

The server returned with their drinks. "Have you decided what to order?"

"I want the filet mignon with a baked potato," Elise said. "Separate checks, please."

"And you, sir?"

"I'll have your salmon."

"Thank you. I'll be right back."

An awkward silence ensued. Elise didn't know what to add to the conversation. *He wanted to see me. Let him say something.*

Zed cleared his throat. "It seems you want to argue with everything I ask or say. Why?"

"What more can I say to you? You disagree with me—and you must do it. You believe what Zed Norris Ministries teaches. I don't."

The server interrupted their conversation when she placed their plates of food on the table. "Let me know if you need anything."

"Thanks," Elise said. She cut her potato and buttered it.

"The problem is you refused Christian counseling and didn't pray God would heal you when you were depressed."

"Bunch of crap."

"Geez, now your language is bad. Listen, we had it good until you lay in bed most of the time. Remember how we used to tease each other and laugh about it? You loved to tickle me, and the sexual banter between us was great. Most importantly, we agreed on spiritual matters. I miss all that. Don't you?"

How much do I want to admit to Zed? Truth. I believe in truth. "Sometimes."

"I don't fully understand depression."

"You had more sympathy for the members in your congregation than you did for me. I imagine you still do. God is supposed to be about love. Your people criticized me when I was down and so did you."

"I didn't understand you. But you must admit when you told some people they were full of crap, you created animosity. They didn't deserve that and neither did I."

"You're right. But I didn't have control of my brain. I apologize."

"I'm glad to hear that, Elise."

"I read on a website that depression might involve a chemical imbalance. They recommended medication if necessary,

74

along with counseling." Zed cleared his throat. "It seems to have helped you. You look brighter. Are you less depressed?"

"Yes. You've made a start in your research. There's more to know. Can I trust you to believe me?" Elise sipped her wine.

"I promise I'll listen without interruption and at least research anything you tell me. I won't give you advice."

"This is confidential. The psychiatrist in the hospital diagnosed bipolar II. That's a milder version of bipolar I, which is extreme on the manic side."

"Oh. I've heard of it. Tell me more about it."

"It's a mood disorder. But instead of normal ups and downs in a person's psyche, depression goes deeper and without cause. The manic side of bipolar I causes many out-of-control symptoms such as promiscuity, bad relationships, gambling debts, or other things. I had light symptoms when we lived together, except for my last bout of depression. When I was manic, I overcharged our credit cards."

Zed sighed. "This is worse than I thought. You're crazy?"

"No. I'm diligent about the prescribed protocol of my drugs. Bipolar is uncontrollable in the brain, Zed, unless I have medication. Even if you learn the complexities of bipolar, it doesn't mean our relationship will be healed."

"Elise, I think if we saw a Christian counselor together, we could save our marriage. When we said our vows, we promised to love and care for each other forever."

"Let's finish our meal." *He's fooling himself about our relationship. He hasn't changed.*

Elise stared at the sidewalk as she walked home and almost bumped into other pedestrians. She had refused Zed's offer of a ride. She trudged up the stairs to her room and threw her Louis Vuitton handbag on the loveseat. *How dare Zed insult me as if he knew anything about bipolar. And why did Mom think it was okay to tell him where I'd be?* She dug her cell out of her purse and speed dialed Janet's phone.

"This is Elise, Mom."

"Honey. I'm glad you called. How are you?"

Elise drew her hand over her mouth and paced the floor. How could she get her point across without hurting Janet? "I wish you hadn't told Zed where to find me."

"He seemed down in the dumps. His voice was distraught when he asked about you. I didn't tell him where you live."

"You told him I was at the fair. He came to see me."

"Oh no. I didn't think he'd do that. What happened?"

"We went out to dinner. He still thinks we can solve our problems."

"I'm so sorry, honey. I wish you could get along."

"You and Dana think the same way, except you don't wear your religious hat. I thought you understood my position about my marriage." Elise sighed. "I don't mean to hurt you, Mom. You and Dad help me in more ways than one."

"I think my problem is that I struggle with what I learned about God and the teachings of the church Dad and I go to. It's like Zed's, you know. It's ingrained in us. And you're my daughter and I want what's best for you. Please forgive my intrusion in your personal life."

"It's okay, Mom. I don't think Zed will bother us again."

ON MONDAY, ELISE drove to Eureka to see Karen. Her conversation with Zed had rattled her. She paced the floor while waiting for Karen.

Karen opened her office door. "Ah, Elise, you'll wear the floor out by pacing. Come in."

"Sorry." Elise sat down. "Thanks for seeing me on short notice."

"I'm glad you called. What happened?"

"It's Zed." Elise related the conversation and sighed. "He doesn't get it. Now I doubt myself. He questioned the way I choose to live my life. I hate myself. Bipolar ruined my life. What if I end up crazy?"

"Didn't you learn about it in the hospital? Don't let Zed's opinion undermine the progress you've made. It's up to him to change—but he might not. Can you accept that?"

"I don't know."

"Why not?"

Elise leaned forward. "I want my life to be the way it was

before I left. I'm confused about everything."

"Your situation is difficult. Some people battle one thing at a time. You must adjust to bipolar. And you need to accept your separation from your husband and your church. You invested years of yourself in them. In time you'll find the right path. Concentrate on painting. Make new friends. There are people with similar interests and problems. If you're authentic, you'll find others that are too."

"I'll try."

"Anything else you want to talk about today? We still have time," Karen said.

Elise told Karen about Dana's reaction to her problems and decisions. "I thought of all people she would support me. I don't know why I think that though. She envied my life with Zed. Dana desired our expensive lifestyle. And she talks about my separation from Zed as if it's easy to resolve."

"Family is sometimes the most difficult when it comes to understanding about mental illness and its impact on a person's life. Does she go to the type of church you did?"

"It's similar. The more I question, the more she opposes what I say. Zed is like her."

"Can you cut her some slack? You've had to change to survive. I take it her life is on an even keel right now?"

"Her only problem seems to be she wants a job but hasn't found one yet. She whines about her lack of one. Her husband said finances are tight."

"Does she seem happy?"

"Mostly."

"Does she push your buttons?"

"Yes. And I usually retort in one way or another. I'm not always diplomatic."

"Instead of being negative with her, what can you do?"

Elise rubbed her forehead. "Maybe I can tell her I'll think about it. Would that work?"

"See if it does. Again, you need some new friends. There are other people who suffer and question life. They'd identify with you." Karen stood. "I'll see you at our regular time."

Elise bit her lip. "I didn't think therapy would be so hard."

The drive home soothed Elise. The beauty of the meadows and the mountains with the evergreen forests made her wonder if a force existed that was greater than she.

AFTER WORK ON Monday, Elise made her way to Nick's jewelry store. She wanted silver earrings that would match her favorite necklace. Perhaps he made handcrafted silver she could afford. She entered the small store.

Nick sat in an alcove in the back of the store at his desk shuffling papers. He looked up when she entered. "Hey, Elise. Have a look around. If there's something you want to buy, let me know. What are you looking for?"

"Earrings."

"Do you have a particular style in mind?"

"No. I think I'll know it when I see it."

"I'm open until six. Take your time."

Elise noticed he kept an eye on her for a while before he returned to his work. She perused the jewelry through the locked glass cabinets. *I can't afford these.* She moved to the jewelry trees on top of the cabinets that displayed the less expensive items. Sets of simple hooped earrings caught her eye, and she thought one pair in particular would go well with her necklace. "Nick, I'm ready."

"You found what you wanted?"

"For now. Thanks."

He met her at the cash register and rang up her purchase. "I'm glad you came to my shop. I wanted to ask you out for coffee the day I saw you. Thought you might consider me too forward though."

"I'm not dating right now."

"It's just coffee, Elise."

"I don't want to date anyone until my divorce is final. I take it you're single?"

"Not my choice."

"Too bad."

"Life is shit sometimes. Would a conversation over coffee violate your principles?"

"I'll have to think about that. Thanks for the thought though." *Maybe my auburn hair and light green eyes still attract men. And I'm thin again.*

"Let me know if you change your mind."

"I will." Elise turned and left the store. *Would it be improper to have coffee with Nick? At least he might be a new friend.*

ELEVEN

Zed

IN HIS OFFICE AT HOME, ZED SHOOK HIS HEAD AND SHIFTED HIS BODY to stand. "Dad, I wish I could convince Elise to stay with me. So far she refuses." He placed his phone to the other ear.

"Why?" His father's voice traveled across the miles from Colorado. "Has she forgotten her vows and your roles in the church? There are too many divorces, and pastors need to lead by example. That's what the scripture teaches, son."

"I realize that. I tried to reconcile with her. Many walls keep us from understanding each other." Zed decided not to share the issue of bipolar. "And she's bitter toward my church. Maybe God too. I went to see her in August and she won't budge. Time isn't in my favor. This is the end of October. It's been seven months since she left me. Is Satan stalking me?"

"You know he can. Mom and I will pray for you. Listen. Fly to Denver and have Thanksgiving with us. We had a good relationship with Elise. Invite her too."

In anger, Zed raised his left hand toward the ceiling, almost dropping his cell phone. "Dad, I don't feel up to celebrating Thanksgiving. I'll go to a restaurant. Tell Mom hello and give her a hug." Zed ended the call and threw his phone on the office chair. The picture of his brick facade church on the wall reminded him he had duties.

His dad and mom had pinned all their hopes and dreams on him because he was their only child. They had raised him in a church affiliated with his and hoped he would be a minister someday. *Did I fulfill their wishes, or did I receive a call from God? Why question that now? I'm ensconced in the doctrine of my church.*

Zed walked out of the house and down the front walk to the mailbox. The perennials Elise had planted in the yard were dead due to a deep frost. He groaned at the sight. They reminded him of his relationship with Elise.

The mail contained a letter from her. His breath became shallow. He ran back to his office and tore the envelope open with shaky hands. There were smeared dry spots on the letter as if Elise had shed tears while she wrote it.

Dear Zed,

Perhaps this letter will be painful for you to read, but I hope you realize it is almost more than I can bear to write it.

When we married, I thought it was forever. I was sure of what I wanted in a man, what I wanted in a marriage, and that I wanted to be part of the ministry of a church. My dreams came true. One of the highlights of my senior year in college was meeting you. Your warm blue eyes and blond hair attracted me. Your steadfast faith appealed to me. Your ability to stay calm in the ups and downs of life—something I had difficulty doing— anchored me when we were married.

It never occurred to me that I would be faced with the choices I have now. I wish that somehow, I could have been diagnosed with bipolar much earlier in my life and that medication had been prescribed. I'm sad my quest for wellness, according to the teachings of your church, was not enough and it led to this point.

You asked if I was crazy when I told you I am bipolar. Your insensitive words sealed my intention to divorce you. The papers are on the way from my attorney.

I cannot ask you to leave the church for my sake.

Elise

Zed covered his face with his hands. Hope fled like a tumbleweed caught up in a flurry of wind. *"God, where are you?"*

MONDAY EVENING DRAGGED as if Zed were on a tractor plowing acres of land. No church meetings, and his parishioners had not disturbed him. He hadn't had time to himself since Elise's letter of a week ago. He positioned himself in his desk chair to browse the Internet. His last conversation with her came to mind and he decided to search for 'new wine.' What was the definition?

He learned yeast was a natural product in grapes, and it fermented the juice as well as what was added by the winemakers. Elise was right. It was alcohol. Conflict seized his mind. Why the teaching, and how had it started? He'd look for the answer to that later.

Compelled by a need to know about bipolar, he again searched the Internet. It revealed several websites, one of which was the National Institute of Mental Health. That sounded credible. He clicked on their link. The length of the article surprised him. He scrolled down the pages as he read. Even teenagers could be afflicted. The enormity of what he read played havoc with his mind. He whispered, "You didn't listen, you fool." He tried to assuage the guilt that swept over him.

How would he have known? Nothing in seminary or church experience had prepared him for this illness. He knew Jesus performed many physical healings. And he had cast out demons. Had Jesus healed people of mental illness?

The thought occurred to him he could study psychology at the local university. It might not help his relationship with Elise. However, the people he counseled in his church might benefit. Could the attacks of Satan and lack of faith cover all the reasons people weren't healed? Perhaps the church didn't know everything after all. How far could he go with new thoughts about psychology with his parishioners? How could he reconcile the differences between psychologists and faith healing?

The next day Zed phoned the registrar at the University of San Francisco, Santa Rosa. "Could I pick up a catalog for the spring semester?"

"You'll find it online, sir."

After that Zed called his friend Joe from seminary days. "It's Zed. If you have a few minutes I want to get your advice about something."

"Of course. What's happening?"

"Did you take college courses to help you counsel your church members?"

"We had some classes in seminary. That's my basis for that kind of thing. Why?"

A shiver ran down Zed's spine. What was he getting into if he went to the university? "I thought I'd take a psychology class or two. I think it might help me when folks come to me for help. What do you think?"

"Be careful what you do. Scripture is the best way to deal with problems. I wouldn't mess with psychology. It leads people astray. Sometimes psychologists and secular counselors tell people to divorce, and they have affairs with their patients. They're off track. It masks the truth of the gospel."

THE DIVORCE PAPERS arrived in mid-December from Elise's attorney. Zed filed them in his desk drawer. Maybe in a few weeks he could muster the courage to sign them. Not now. Enthusiasm for Christmas and the special activities at the church evaded him. He had heard about the blues people experienced at Christmas. Until now, he had thought it was nonsense.

He searched his files of sermons on his computer and found some that centered on the birth of Christ. The one he had preached four years ago caught his attention. He doubted anyone would remember the specifics.

The Christmas pageant on Christmas Eve comprised of young children and live animals. He had asked the deacons to prepare a small bag containing candy and a scroll of the Christmas story for each participant. His lips turned up slightly with the thought of doing that. Children loved special treats from their pastor. He would give them the bags after the service.

ON CHRISTMAS EVE, Zed stepped behind the pulpit, and with his customary enthusiasm, greeted the congregation. Full house. He had put his depression behind him.

The children played their roles well. Mary sat on a bale of hay and held a live baby on her lap. Joseph stood next to her. The wise men knelt before the Christ child with their gifts. Angels flew through the air, manipulated by the stage crew. It was a great night for celebrating the coming of Jesus to save the world from sin.

"Merry Christmas everyone. Thank you for coming to this important celebration of Christ's birth. Glory to God in the highest and peace on earth. You know, this world tries to take Jesus out of our blessed holiday by greeting others with the words, happy holidays. If we do that, we are ashamed of the Savior. God's intent in sending Jesus was to save us from our sins and bring the message of Christ and his blessings to the world.

"Let me remind you that the wise men brought gold, frankincense, and myrrh to the baby Jesus to worship the newborn king. We need to give way and above our tithe to honor Christ. There are people less fortunate than us, and the blessings of Christ must be shown to them. Use this Christmas season to reveal to people the richness of our Lord."

Why doesn't Elise see this?

"Let's pray. Father in heaven, there are folks here who need a new house, car, and money to pay their bills. They have health problems. We know if they confess your positive words of scripture and claim your promises, they will receive abundance beyond what they think or want. In Jesus name, amen. Let's stand and sing 'Joy to the World' as we leave this service. God be with you."

At home again, Zed walked into his living room. He hadn't put up a Christmas tree because there was no one to share it with. His sermon had been meaningless to him.

Elise's family would celebrate together. He hadn't wanted to go to Colorado to be with his parents. And even though he loved Joe and his wife, who had invited him to spend Christmas day with them, his enthusiasm had waned. He hit the wall in his living room with his fist. Elise had taken the joy out of the holiday season. It was muddied with depression, and he wished it was behind him.

On Christmas day Zed drove across town to his friends' home. Joe and Mary greeted Zed at the door and invited him to join them in their spacious family room. A green sectional sofa with pillows decorated in Christmas themes brought it to life. The Christmas tree was covered in glass ornaments of every color and shape. The coffee table in front of the couch held fudge, divinity, and caramel drops along with chips and dip.

"Have a seat and help yourself to some goodies, Zed," Mary said. "May I get you a cup of hot spiced cider?"

"Sure. And thanks for the invite. I didn't want to spend Christmas day alone."

"No problem," Joe said. "Glad to have you. Sorry Elise isn't here. We've been a foursome since you were first married. Any news on that front?"

Zed swallowed a sigh. Joe's candor, which Zed usually found refreshing, irked him today. Why talk about Elise? He decided to dodge the answer. "Not much. It's the holidays, you know."

THE MIDDLE OF January came too soon. Zed entered the grounds of the one-hundred-year-old university. Aged buildings mixed with the new. He thought about what he had done by enrolling. *I'm toying with Satan by opening myself up to the idea of God not healing mental illness*. The Abnormal Psychology class overwhelmed him. The list of psychiatric disorders in *The Diagnostic and Statistical Manual of Mental Disorders*, which was the psychiatric bible, extended into the hundreds. He thought the Bible gave all the answers to life.

Could the scope of this book be accurate? What is my response to it? Where does demon possession fit in these disorders?

At home after class, Zed decided to call Joe. "Do you have time for a question or two?"

"You bet, buddy. What can I do for you?"

"We both practice Christian counseling, and I'm wondering if we deal with mental illness like we learned in seminary. How do you handle that when you're in session with people?"

"We know the Bible is true. I quote verses about how Jesus healed the sick and practiced exorcism. Once in a while, I conduct one myself."

"I've never done that," Zed said. "What was the outcome?"

"If they dedicate their life to God, the devil leaves them."

"What about normal problems, such as relationship issues with couples or their children?"

"Don't you quote scripture, Zed? This is basic seminary stuff. What brought up these issues?"

Zed didn't want to betray Elise, so he said, "I have some tough issues with a couple. I wanted to confirm I'm on the right track with them."

"You are if you're showing them the right scriptures. Keep it up and you'll see positive results. It takes time for people's faith to change."

"Thanks, Joe. I needed reassurance."

The puzzle grew in Zed's mind. Elise, even though she denounced church, had confessed to less depression due to medication. He wished he had someone else to talk to. No one came to mind.

THE DIVORCE PAPERS plagued his mind every time he opened his desk drawer. He had until mid-June, two more months, before he had to sign the papers and get them to Elise's attorney. Zed wanted more time. But Elise's letter had said it all. He didn't know how to refute what she said about him. He was the pastor of the church she now hated. He decided to hire a divorce attorney for professional guidance.

ZED'S HANDS TREMBLED when he opened the door to the office of his legal counsel, Mr. Sanders. His white hair contrasted with his navy blue suit.

"Welcome, Reverend Norris. Have a chair. What can I do for you?" he asked.

He sat opposite Sanders in a cushioned straight back chair and looked at the two walls lined with bookshelves filled with law books. He shivered. This was real. Not pretend. "My wife and I separated, and she initiated a divorce. I was served with these legal papers. I want you to look them over before I sign them. Perhaps you can verify whether they're consistent with the laws of the State of California. I want to give Elise a fair settlement, nothing more."

"Is this an amicable divorce or contentious?"

"Both. We go back and forth between the two."

"I'd advise, for the sake of my fee, that you make it amicable. I'll need some time to look them over. Are you in a hurry to get this resolved?"

"I've had the papers since December. I don't have much time left."

"One month sound okay? Not longer, unless something major materializes."

"Sure. Thanks for your time." Zed pushed back his chair and extended his hand to Sanders. "I'll look forward to a call from you."

On his way home Zed's mind focused on what he imagined he would hear from his board and congregation when he told them the divorce was in process. Some would chastise him and quote him scripture in the same vein as his father. Single members might sympathize. In the meantime, he needed to speak to his psychology professor.

ZED SAT IN the small office of Dr. Steinhouse who taught his abnormal psychology class. The professor was dressed in his usual haphazard way—his shirt hung halfway out of his pants, and his face showed a day's growth of whiskers. Books and papers were stacked everywhere. Zed introduced himself and said, "I'm one of your students and I'm also the pastor of a church. I have some questions and thought you might give me answers."

"I'm interested in your story."

Zed explained the position of his church on mental illness. "Have you seen people healed from psychiatric problems?"

"If you mean faith healing, no. Depressed people need therapy and medication. Once they work out their problems, they can stop treatment. This is not true for people with illnesses such as bipolar or schizophrenia. They'll need drugs and often counseling the rest of their lives. And they must understand how important that is. There's no cure. I consider these things forms of healing. What prompted you to take this class?"

Zed described Elise's illness. "I counsel members of my congregation if they come to me with their problems. I train church deacons to help me. We use scriptures to guide people. My inability to help my soon-to-be ex-wife troubles me. And I feel guilty." He lowered his head.

"Sounds as if you made an honest mistake. People often do when they try to help the mentally ill. The beliefs of your church hindered too. What do you intend to do with the knowledge you gain from these classes?"

Zed scratched his head. "I . . . I don't know. My goal was to understand Elise and members of my congregation. This goes against the training I had and the beliefs I've held dear my whole life."

"Are you afraid you'll sin if you study psychology and its methods of treatment?"

"I don't know. It's foreign to me."

"I'd suggest you continue to study. Complete the course and see what you think later. I know some counselors who could help you clarify your thoughts and beliefs. They wouldn't try to change you, only help you define what you believe."

"Interesting. Thanks for your time." Zed shook his professor's hand and left the office.

He drove the few miles to his church. He hoped no one wanted to schedule a counseling appointment. He didn't know what to say anymore. His secretary greeted him and handed him some messages. "Nothing too important, Pastor."

"Good. Don't direct phone calls to me until I tell you. I want time to read my Bible and pray."

Zed sat at his desk while he leafed through the gospels for a quick refresher of the stories about Jesus healing people and casting out demons. Jesus raising Lazarus from the dead stood out in his mind. Had that happened? He didn't know of anyone in modern times who had experienced it—especially after they had been dead four days. Yet Jesus had said, "The works that I do shall you do also, and greater works than these will you do." Near-death experiences weren't the same thing. *Why did Jesus wait so long to heal Lazarus?"*

The prayer Zed thought he would pray didn't emerge from his mouth. Instead, he hit the seat of his chair with his hand, fell to his knees, and cried for the first time since Elise left.

Why God? I don't understand what I believe. I want off the emotional roller coaster.

TWELVE

WARFARE ON SPIRITUAL IDEAS RAGED WITHIN ELISE. WHERE DID truth fit in with what she had been taught all her life? She decided to visit St. Mary's Episcopal Church on Easter Sunday.

She climbed the steps of the old gray wooden church built in 1928. She slipped into a pew in the nearly full sanctuary. The garb of the robed priest was foreign to her. Zed always wore an Armani navy blue suit. The adult choir filled the sanctuary with song. It stirred her to tears.

The sermon caught her off guard. Reverend Andrew McDonald preached about the resurrection of Christ. Some scholars thought it was spiritual, not physical, he had said. Elise had squelched a cry of disbelief. And he taught that the execution had come at the hands of people, not by the design of God. He said, "Would a loving father cause his son to die?" The question evoked more questions from Elise. Where did this perspective come from? Her former church taught the scriptures were the literal word of God.

After the service, the Reverend McDonald gave Elise a warm welcome, as did the other parishioners. Several invited her to coffee hour afterward. "No, thank you," she said as she glanced at her watch. "My family is waiting for me to join them for Easter brunch. I appreciate your kindness." Elise knew from experience that sometimes people tried to convince newcomers to attend the church regularly.

At home, she relaxed in her room about fifteen minutes before she headed to Dana's house. Elise covered the hot cross buns she had made yesterday in her allotted time in the kitchen, which she shared with the owners and the other renter. The promise of Dana's homemade potato salad and Janet's honey cured-ham lured Elise away from the apartment.

Cliff opened the front door. "Ah, a beggar."

"No, I brought my share of the food, you brute." She playfully tapped him on the arm.

"Okay, okay. Dana and your mom are in the kitchen, and your dad's reading in the living room. I'm going to check on the kids while you women finish the meal preparations."

He stepped aside, and Elise headed to the kitchen. "Wow, the smell of the ham heating in the oven makes me want to eat all of it."

Dana laughed. "You're in a good mood. Are you feeling better?"

"Sometimes. My legal counsel mailed the divorce papers to Zed in December. I cried." Elise bit her lip. "I haven't heard from his attorney. I'll have to call Zed. I hoped he'd do it without a reminder from me."

Janet joined the conversation. "Why did you wait until now to tell us?"

"I hate to burden you and Dana with my continuing saga with Zed."

"Please don't keep us in the dark, Elise," Janet said.

"Okay. By the way, I went to the Episcopal church this morning."

"What did you think of the church service?" Janet asked.

Elise squeezed her eyebrows together. "Well, the priest and the people were friendly."

"And?"

"To think I'd go there all the time, well, I don't know." Elise explained the essence of the sermon.

"He sounds radical," Dana said. "You're walking in dangerous territory. You'll lose your faith."

"At least the priest gave me something new to think about."

"I heard he conducts divorce recovery workshops. I don't agree with you going to one, but since you're insistent on leaving Zed, I think you should consider it."

"I'm surprised you'd suggest that since you're concerned about my beliefs."

"Ask about it," Dana said.

"I don't think I want to attend something a church sponsors. What if the leader tries to convert me? I'd get up and walk out."

"I've heard the Reverend McDonald leads it. Negative gossip about the workshop hasn't crossed my way. Go see him. Ask him how he conducts the program. Doesn't hurt. You haven't listened to me so far."

"Zed's apology helped me somewhat. After all the angry things we've said to each other, I didn't expect it. You know how it is, in the heat of the moment, your brain goes to the dictionary and finds a string of words for you to sling at each other and you don't even mean them."

"I know. Sometimes Cliff and I go at it, and then we're sorry afterwards. We're trying to learn to talk it out instead of getting mad. It isn't easy. Anyway, let's eat. Mom, please ask the guys to come to the table."

The children, her dad, and Cliff entered the dining room.

"Hey, Mark and Sammy," How are you?" Elise asked.

"Aunt Lisi, the Easter bunny gave us lots of candy. See my chocolate bunny?" Sammy asked.

"Hmm. My favorite. Do I get some?" Elise watched his smile widen as he nodded his head. "And Mark, what about you?"

"Yeah, but he gave me a Lego set too."

"Wonderful. How do you know the Easter bunny is a boy? Maybe it's a girl."

"Nah, who wants a girl Easter bunny?"

"Maybe I do."

"You're too old."

Cliff laughed. "Don't ever say that to a woman. They don't like it."

"Why?" Mark asked.

"They never tell their age. Let's eat."

Once they were seated at the table, Cliff blessed the food before they ate.

After the meal, Stephan said, "Cliff and I'll clean the kitchen. Right?"

"You bet. You women can go to the living room to visit. And Mark and Sammy, off with you to play. Save some of your Easter candy for your grandpa and me."

"Do we have to?" Mark asked.

"Of course."

Elise stood to go to the living room and gave her dad and Cliff hugs. "You're both great. I owe you one for this."

"Another bottle of wine would be great," Cliff said. His eyes twinkled.

"Since when do you drink?"

"Oh, we looked at scripture after we knew you imbibed. We agree with you. Because of the kids, we don't do it often."

"I'm truly surprised. I'll bring it next time I come," Elise said. She followed Dana and Janet into the living room by the fireplace.

"Elise, give us the scoop," Janet said. "What did your letter to Zed say? You've never told us."

Elise repeated a small version of her correspondence to Zed. "And he's a pastor. It's his calling and unless he changes his beliefs about faith, prosperity, and healing, I can't imagine reconciling with him."

"Honesty is the best way to live," Janet said.

"I think so. This is the first part of April. He needs to return the divorce papers by mid-June. I've waited long enough, and I have no hope of reconciliation."

"Since we're being candid, I want to discuss something with both of you," Janet said. "This isn't a final decision, but you need to know. Dad and I are considering attending a different kind of church."

"What the . . . ?" Dana said as she stood. She raised her voice. "Why? Has Elise influenced you?"

"Calm down, Dana," Janet said. "This isn't a final decision."

Dana gesticulated with her hands. "It's Elise this and Elise that. I heard it growing up."

"Dana," Janet said. "We've given you the same attention we always gave Elise. Please sit down."

"As you wish."

Elise looked to Dana and then Janet. "Why do you want to change churches?"

"Your time in the hospital petrified us. You almost died. We researched bipolar disorder. There's no cure. The way our church teaches, healing doesn't fit with what we found."

"There're consequences, Mom. Don't be hasty," Elise said.

AT THE BEGINNING of June, Elise phoned Zed. "It's Elise."

"I suppose you're wondering where the divorce papers are."

"You've had them long enough."

"I had my lawyer look at the papers. And he reviewed the financial settlement with me. We need to sell the house and divide the equity."

"I haven't received papers that require my signature to sell the house. Where are they?"

"My attorney will send them. You'll get half of everything we own. But I want us to work on our issues. We'll see a counselor together. A non-Christian one if you want."

"If that was the only issue, I'd go. You know it isn't, so sign the damn papers and let us both go on to other things. I want my share of the money. And you need to see reason."

"Do you love me, Elise? The Bible says love is the most important thing—love of God, others, and ourselves."

Zed's words sounded familiar. They were the voice of a pastor coaching a parishioner, not a wife. "I've heard those words before, Zed. I want the details of the divorce settled. You'll hear from my lawyer again. And sign the damn divorce papers." She clicked off her phone.

ELISE LEFT GOLDEN Gait Mercantile after work and enjoyed the pansies the merchants had planted in pots outside their stores. She ambled down the street a few doors and entered Nick's Silver.

"Hey, how's it going?" Nick said.

"All right. How about for you?"

"I've only seen you to say short hellos, and you haven't come back to the shop."

"I'm busy working and doing other things. So, well, you invited me to go with you for a cup of coffee months back. Is . . . is that offer still good?" Elise chewed her lip. She wanted a friend, someone who would listen to her. She hadn't met anyone else. Maybe he already had someone. *What more do I want from him, if anything?*

"How about Chinese at the new restaurant after I close the shop? If you're free, that is."

"Love to."

"Hang on a minute while I shut down my computer and put the closed sign in the window." Nick's quick movements had the tasks done without delay.

He talked very little while they strolled to the restaurant, which gave Elise time to reflect.

Nick opened the door for her. "Right this way, Miss."

"I wish that were true," she responded.

"No divorce yet?"

"Soon."

"Let's sit down." Nick pulled out a chair for Elise. "We can talk more after we order. What sounds good to you?"

"I don't know. Maybe honey walnut prawns."

"I like mu shu pork. Isn't the décor great? Even the Buddha, with the offerings to him, appeals to me. See the red lanterns hanging from the ceiling? I think it's meaningful to them. Not sure why though." After they ordered, Nick said, "You're still waiting?"

"Unfortunately."

"Unlike Zed, my ex and I wanted it to be over," Nick said. "She stepped out on me and I didn't want to see her again. They left town."

"Why did you leave Los Angeles?"

"I came back here to get away from the big city. I sold more jewelry there, but I hated the way a lot of people cater to Hollywood. Your auburn hair is beautiful, by the way. A lot of bleached blonds where I came from."

"It's natural. Maybe when I turn gray, I'll dye it. Here's our food. Do you want to share it?"

"No thanks. I like my mu shu pork. Dig in. Where are you from? Most recently, that is?"

"Santa Rosa. I was there several years. I'm glad to be back home. The tight community spirit here appeals to me. And the Victorian architecture is delightful."

"Don't you mind that everyone knows your business?"

"Sometimes. Since I've been away, new people have settled here, and I don't know who's friends with who. Overall, it's okay." Elise gathered her thoughts. Nick seemed like a nice guy. Time would tell whether she would go out with him again. "I learned there's an art association here," she said.

"There is. The Ferndale Art Guild. Your art must be reviewed by a panel of judges. I'm a member. It takes a while to be accepted. They want quality work and I don't blame them. I can get you an application if you want."

"I'm not ready for that. I hoped for a less formal group for now."

"You're in luck. We have that too. We call ourselves Aspiring Artists. Do you have a business card? I can contact you when we get together next."

"I don't have one. I'll give you my number and email."

"I knew there was a way to get your number." He winked. Nick typed them into his cell phone. "We're always looking for new members to help promote the arts."

"Thanks. I'll look forward to your call. I'd enjoy the group." Elise looked at her watch. "I need to go home. I want to do some research on the Internet."

Nick signaled for the server. "May we have our bill now? To Elise he said, "Let's do it again."

Elise twisted the end of her hair. "Yes. And thanks for the food. Delicious."

Nick reached for her hand. "I enjoyed getting better acquainted."

"Me too."

At home, Elise switched on her computer and searched the Internet. Was Jesus' resurrection spiritual or physical? Sources she hadn't dreamed of materialized. She noted that some websites originated from Christian fundamentalists. She looked further. An Episcopalian bishop had written a book on the subject. Elise found it on Amazon. She used the "look inside" feature and perused the table of contents. Interest grew. The website brought up other books on related topics, and she put some of those in her Wish List. She ordered the clergyman's book on resurrection and put a rush on the shipment. A warm glow filled her. At least this might educate her on what others believed.

THE NEXT DAY Elise phoned the Episcopal church office. "Hi. This is Elise Norris. I need some information about the divorce recovery workshop you conduct."

"I'll connect you with the priest. He teaches it."

"Thanks."

"This is Reverend McDonald."

"I'm interested in your divorce class. Is it open to the community? And if so, do you try to convert people to your faith?"

"Anyone can attend. And no, I don't proselytize. I use a secular book on grief. Everyone receives a workbook and homework assignments. Does that help?"

"Do you talk about God?"

"Not unless a participant raises a question, then I give my opinion. The emphasis of the class is on healing the wounds of divorce. How each person does that is a matter of personal choice."

"So, you don't talk about God on a regular basis."

"No. My purpose is to lead people out of their suffering to a place of wholeness. Some who attend never go to church."

"That doesn't bother you?"

"No. God is in charge of people's lives. Not me. I hope you'll come to class."

"When does it start?"

"Tonight. Seven-thirty."

"That's timely. I'll think about it."

After dinner, Elise walked the few blocks to the church. The fog had rolled in from the coast, and she pulled her coat collar up. Her stomach churned. She hated new situations.

The class was held in the church's Community Life Center. She opened the door and walked toward an open door across the hall. She almost fell over when she saw Nick. He waved and offered her a chair next to him. It was the only chair available in the small circle of five people. Elise coughed. Anonymity was no longer an option.

Reverend McDonald led the discussion. "I want to establish the rules of this group in our first meeting. I expect everyone to understand this is a confidential meeting. Don't discuss the problems or issues presented in the group with anyone outside these walls. Do you have questions about that?" No one spoke. "Let's begin with introductions. State your first name and how long you've been separated or divorced," he said with a smile.

Elise cleared her throat. "Elise. Separated. I've lost track."

"Margaret. Three years." Her words were tight and controlled.

"Shelly. Two and a half years." She dressed in sloppy clothes and had a stringy ponytail, no makeup, and a few wrinkles.

"Kathy. One year." She talked through clenched teeth and admitted she was bitter.

"Nick. One year."

"I'm divorced and remarried," McDonald said. "I know many of the feelings you've experienced or will. I'm using a book, which you all get a copy of, called *The Stages of Grief: A Means to Heal from Divorce.* They are denial, anger, bargaining, depression, and acceptance. These are also the stages people go through who experience the death of a loved one. I want to emphasize that people do not experience these emotions in sequence. You might start with depression or maybe denial instead. The point is to deal with each emotion as it comes."

Elise looked around as the other four nodded their heads.

"We'll talk about depression tonight, which brings symptoms of sadness, hopelessness, despair, and other feelings," McDonald said. "My belief is that when we experience any of these emotions for two weeks or more, we need medication and counseling. If you haven't availed yourself of treatment, please do so. Often, people experience depression along with the other symptoms until they accept their divorce. That brings true freedom.

"Plan to do some emotional work in this class. That's the hard part. Read the chapter about depression before the next class and answer the questions at the end. We'll use your responses as a springboard for discussion next week. Please join me for coffee and cookies, and if you don't know each other already, I suggest you introduce yourselves since we'll be in class together."

The small talk among the class helped, Elise thought. After she finished her refreshments, she waved goodbye to Nick. However, he joined her at the door. "May I walk you home?"

"Sure." Elise looked up at the sky. "Too bad it's foggy. Otherwise, we'd see a multitude of stars. The universe makes my problems seem small."

"True. So, what do you think of the class?"

"It's nice to know I'm not alone in my struggles. At least the Reverend has experience in what he teaches. I'd hate to sit in this class if the instructor had textbook learning only."

"Yep. I like that too."

They walked the few blocks to Elise's home. "I have a room here, Nick. See you next week in class."

"Hold on." He took a step forward and placed his hands on her shoulders and kissed her. "Sleep well."

"Nick, I—"

"Don't speak. See you soon."

Inside her room, Elise poured herself a glass of wine and sat on her loveseat and reflected on Nick's kiss. She liked the intimacy and glow of it. She felt special for the first time in a long while.

A kindred spirit flowed through her as she thought about each person in the class. There were thousands of divorced people in the world and meeting some of them gave her a sense of belonging. Regrets. She probably wasn't the only one who said, "If only. What might have been?" She knew she needed the group and was glad Nick attended too. Perhaps they could be friends. Maybe more.

ON HER WAY to Eureka to see Karen on Monday, Elise hit the accelerator and the speedometer rose to eighty miles an hour. Damn, if she wasn't mad at Zed. Why did he think she would come back to him if he prolonged the divorce proceedings?

She heard the siren before she saw the patrolman behind her. Another damn escaped her lips. An excuse formed in her mind and she knew it would be a lie. Damn Zed. Damn, damn, damn. She pulled over on the shoulder and lowered the passenger side window when the officer approached. "I'm sorry, sir. I know I shouldn't speed." She started to tell him that her grandmother was dying in the hospital.

"Your driver's license, ma'am, and car registration."

"Yes, sir." She dug around in the glove box and retrieved the registration from a folder. She pulled her license from her wallet. The officer took them and walked back to his car. Elise wondered if he thought she was a criminal. She looked in her rearview mirror and saw him come toward her.

"You have a clean record, Ms. Norris. I'll give you a warning this time. If you do it again, you'll pay a large fine. You've been driving long enough to know how dangerous it is to speed."

"Yes, sir. Thank you." The policeman walked away. Drops of sweat ran down her face. She sank against the back of the seat and blew out a breath. She needed to talk to Karen.

AT KAREN'S OFFICE, Elise drew a deep breath. Honesty again.

Karen opened her door. "Elise. Come in and sit down."

Out of habit, Elise chose her usual chair. She crossed and uncrossed her legs and picked at imaginary lint on her slacks.

"How are things, Elise?"

"I'm so mad I could spit. I woke up angry. If Zed stalls this divorce again, I don't know what I'll do. I had to call him to find out why he hadn't signed the papers. He wants me back. He can't seem to get it through his dinosaur brain that I want out of this marriage. And I almost got a speeding ticket on the way here. Not good."

"Not to mention you put yourself in danger," Karen said. "If you wake up angry, beat a pillow, or scream into it when that happens. Anything that's safe. Don't injure yourself or anyone else. You need to journal it too. Write when you get home this evening."

"I know you're right. I'm furious though."

"Have you felt this way before?"

"Only with Zed. It terrifies me."

"You have to get it out. Why do you think Zed is stalling the divorce?" Karen asked. "He says he wants you back. Is that all? Or is there more?"

"I imagine his parents put him under pressure to reconcile. And Zed's a strong believer in what's right according to God's word. His parents take it to the extreme. Maybe he's ashamed that he can't straighten us out, or me, to be more exact. Besides all that, he's a procrastinator. Drives me nuts."

"What are you going to do about it?" Karen asked.

"I think he'll concede in the end. If he doesn't comply, I'll drive down to see him."

THIRTEEN

ELISE'S CELL RANG. CALLER ID SHOWED IT WAS NICK. "HI."

"Hey, yourself. Have I caught you at a good time?"

"I just finished dinner."

"The next Aspiring Artists meeting is next week. Any chance you want to attend?"

"I'm not sure I qualify. I've painted a couple more pictures, landscapes of the scenery between here and Eureka, but I'm not sure they're good."

"It's an informal group, not a juried show. Come on, don't say no."

"Are the people friendly?" Elise asked.

"Most of them. Ginny comes across as abrupt at first. She loosens up once you get to know her. So, how about it?"

"Where, what day and time?"

"Next Tuesday evening at the Episcopal Community Life Center. They're great about letting us use a room. I'll meet you there, say seven forty-five."

"I suppose this is the best way to meet more people."

"Yes. Change of subject. See you tomorrow night at the divorce workshop?"

"We're talking about denial, right?" Elise asked.

"Yep. I'll pick you up, if you don't mind."

"You don't have to do that."

"See you at seven-thirty. Bye," Nick said.

Elise heard the click before she could refuse. She thought of the artists' meeting and bit her nail. What if they didn't accept a former pastor's wife as one of them? She rubbed the back of her neck. Sometimes people quit swearing in front of her when they found out she was a minister's wife. The ones who didn't apologize for their behavior or speech obtained her approval.

Elise grabbed her new book from Amazon on spiritual resurrection and decided to read in bed. When she put on an old nightshirt, she thought of Zed. He would hate this crappy torn cotton gown. He had enjoyed the sexy transparent ones she had worn. Everything had to be classy as far as he was concerned, even if it wasn't comfortable.

She had trouble concentrating on the book and set it aside, hoping sleep came soon. However, her stomach knotted, and her mind shifted to Zed, the impending divorce, bipolar, therapy, spiritual issues, and the condemnation from Dana. Would the artists think she was a nutcase if they knew her story? They might fall into the same category as her sister. Karen's empathy and that of Janet's encouraged her. She paid a counselor to listen, and well, mothers loved you no matter what. At least hers did.

The alarm on her cell phone blasted Elise out of her semi-conscious state the next morning. She fumbled for the unwelcome sound and pressed the off button. For a couple of minutes, she thought about calling Ed to plead a vicious headache and take the day off. She half rolled out of bed and struggled to find her robe. Coffee. She must make coffee.

Once the instant coffee made its way to her stomach, the thoughts of the night and the havoc they had played in her mind lessened. She knew that the upcoming Divorce Recovery Workshop that night explained some of the reasons for her restlessness.

AFTER WORK, ELISE chose khaki pants and a pink knit top for the workshop. Her hands shook when she inserted her gold earrings. She didn't want to look troubled. A good image often projected confidence and well-being.

At Nick's first knock, Elise answered the door. "Hi, Nick. What's this?" she said as he handed her a bouquet of red and white carnations.

"My way of saying thanks for your good company. That's all. I'll wait here at the door while you put them in water."

"No, have a seat." Elise motioned to the loveseat. "I'll get a vase and then we can be on our way. You didn't have to do this you know. Thanks."

As she put the flowers in a vase, Nick said, "Are you okay? You have dark circles under your eyes. Did you sleep well last night?"

Elise's eyes widened. She forgot to mask them with makeup. *Stupid mistake.* "I'm okay."

"Are you sure?"

Offended by his attention to her eyes, Elise stiffened her shoulders. "I'm sure. Shall we go?"

"If you're ready." He opened the door and Elise walked through with her head held high. She didn't want him to know she had almost changed her mind about the meeting.

At the workshop, Nick led Elise to a chair and sat in the one next to it. Elise whispered, "Maybe we should separate. People will get the wrong idea about us."

"That's okay with me." Nick's face lit up as bright as a full moon. "Time to start."

The Reverend joined them in the circle of chairs and started the meeting. "I'll define denial first. Then we'll talk in groups of two. I prefer you choose someone you don't know."

"Denial is the refusal to acknowledge truth or reality. This can be the truth about yourself or about others. In divorce, both parties often fall prey to this. Especially when a spouse says, 'I never loved you,' the injured party often denies this is true. And thus ensues an accounting of the way love was shown." McDonald continued. "There are, of course, myriad reasons for divorce. Each of you has yours. Questions? No? Let's pair off for discussions on denial."

Elise saw the lady with the messy hair and sloppy clothes

who kept her head down. Maybe she would talk. Elise could sit and nod her head instead of revealing her inner secrets. "Hi, I'm Elise. I've forgotten your name."

"Shelly." She didn't look at Elise.

"What did you think of the definition of denial?"

"Not much. You?"

Great. What next? Another tactic. "Are you separated or divorced?" Silence. "Did you leave your husband, or did he leave you?"

"He said he loved someone else," Shelly said. "I don't believe it though. I don't care what Reverend McDonald says."

"Why do you think he still loves you?"

"We grew up together. We were neighbors. We attended the same church. We dated through high school and college. We did everything together. How can he not love me?" Shelly finally raised her head and looked at Elise.

"I don't know. Are you in denial?"

"No!" Shelly said, loud enough for everyone to hear.

Elise wanted to crawl under her chair. "Well, I guess we don't have anything to discuss."

Shelly answered. "You didn't say anything about yourself. That's not fair."

"You're right. I left my husband."

"Why?" Shelly's eyes bored into Elise's.

"He didn't understand me."

"Why?" Shelly asked.

Elise shifted in her chair and felt her legs twitch. She couldn't talk to Shelly. Her whys made Elise uneasy. *I want a different partner.* "Don't know. He wants me to come back. Thinks we can work things out."

"Why?"

Why the whys? How about a different word? "Says love is more important. Maybe he's in denial."

"Are you?" asked Shelly.

"I don't think so. I want a divorce."

NICK MET ELISE at the bottom of the stairs in the Golden Gait Mercantile at noon the next day. "What are you doing here?" she asked.

"Nice greeting for a friend. I thought we'd go to lunch together."

"Oh?"

"I thought we were friends, Elise. What's the matter?"

"You surprised me. Sorry. I had another night of insomnia. I'm annoyed with myself."

"Lunch with a friend might help," Nick said.

"Could we grab a sandwich and go to Fireman's Park? Maybe the fresh air would do me good."

"Sure. The deli has great sandwiches," Nick said.

They walked down the street and into the deli. At the counter, Nick asked, "What do you want?"

"The turkey with cranberry sauce looks good. What about you? By the way, I'll pay. You have to put up with my crabby personality today."

"I invited you. What do you want to drink?"

"Diet Coke."

Elise opened the door and they made their way down Berding Street and walked the short distance to Fireman's Park. The green grass and picnic tables invited adults and children to enjoy the summer sunshine. A baseball diamond, basketball court, and bocce ball lanes provided entertainment for the adults. The children's play center was full of youngsters. Their mothers talked among themselves as they watched their kids.

Elise said, "I love the smell of fresh-cut grass." She breathed deep and let the peaceful view engulf her. "Let's sit at this table. We can see most of the activity."

"Fine with me."

Nick scooted up by Elise on the bench. He leaned in and kissed her.

Caught off guard, Elise breathed deep. "Nick. I—"

"Don't say anything. Let's eat."

"Nick, let's cool it a little bit."

"Sorry. Your soft full lips entice me. And you smell of

lavender. I can't resist you." He winked at her.

Elise couldn't help enjoying his good nature and humor. And the kiss? Her lips had tingled. She grinned. "Tell me how your conversation went with the person you paired with at the workshop last night."

"I told her I'm still angry with my ex. The denial part didn't resonate with me at this point. It would have when my wife first left. I thought she'd come back to me then. I asked her to go to counseling and she wouldn't. What about you?"

"Zed still wants to reconcile. I can't and won't. He says he understands me a little better. A *little* isn't enough."

"Did you leave him?"

Elise hesitated. *How much do I want to reveal to him?* "Yes. I was ill, and he thought God would heal me."

"Why would that cause a divorce?"

"It's a long story. We don't have time over lunch. I need to get back to work."

"Come on. You have twenty minutes yet. Spill."

Elise squared her shoulders. "My husband's a minister—"

"You're joking, right?" He touched Elise's arm. "I can't imagine."

Elise slipped off the picnic bench. She stood. "I thought we were having an honest discussion. Did I miss something?"

"Sorry. Please sit down."

"Okay. I'll give you a brief synopsis." She chose to leave out her bipolar disorder and that she was seeing a therapist on a regular basis.

"So, you're home trying to figure everything out. Right?"

"At least some of it. I do know I won't go back to Zed."

THE WEEK HAD passed. Elise practiced short sentences that described who she was and what she did while she made her way to the Aspiring Artists meeting. A soft breeze from the west cooled the summer air, and she breathed deeply. Out loud, to herself, she said, "Hello, I'm Elise Norris. I work at the Golden Gait Mercantile and paint oils in my spare time." Perhaps she could get others to talk about themselves. Most people loved to do that. She had avoided personal questions during her duties as a pastor's wife with that technique.

Elise opened the main door to the Community Life Center. The room down the hall was open and she heard laughter. She stumbled and then righted herself. *Calm, be calm.* She broke out in a sweat and wiped her forehead. *Silly me. Nick said everyone is nice except Ginny. What am I worried about?*

Nick stood in the doorway. "Elise, I'm glad you made it."

"Nick. Hi."

"Come in. I'll introduce you to a few people before we get started." Elise felt the pressure of Nick's hand on her back.

"Don't touch me, Nick. Remember what I said?" Part of her wanted the intimacy. It had been so long since Zed had responded in that way.

"Sorry. When you're ready, say so."

Elise sighed. "Okay. Now introduce me."

"Follow me." He led Elise to a woman, maybe late twenties, in hiking boots and khaki carpenter's shorts. "Ginny, this is Elise Norris. She grew up here but moved away. Ginny is a great photographer. We have show and tell at our meetings. Did you bring a photo, Ginny?"

"Yes." To Elise, she said, "What's your field of interest?"

"Oil painting. Landscapes for the most part. I've done a portrait or two."

"Did you bring one tonight?"

"No. Nick didn't tell me about that part."

"I thought I'd let her off the hook the first time here. She won an award at the county fair last year for a painting."

"She should go home and get it," Ginny said. "The purpose of being here is to show your art. Why didn't you explain that, Nick?"

"Ah, Ginny, she doesn't have time to go home. Give it a rest."

"Sorry. I'm too abrupt sometimes. What brings you to Ferndale?" Ginny asked.

"My parents and sister live here. How long have you been in town?"

"About four years."

"Almost time to start," Nick said. "Let's get some coffee, Elise. Excuse us, Ginny."

"Fine with me. Nice to meet you, Ginny."

They walked to the counter and chose a couple of raisin cookies. They stood a moment conversing. "Why is she rude, Nick?"

"I don't know. Don't let her get to you. Wait until you see her photos. Let's sit down."

"Hey everyone, let's welcome a first-timer, Elise Norris," Nick said. "Hopefully, she'll be back."

Elise's cheeks flushed pink. She looked at her peers in the circle. "Oh, I know Jimmy. Hey, remember, we were in econ together. Nice to see you."

"I didn't know you were an artist."

"I studied it in college, and I dabbled in painting from the time I was in middle school."

She continued her search. "And Tyler. Is that really you? You've let your hair grow. I remember a short style because you played basketball."

"Yeah. I like longer hair now."

"I'm sorry, I don't recognize the rest of you. Anyone else know me?" They shook their heads. *Glad that's over.*

Nick continued. "As usual, we'll make the rounds. There are ten of us tonight, or nine, since Elise isn't showing. We'll give our honest comments to each person. Ginny, let's start with you."

Ginny pulled an eight-by-ten color photo out of a folder and passed it around.

Elise studied the picture when it was handed to her. "Damn," she gasped, then held her head down. *Why did I let that out of my mouth?* Teenage girls with short skirts and stilettos stood on a street corner. Some were smoking cigarettes and their faces, plastered with makeup, had a come-hither look. Prostitutes. Where did Ginny get a group of girls that allowed that kind of photo of them to be taken by a stranger? Elise looked at Ginny, who lifted her head and shrugged her shoulders.

"What's the matter, Elise? You've seen hookers before."

"I haven't. I've, well, I've avoided that side of life. Why did you take their picture?"

"My art is the realism of the streets."

Nick intervened. "We don't need to explain or defend our art here. Please limit your remarks to the quality of the work. What do you think, Elise?"

"I'm sorry, Ginny. This photo jarred me into a different world. I imagine that's the effect you wanted."

"That's right."

"Any other comments?" Nick asked as he looked around the circle.

Most of the people awarded the photo accolades. One man said, "You nailed it, Ginny. You always do."

Elise paid attention to the quality of work the others in the group showed. Some people were beginners. One person painted with watercolors and others with acrylics or oils. The herd of Roosevelt elk in the meadow farther north of Eureka made her long to drive there and see them again.

"My turn," Nick said. "I'm working on a set of jewelry. I finished the earrings, but I still need to craft the necklace and bracelet. Maybe next time."

"Bring the oil of the lighthouse next time, Elise. It's good enough to show."

"I'll think about it."

Elise hurried out the door before Nick had a chance to escort her home. She wanted to think about their relationship.

AFTER WORK THE next day, Elise hurriedly sorted the mail on the kitchen counter. A letter from Zed.

Dear Elise,

My attorney is mailing you the papers for you to sign to sell our house. I'll put the house on the market, and you'll receive half the equity. I think we'll receive a good price since you decorated it with neutral colors. The upgrades on the air conditioning and furnace should help, and so will the updated kitchen. The realtor said the granite countertops will clinch a sale.

I have to say one more time that I love you. Perhaps it's too late to save our marriage. I'm continuing to study psychology. I hope to understand my church members better. I want to be a better listener too.

I didn't want to sign the divorce papers, but I did.

Write to me from time to time.

Love,

Zed

Elise sat in her rocker and stared at the letter as if it were a puzzle to be solved. She had what she wanted, didn't she? Nothing seemed right.

FOURTEEN

Zed

ZED SAT AT HIS KITCHEN TABLE AND REFLECTED ON THE UPCOMING annual business meeting of the church. His throat closed as dread built within him.

His recent sermons had caused dissension in the congregation. He waffled on the ideology that faith and money led to a prosperous life and good health when he preached.

One parishioner, Mary Walker, had said, after he preached a sermon on suffering being part of life, "I'm relieved you sometimes preach that Christianity is not the great fixer of all problems. I've had two heart attacks and had to retire from work. I read the Bible and found that Paul the Apostle suffered and so did Job. I almost quit coming to church over your health and wealth sermons."

But some of the most vocal congregants opposed his teachings about difficult lives even though he used scripture to back up his points. They were the big contributors to the church in terms of both money and volunteer work. *Maybe the psychology classes have influenced me too much.*

Zed had taken time, though it was painful, to read books on suffering. His experience with Elise showed him not everyone was healed. His pat answers to people's problems hadn't helped them.

Zed put his head in his hands. *God, I've taught that you supply every need if we've given of our talents, money, time, and love. I don't know what truth is anymore. I wonder what you think of me.*

He drew his hands down his face and muttered, "I still don't understand Elise. Can depression put a person in bed and take away the will to live?"

He used to count on Elise sitting in the congregation. Her soothing words at home and her hugs and kisses helped him get perspective on troublesome problems.

Zed tilted his head and pursed his lips. Before he had changed his ideologies in his sermons, the issues at the business meetings had more to do with what color to paint the church or whether to serve communion every Sunday morning. These things weren't as important as helping hungry people or victims of a disaster.

The main focus of the church was to lead people to Christ. Disappointment settled around him like dense fog. Many of the homeless people who ate in the soup kitchen did not change their ways or believe in Christ. When he asked homeless Rick if he wanted to go to a shelter, the answer surprised him.

"Hey, man, are you kiddin' me? I can't use drugs if I go there."

"Don't you want a better life?" Zed had asked. "Intelligence shines from your eyes. Do you have an education?"

"Maybe. I ain't sayin'."

"Turn your life to Jesus. You'll have a home and a good job. That's all you have to do. Christ honors our faith," Zed had said.

"Yeah, maybe someday. I ain't ready yet."

Zed couldn't believe it.

His church had had a missionary to Africa speak about the poverty, civil war, and AIDS that ravaged parts of the continent. He had said in his sermon on a Sunday morning, "I want to see that change. I know God can help us."

"Amen," the congregation had almost shouted.

He had continued, "I've watched so many die. I concluded

the people needed education, jobs, and good health care in order to thrive. I still believe in the message of salvation, with the caveat that it should be accompanied by practical improvements. If God speaks to you about doing something in Africa, think about giving to my mission in Ethiopia or a similar one that also teaches people how to improve their lives."

No amen. Dead silence. Zed rubbed his jaw. *What was I thinking, bringing in a missionary like that?*

Some changes in his way of thinking since Elise left had occurred. However, she still censored him, as did a growing number of people in his church, though for different reasons. Elder James Prescott shunned Zed except when the board convened. Zed worried how James would act in the upcoming church business meeting.

THE BUSINESS MEETING took place in the church's sanctuary. Out of the 1,500 who attended church, more than 800 members were in attendance. James Prescott, clad in a Gucci gray suit, opened in prayer. "God give us your wisdom in the decisions we make tonight. May your will be done. In Jesus name I pray. Amen." He handed Zed, the moderator of the meeting, the microphone to call the meeting to order and sat down.

Zed looked out at the congregation. "We have a quorum. Thanks for coming." Then he perused the five-point agenda. The final item was an open forum, which invited people to ask questions or bring new business to the floor. Based on the rumblings he had heard, Zed thought that at least one of the elders, at the prompting of several people, would quiz him on what some called his socialistic stance.

To Zed's relief, the first part of the meeting was calm and routine. Finally, with reluctance, he said, "We're ready for the open forum. Keep your statement short. We'll then open it for discussion. If someone wants to make a motion to bring a new item for a vote, they can. It would, of course, have to be seconded, discussed, and then voted on by a show of hands."

James's hand shot into the air.

"Yes, James," Zed said.

"Some of us are concerned about some of your teachings of late. You've preached that the message of riches in modern Christianity needs to be balanced with scripture that teaches we'll have problems of various kinds in our lives. Jesus' death on the cross did away with the human condition if we believe. God doesn't want us to be poor or sick. That missionary from Ethiopia is wrong. I don't know why you invited him."

Zed was glad the contention revealed itself. He didn't want the congregation to split over his teachings. He asked Prescott, "What is your definition of prosperity?"

"You . . . you're putting me on the spot, Zed."

"It's good to get an opinion from you, and anyone else who wants to speak. Then I'll follow with mine."

"I'd rather not answer. However, I will. It means affluence. It's to show nonbelievers they need Christ."

"Anyone else want to respond?" No one replied.

Zed continued, "In the parable of the rich man, Jesus asks him to give up his riches and follow him. Was that a literal command Jesus meant for all of us to follow? Perhaps opulence got in the way of the wealthy man's ability to follow Christ's teachings. Does wealth get in our way? Do we sacrifice relationships with others for success? I think the Bible asks us to be responsible for the quality of time we spend with our families. If that means we earn less money to accomplish this, let's do it."

"Your marriage failed, Pastor," James said. "You're not a good example. Where's your faith?"

"That's personal. I asked Elise to return to me. She won't. I admit I didn't understand her sometimes. I've asked her to forgive me." Zed paced back and forth across the front of the church.

"Let's think about faith healing for a moment. We know some people are healed through medicine. However, it isn't the type of miracle we see in the Bible. And Jesus said he didn't want to be followed because he performed miracles. He desires that we love one another.

"I believe God has the power to change lives that want to be changed. The keyword here is want. Does the drug addict want to kick his habit? Does he want to enter a rehabilitation facility and do the required work? As you know I've been taking a psychology class. I've done this for two reasons. I want to understand Elise better and improve my pastoral counseling."

James Prescott interrupted. "Are you going to say you think all problems are psychological and not spiritual?"

"No. Please let me finish. I think all of us need to adhere to the teachings of Jesus as well as the Ten Commandments. Christianity would be easier to follow if it were made up of black-and-white answers."

"What happened to your faith?" Prescott asked.

"You're out of order. Please be courteous in any comments you make."

On the other side of the aisle, a woman raised her hand. Zed acknowledged her. "Yes, Nancy."

"I'm wondering what James thinks of me? Um, I have diabetes. I believe God could heal me. Until he does, though, I'm going to take the insulin. Otherwise, I'll die. And what about the missionary who talked about Ethiopia? I like what he said."

James stood, red in the face. "Maybe you don't have enough faith," he said. "And I think the Africans need to believe God for a better life. Maybe they need to give more money. The Bible says God will prosper us if we give our offerings to him."

"Order," Zed said, raising his voice. "Let's not let this degenerate into something that we'll be ashamed of later. I believe each of you made a point."

Amos raised his hand. "I've been in this church for twenty years and volunteer doing maintenance on our building." He worked as a contractor and was well respected in the community. Zed motioned for him to continue. "Well, I've been thinking, Pastor. Elise put you through hell. Seems to me that this summer you need to take a two-week vacation, plus go to the retreat for ministers. You could think about how you want to lead this church. You, know? I make a motion to that effect."

Zed's throat tightened. He didn't want to go on vacation by himself or attend the upcoming ministers' retreat. He decided to go along with it to keep peace. "Is there a second to Amos's motion?"

"Second," Prescott said.

"Let's see what others have to say on this," Zed said. "Yes, Kyle."

"I think James and Amos are right. Elise came close to ruining your career, and I think you need a break to sort things out. You've been a good pastor, and most of us think you got the raw end of the deal."

Kyle irritated Zed. Rather than having opinions of his own, he voiced what others said. "Is there any other discussion?" Zed said. He looked around at the audience. No one raised their hand to speak.

"Okay," Zed replied. "Those in favor, raise your hand."

Two-thirds of the congregation raised their hands.

"Those opposed, raise your hands. It is carried. Thank you for recognizing my needs. I appreciate it."

"On a different note, let's take a straw vote. By a show of hands, who opposes my current teaching about suffering?"

Zed's mouth dropped open. Almost three-fourths of the congregation raised their hands. He had estimated one-third.

AN HOUR LATER Zed pulled into the three-car garage of his five-bedroom home. He opened the door to the kitchen from the garage and slammed it hard. "Hell! I. Won't. Go." *Where did the swear word came from?*

"See what you've done to me, Elise?" he raged. "I'm irritated, and I want to use ugly words when I think of how you left me. If I weren't a minister, maybe I'd swear more, or throw things. I know I misunderstood you. Please, please, why couldn't we have worked this out?"

He had always had Elise at his side at retreats. This would be his first one without her. Sometimes married pastors and their wives ignored single ministers due to their fear of sexual misconduct.

And vacation? He and Elise had enjoyed their trips. They both loved nature and had cruised to Alaska for ten days. The sights were spectacular, their lovemaking, passionate. Her mood was up on that trip, and it showed in the glow on her face. On formal dress night, his black tuxedo complemented her ocean-blue dress. She loved the flow of the waltz and wanted to dance. They were raised to believe that dancing was evil because it led to sex. Even though married couples could dance, they didn't know how. He didn't want to make a fool of himself so he told her no and saw her face droop. Elise liked to go with the flow too much.

Zed enjoyed being married most of the time. Elise had wanted children and grand-children. She had seen a fertility specialist because they had no children after five years of marriage. Her tests were normal.

The doctor had asked him to come in and be tested. He had refused because he knew it wasn't his fault. Elise had cried. Her letter made him question some things that he had not let surface before he received it. His emphasis had been on making her want to come back so they could go on with their life the way it was. Now he was questioning his behavior, and it didn't feel good. He had always been confident he was right. He followed God and served him to the best of his ability. Not that he didn't make mistakes. Here he was living the single life without the benefit of dating or the hope of finding a partner again.

He hit the wall and made a small dent on it. "Hell and damnation, what am I going to do?" he yelled.

Elise thinks she lost a lot. She at least has the option of getting married again. "I have to live the rest of my life going to church affairs without a spouse, always on the outside of the circle of married people because my church says I can't get married again," he said aloud.

Exhausted, he made a cup of instant coffee and took it into the living room to drink. What had he learned from fellow ministers? After a big loss, there was a time of grieving.

Sleep eluded him until four in the morning. Zed groaned as the alarm sounded at seven o'clock. He shut it off and got out of bed. Perhaps he needed a therapist too. He realized now that he had delayed the inevitable by thinking Elise would come back to him once he understood her. Where was his life headed now?

FIFTEEN

Elise

ELISE FIDGETED IN THE CHAIR IN KAREN'S OFFICE, BOWED HER HEAD, and bit a nail. She slapped her hand. *Bad habit.*

"What's happening, Elise?" Karen asked.

"I paint, go to the divorce recovery work-shop, attend Aspiring Artist's meeting, and see Nick on a regular basis." Elise avoided Karen's eyes.

"What's the topic of discussion in the recovery workshop now? You've covered depression and denial." Karen lowered her head to catch Elise's eyes.

"Oh, I don't know. The usual stuff." Elise raised her head.

"And?"

"That's about it." Elise crossed her arms as if to hold Karen back. The tension seemed audible.

"Oh?"

"Not much to say."

"You're being evasive."

"I think I've spilled my guts enough. I don't need counseling anymore."

"Why do you think you're ready to stop?"

"Therapy's damn hard. I don't deserve this." Elise chewed on the inside of her cheeks.

"Does anyone? What's bothering you?"

"It's not important."

"Elise?" Karen leaned forward. She touched Elise's arm and then withdrew her hand.

The story came out in one big whoosh. "Okay, okay." Elise's shoulders drooped. "My former church doesn't ordain women. I was a teenager when God called me to be a minister. I met Zed when he was in seminary, and we fell in love. He became a pastor. Being his wife was the closest I came to fulfilling my call. I loved my life. It was my whole identity. Now I don't know who I am anymore." Elise covered her face. The weight of it all crushed her as if she were covered by sand on a beach.

"Another big hole in your heart. You've waited many months to tell me this story. Do you know why?"

"It's all been a jumble—mixed up and crazy in my mind. In the last couple of weeks, I realized I don't receive much satisfaction from my life, except in painting." Elise wrung her hands. "At first I was desperate to get away from Zed and the church. I suffocated from both."

"So, now your loss of the ministry bubbled to the surface."

Elise blew her nose.

"What are your thoughts about your previous life?"

"I loved Zed . . . with all my heart. I enjoyed marriage and going to church. I loved God."

"What do you want from life now, Elise?" Karen looked at her notes.

"I don't know. I'm in a deep chasm. I can't climb out. However, I'm still skeptical about God. And I need a career. I don't want to be a secretary the rest of my life."

Karen shuffled her notes on Elise that were in the file folder on her lap. She made hurried notes on her yellow pad before she said, "Let's talk about the loss of your call to the ministry. It created a vacuum in your life. Your time with Zed didn't quite fulfill what God wanted from you. You started a soup kitchen. It shows leadership skills. I believe you have the ability to find a new direction for your life. You're not the only one who searches for significance in their life."

"I'm not?"

"If you're interested, I'll loan you a book about a nun who

got pregnant. She went through hell in the convent and they kicked her out. Want to read it?"

"Maybe."

Karen retrieved the book from the shelf and handed it to Elise. "Back to your calling. Did you know Episcopalians have women priests? Talk to Reverend McDonald about your situation."

"I don't know if he'd understand." Elise rocked back and forth in her chair.

"He might not. Based on what you've said about his empathy in the divorce workshop, I think he'd be kind. At least give it some thought."

"All right."

"You've been working hard. How about a fresh cup of coffee? I brewed a pot just before you came, and I'm dying for a cup."

"Sounds great." Elise stood. "I think I'll take a closer look at your pictures. Monet is probably my favorite artist. The subtlety soothes my spirit."

"Yes. I relax when I look at them," Karen said. "These are prints. Can't afford the originals. Here's a funny story. I went to an art show in Southern California where they were selling the work of the peers of the great Impressionists. They thought I had money and were quite attentive. They dropped me when they realized I wasn't going to buy. The prices were thirty thousand and up. I laughed and left."

"Zed and I paid as much as twenty thousand dollars for some of our art. Now it seems ludicrous. That money could have helped the poor. Zed Norris Ministries is more interested in showing its wealth than helping people."

Elise sipped her coffee. "Love the taste. What kind is it?"

"Black Thunder. Is it too strong for you?"

"Just right."

"Well, back to work. Shall we?" Karen asked as she sat down. "Have you journaled about your loss of the ministry and the kinds of things you saw that went against your principles?"

"No."

"Try it. You might make some decisions based on what

you write, and you'll understand yourself better." Karen jotted down some notes.

"I don't know if I'll ever recover."

"Look back and see how far you've come. You'll have setbacks. The thing is, you're still better than when I first saw you. Someday you might want to read what you wrote. You'll be amazed at your recovery. Do you know there are art therapists? Their clients use different forms of art to express their emotions. What story would you tell in your paintings? You know, something people could relate to."

"Pain. Damnable pain," Elise said. "Who wants to see or buy that?"

"I don't know. The paintings would be for your benefit, not others."

Elise smiled. "I'll think about it."

"Good. We have a little time yet. Tell me how things are between you and Nick."

"I'm attracted to him, but I don't know if I want more. He's handsome in his own way and kind." She smoothed her hair. "Since he's divorced, we struggle with similar feelings even though our reasons for divorce are different."

"Does your love of Zed stand in the way?"

"Probably. Nick kissed me a few times. At that point I wasn't divorced, and I told him not to do it again. But I enjoyed it."

"Is it wise to see him?"

"Sometimes I ache for a close relationship with a man." Elise hugged herself.

"You're both vulnerable right now. I hope you won't rush into something new." Karen looked at her watch. "You've done well today, Elise. You didn't want to be here, and yet you revealed a significant problem. I want to see you in one week instead of two. We have a new issue to delve into."

Elise seethed on the way home to Ferndale. She screamed. "Why is life so hard?" Perhaps she shouldn't pop into Nick's shop or invite him to lunch or dinner, but she needed a friend.

That evening Elise sat on her loveseat with a notebook and pen. The words flowed.

God,

If you exist, why did you call me to the ministry? I promised to spend a lifetime in church work. I thought you wanted that. The Bible tells about people who served their whole lives. The disciples served Jesus until they died. I'm lost. I don't know who I am or what to do. What does it mean to serve you?

Elise

BY THE TIME Elise met Nick for dinner a few days later, she had researched Judaism, Christianity, and Islam via the Internet. She agreed with some theological ideas in each religion. She steamed with anger about some beliefs. Orthodox Judaism was still patriarchal. Islam said women were important. Yet the teachings made most Muslim women subservient to men. Some factions of Christianity believed women shouldn't do anything in the church. The three religions shared some beliefs, particularly in the Old Testament. Abraham was important to all of them. *If more people emphasized their commonalities, there might be less misunderstanding among them.*

On other dogmas she was neutral. How did a person live with the ambiguities of life and maintain any kind of faith in God? The black-and-white answers were the easiest to believe. Then she, and others, could condemn everyone else to hell.

THE CAFÉ WAS busy. Nick sat at a small table tucked away in the corner. She saw a bottle of wine on the table, which made her nervous. This wasn't a romantic dinner as far as she was concerned. It was a search-for-answers time.

"Hi, Nick," she said when she sat down. "This table might be quieter than the other ones."

"Yep. I ordered a bottle of wine. You mentioned once you favor cabernet, and they happen to have a nice one on the wine list."

"I'm not sure wine is a good idea for a serious conversation."

"It's Friday night, Elise. You can relax. I'm not going to

seduce you in public," he said with a grin. "I might give it a try later."

"I like you, Nick. And enjoy your attention, but our relationship is about friendship for me."

"I have selective hearing. Anyway, let's order."

Once they received their salads, Elise elaborated on what she'd learned from her research. "Nick, I can see why you don't want to go to church. There's a great division between some religions. I'm confused as to what I believe. I'm not sure there's a god. I want to mesh my new research with what I once believed."

Nick rubbed his forehead. "It seems to me that if you want to go to church, you'll need to find one that is at least tolerant of other religions. Have you ever asked yourself how a righteous god can send millions of people to hell? Did you know that if a person is born into a religion, it is rare for them to change the way they believe?"

"I've never thought about that," Elise said. "I was taught that Jesus is the only way to God. Maybe I need to rethink that issue."

"Most religions believe their way is the only one. I told you from the beginning I'm not a spiritual person."

"You don't seem opposed to God."

"I've never gone to church. Don't intend to. Leave it at that."

Elise realized she had overstepped her bounds and was relieved to see the server bring their entrée. "I'm famished. The wine will go well with the spaghetti." She sipped the cabernet and then put her fork into the pasta and twisted it on the spoon. Nick seemed intent on his food. "Did I offend you? I didn't mean to.

"I don't want to talk about religion. I only know a little bit, and the subject isn't my favorite. I've seen good people hurt by it, and you're one of them. Maybe I'll be interested in God when hell freezes over."

"Oh, I'm sorry."

"Not a problem. Just promise you'll see me again," Nick said and winked. "Let's do something fun next time."

Elise laughed. "Depends on what you mean by fun."

ELISE TOOK A deep breath and knocked on the door to Reverend McDonald's office.

"Come in. You're right on time," he said.

"I'm always prompt." Elise slid into the chair at the side of his old oak desk and waited for the priest to speak.

"You didn't say on the phone what you wanted to talk about. How can I help you?" Reverend McDonald folded his hands as if in prayer.

"I have some questions about God's call to the ministry. What would you say to someone whose vocation ended with divorce?"

"Are you talking about yourself?"

"Myself and others." Elise probed his dark brown eyes for possible wisdom.

"Tough question. Were you a minister?"

"No, but my ex-husband is, and I had a major role in helping him." Elise related her part in Zed's ministry. She held back her tears.

"Did you feel called to the ministry?"

"When I was a teenager, I did. I miss my role in church, but it ended before we divorced."

"Some churches ordain women. Have you considered going to seminary to qualify for the ministry?" Reverend McDonald asked.

"I believed a woman's place in the church was teaching Sunday School or working in the soup kitchen. It doesn't matter now. I don't believe in God anymore."

"So why are you questioning this now?"

Reverend McDonald's kind voice appealed to Elise. "Well, I think it's because I'm not helping people with their problems. And I wonder if God really called me to the ministry. My emotions are mixed."

"Did you think of this as a lifetime call?"

"That's what my ex-church, as well as others, teach."

"The Bible usually doesn't give the age of the priest or the preacher as to when they started their ministry or at what age they may have died. The word of God is vague on this issue. Since you were taught it was a forever career, maybe you could rethink that teaching."

"That's hard, but I'll give it some thought," Elise said.

"I suggest you find another outlet for service. Eureka might be a good place to start. They have programs for homeless people and drug addicts. There are other needs too."

"Do you have information you could give me about the opportunities?"

The reverend opened his desk drawer and handed Elise several pamphlets. "Maybe these will help."

"I like what you said about a call to the ministry. I'll think about it."

"Good. Do you have other questions?"

"Not right now. Thanks for your time." *I don't think I'm ready to reach out to people, but at least I can call some of these places and see what their requirements are for someone like me.*

Back in her one-room apartment, Elise pulled a bottle of wine from the electric cooler she had bought. Isolation overwhelmed her. A year had passed. Time hadn't lessened her loneliness at night.

SIXTEEN

ELISE GAZED AT THE SIDEWALK AND LET HER HAIR FALL IN FRONT OF her face as she walked the five blocks to the Aspiring Artists meeting. Nausea threatened. She clutched the painting of the Cape Mendocino lighthouse. What would the other creative people have to say when they judged her painting? The crisp ocean breeze failed to refresh her anxious mind.

She entered the community building and saw Ginny and another woman just inside the door of their meeting room. "Hi Ginny," Elise said. She nodded at the other woman who wore tight jeans and a shirt splattered with paint. "I'm sorry, I forget your name."

"I'm Angela." A smile crossed her face. "I see you brought a painting. That's great."

"Yes. I'll see what everyone thinks of it."

Ginny said, "Could we get a preview? Sorry I was rude the first time we met. I was frustrated about something that happened."

"That's okay," Elise said. She turned the painting around, which she had held close to her body.

"It's good," Ginny said. "I didn't know what to expect. Sometimes Nick overstates the quality of a person's work if he's interested in them."

Angela chimed in. "The thing is, we all improve with time, Nick included."

"I know I need help with my art," Elise said as she chewed her lip. *I hope they're kind in their criticism.*

Ginny said, "Are you scared to show the group?"

"Somewhat. It's hard for me to take criticism."

"It's as if someone tells you your child is inadequate. We work hard to make it our best, and then someone tells us it's not good enough," Ginny said.

Angela said, "She's right. Well, I'll leave you two to talk. I want coffee before we start. Hey, Nick just came through the door."

"I thought you'd come with Elise," Ginny said.

"I had a late customer. How are you, Elise? Sorry I couldn't swing by to pick you up."

"No problem. I'm getting better acquainted with Ginny and Angela."

"Almost everyone is here," Nick said. "Let's start."

Elise bit a fingernail and chose to sit between Ginny and Angela instead of by Nick. *Cool things off a bit.*

Nick raised his voice. "Let's seat ourselves. We'll visit later. Let's tend to business first. How many of you will be at the next meeting? It's vacation time." About half raised their hands. "Shall we skip next month or continue as usual?"

"When we started the group, we said we'd meet regardless of the number," Ginny said. "I want to enter a photo in a contest."

"Anyone object?" No one responded. "Let's get started. Any good news to share?"

Angela raised her hand. "Three people bought my art cards. They found me through my webpage and blog."

The group applauded. Nice, Elise thought. *They support each other. I think I'll enjoy these people.*

"Who has art to show?" Nick smiled.

Elise's throat closed part way. "I'll sh . . . show mine. It's not very good though." She held her painting up for all to see. She held her breath. "Any comments?"

"I'd make the lighthouse colors more vivid. And strengthen

the sunlight showing through the lens," one person said.

"I agree," Ginny said. "And since it shows sunshine, I'd deepen the blue of the ocean. The perspective of the painting is good. That's all I'd change, which is simple enough."

The others in the group agreed with the nod of their heads.

"Thanks. I see what you mean," Elise said. "You've given me some good things to think about. I'll try to have another painting ready for the next meeting. And I'll bring this one back after I touch it up."

Elise watched as others displayed their art. The comments were helpful, not rude. After the last person took their turn, Elise slipped out of the meeting. She didn't want Nick to choose her over the others to converse with.

A WEEK LATER Elise listened to Reverend McDonald open the meeting at the Divorce Recovery Workshop. He said, "If you did your homework from a week ago, you know we'll discuss bargaining tonight. Sometimes we plead with our spouse before the divorce not to leave. We promise we'll change, or we ask him or her to go to counseling. We know it didn't work for anyone here. Right?" Everyone nodded. "Also, we often negotiate with God to prevent the split. What did you do? Are you still pleading? If so, let's discuss the issue. Anyone want to volunteer?"

Elise raised her hand. "I didn't bargain because I left my husband. Not too long ago he tried to tell me he had changed. I don't believe him. One of the reasons I left him is he didn't help me when extreme depression suffocated my mind. Zed's church says God heals everyone. I couldn't take it anymore."

"Your husband is the bargainer," Reverend McDonald said. "How does that make you feel?"

"Conflicted and angry. He doesn't understand me. And yet, when he says he's sorry or that he's changed, I think I'm wrong and should go back to him. He can't change what he preaches though. The church might fire him."

"I can see why you're frustrated," Reverend McDonald said. "Anyone else want to share?"

"My wife had an affair," Nick said. "I didn't bargain with

her. I was so angry I wanted her to leave after she refused to go to counseling with me."

Shelly said, "I've pleaded with my husband to come back. We've been together since we were teenagers. He says he doesn't love me. It's not true. The divorce isn't final, and he has a girlfriend. I don't understand. I've told God I'll do anything he wants me to do if only he'll bring back Ted."

"Has it helped?" the Reverend said.

"Not yet."

"I think bargaining is a way to control or manipulate a situation or people. I'm not speaking of negotiation. That includes both parties working toward similar goals. What happens when we bargain with our spouse before our divorce or even afterward? Do we receive what we want? For instance, maybe I divorced my wife because she had affairs. She bargains with me. Says she won't do it again. I take her back and she does it again. I'm the loser. I should have accepted that I couldn't fix her. Who else wants to speak?"

Bob raised his hand. "I'm just an old dairy farmer, but I love my wife. She's a good person. Our personalities clash, and we fight all the time. How can I get her to go to counseling?"

"Is she willing to go?" the Reverend said.

"No. She wants out of the marriage. Our children are suffering though. I want to fix it for them."

"What are your options?"

"None, I guess."

"That brings me to next week's discussion. Acceptance. Do your homework, which will make you analyze why you have or haven't come to that point. Let's have our refreshments."

Elise said hello to Shelly and out of the corner of her eye saw Nick approach. *What shall I say to him?*

Nick said, "Excuse me, Shelly, I want to speak to Elise."

"Sure."

Elise stepped a few feet away and looked at Nick.

"You didn't sit with me at the art meeting and you didn't tonight. What's going on?"

"Now isn't the time to talk about it. Walk me home and I'll fill you in."

"You ready to leave now?"

"Yes." Elise caught the attention of Shelley and the Reverend and waved goodbye.

Once outside, Nick said, "Spill. What's wrong?"

As they walked to the house Elise stayed in, she said, "I believe you want more than friendship. I'm not ready for that. I think we should cool our relationship."

"I feel chemistry between us. You responded when I kissed you."

"Most women would. You're a handsome man with a good personality. Quit pushing me. My problems are complicated, and I don't want them muddied by a romance with you. Can you understand that?"

"Maybe. You can't accept what happened to you."

"You might be right. If you decide friendship is all you want, call me." She turned away from him. "I think we should call it a night."

"Wait a minute, Elise. Let's talk."

"Okay."

"Give me another chance. I think we're good friends too. Let's not throw that away."

"You're right," Elise said. I'll see you at the next Aspiring Artists meeting."

THE NEXT WEEK Elise punched in the phone number of Ginny Channing. She got voice mail, and with a slight hesitation, invited her to have snacks. "If you don't mind, I want to pick your brain about art, and especially the kind of photos you take. If you don't mind eating off my coffee table, I'd love to have you come to my one-room apartment. Give me a ring."

Elise slid onto her stool and worked on her new sketch—another drawing that would turn into a painting. Her cell phone rang, interrupting her. She said, "Ooh, just when I'm getting started." She grabbed the phone and said in a clipped tone, "Elise."

"Hi, it's Ginny. I'll bet you're working, and I disturbed you. I can tell by your voice."

"Oh, I didn't mean to sound abrupt. You're right. I'm in the middle of a sketch. I'll stop for a few minutes."

"I don't answer when I work. Anyway, I accept your invitation. When and what time?"

"Does next Thursday work for you?" Elise asked.

"Yes."

"Seven okay?"

"Fine."

Wow, as easy as that, Elise thought as she shut her phone off. She went back to her sketch. *What would represent emotional pain?* To show her paintings, even to the group of Ferndale artists, meant exposing herself—naked in a world that might not understand.

She felt a power surge through her hands. An image came to mind, and she picked up her pencil from the easel shelf. She drew the face of a young woman. Her eyes were squeezed shut, and tears coursed down her cheeks. The lips formed an O as if someone had plunged a knife in her back.

Elise sat back and looked at the sketch. Her cheeks were damp, and she wiped them with a paint rag.

THE NEXT NIGHT Elise surveyed a new outline of a picture. The idea had come to her in the shower that morning. She imagined a church building, which stood in the background, quite small, with a dilapidated frame. A few shingles from the roof lay on the ground. The wood siding was bare. A minister, in a suit of black, holding a Bible high over his head, stood on the dirt path leading from the church. His cheekbones were prominent, like President Lincoln's, and his lips dragged at the corners. He pointed at an old woman with a wrinkled face, white hair, and a hunched back. She wore a faded dress and scuffed shoes. The caption over the preacher's head said, "If you don't give your tithe to the church, God won't bless you." The woman said, "But Pastor, I have little food and can hardly pay my rent."

Elise stood and backed away from the sketch. Many pastors made giving money a requirement of membership.

They said people everywhere are going to hell. Give to this church so others can be saved. *What kind of Christianity was that? Guilt, always guilt in one way or another.*

GINNY'S KNOCK ON the door caused Elise's heart to beat faster. "Hi. Come in. I made a tray of goodies for us." An army-green tee hugged Ginny's muscular body. It was paired with brown cargo shorts and heavy hiking boots. Her hair, brown with blond highlights, was cropped. Elise felt overdressed in her white knee-length shorts, black V-necked knit top, and black flats. Ginny plopped down on the loveseat in front of the TV tray.

"I'm a bit hungry. How did you know I love slightly melted brie with honey and walnuts? The honey smells like clover."

"I didn't, but it's a favorite of mine."

"What sounds good to drink? I have wine, Coke, and iced tea."

"The tea."

"Sweetened?"

"Plain."

Elise munched on grapes while she thought about what to say next. *Should I plunge ahead with my questions or let the conversation develop?*

She didn't have to say anything. Ginny talked. "Good use of your space by placing your easel to receive the best light from your window. I use my big screen computer to edit my photos."

"I paint on weekends during the day. As you can see, I have lamps placed in strategic places in case it's gloomy. Where's your studio?"

"Second floor of my home in a large room. I added two more windows for better light after I print the photos. And I use my computer to edit them in Photoshop. I do little of that because I want the natural effect."

"Great!" Elise said, trying to sound enthusiastic even though jealousy stabbed her heart. She wished she had a separate room to paint in. "Do you support yourself with your photos of street people? Or is that an impertinent question?"

"I subsidize my income with a small inheritance from an aunt. I'm greedy for more though. I want to raise money for a project in Afghanistan to stop the growth of opium. The farmers are slaves to the stuff. It's their bread and butter."

"You're ambitious. What holds your interest in the subject?"

Ginny stood and paced the floor. "My brother's a druggie. Stoned most of the time on the streets of Eureka."

"How awful. What gave you the courage to tell the story of drugs?"

"Pure anger. So much damn anger I could spit. Oops. Sorry for the language. I'll bet you don't swear."

"Sometimes."

"You look innocent," Ginny said, her angular chin softened by a smile. "Now, it's your turn. Show me your work if you want an honest opinion. I don't mince words. You already know that though."

Elise flinched. Ginny was abrupt about everything. Elise chewed her lower lip as she got up and walked to the easel. She uncovered her two sketches and handed them to Ginny. She saw her eyes move from side to side and up and down her work. Ginny gave them back to Elise and walked to the window. She stared down at the sidewalk before she turned back to Elise.

"Damn it, you're angry too. You have a theme, and if you expand it, I think you could sell these if you're in the right place. They show more passion than the landscape I saw. What's your story?"

"It's a long one. I'll give you the short version. Painting about it is my newfound freedom. I'm not sure I have the courage to sell my work," Elise said, looking at her feet.

"Look at me, Elise. There's a price to pay for working through pain. Recovering drug addicts work hard to make a new life. Then the rewards come. Depends on how bad you want it. I'll help you."

For the next half hour, with Ginny leading, they talked about politics and the economy. Elise changed the subject during a lapse and asked, "How did you get a following of your work?"

"I started a blog. Have a website, too, which a professional in Eureka set up for me. I get a lot of hits and sell quite a few photos. Keeps me busy. Through all that I got connected to an art gallery in San Francisco."

"You're amazing," Elise said.

"No, I just work my butt off. You can too."

They finished dessert and Ginny laid her dessert plate on the coffee table. "Sorry, I have a meeting to go to—Narcotics Anonymous. I used to do drugs, and it helps me keep my perspective about my brother." She walked to the door. "I'll be in touch."

Elise carried the leftovers and dishes down to the kitchen. *How do I work through the pain? I hate doing that. It hurts. What would my former compatriots in church think of my art? Do I have the nerve to expose myself?*

IT WAS HARD for Elise to believe another week had passed. The topic for the Divorce Recovery Workshop tonight was anger. Elise had thought about staying home. When Ginny had seen Elise's two sketches, her reaction had stunned her. 'You're angry too, Elise.' The words haunted her. She recognized how her deep anger had led to her current life.

Except for Reverend McDonald, Elise was the first to arrive at the Divorce Recovery Workshop.

"Hi, Elise," the Reverend said. "Coffee's ready if you want some."

"Thanks." Elise helped herself to a steaming cup and poured a little cream in it. She sipped it on her way to a chair.

"How are you doing?" McDonald asked.

"Oh, I'm confused about anger."

"Do you want to discuss it before the others come? We have about ten minutes."

"Anger is a religious issue for me. I grew up believing it was evil. And that we had to resolve it before going to bed at night. It seems like I squelch it, and then suddenly I erupt in unhealthy ways."

"Were you taught Jesus never got angry?"

"Oh, definitely. He supposedly had righteous indignation instead," Elise said.

"And you're questioning that?"

"Right."

"I think Jesus was angry at times. As you know, besides fuming interactions with the money changers at the temple, his wrath with the Pharisees is obvious in the New Testament."

"Where did he show anger against them?" Elise asked.

"When the Pharisees came to him to be baptized in Matthew's gospel, he called them a brood of snakes who were depending on their lineage from Abraham to help them escape God's wrath."

"I never thought of any of those things," Elise said.

"Anger is a normal reaction to various people or circumstances in our lives. It serves us well when it spurs us to positive action, but destructive behavior to ourselves or others is a sin. You mentioned not going to bed angry. In the book of Ephesians in the New Testament, there's a verse that says, 'Be angry, but do not sin.' This indicates it's okay to be angry if we don't hurt anyone, ourselves included."

"Thanks. Your explanations help me. I often feel guilty when I'm angry. And I do know I've hurt others with my hateful words."

"That's quite an admission. I'm glad we discussed this, Elise."

"Would you mind if I skipped the session tonight? I'd like to go home and look at the scriptures you alluded to."

"Not a problem for me. Here's something you might want to consider too. Read the scriptures about Jesus being reluctant to heal the sick sometimes—and when the Syrophoenician came to him for healing, he called her a dog."

"Are you sure he was like that?"

"We always want to view Jesus as the good shepherd. But he was human as well as divine. It's a difficult dichotomy."

"I'll research what you told me. It gives me something new to think about. I'll see you next week."

Lost in thought, Elise left the room as the other workshop

members started to arrive. She stumbled against Nick.

"Elise, what's up?"

"Oops. Sorry I bumped into you. I'll be at the next workshop." She hurried toward the door of the Community Center, unwilling to stop for anyone else.

At home, Elise grabbed her Bible from her small bookshelf and used the concordance in the back of the holy book to find the scriptures Reverend McDonald had mentioned. She worked until midnight reading every instance of anger and healing she could find. *Maybe it's time I thought of Jesus being human.*

SEVENTEEN

Zed

ZED BOARDED THE PLANE AT SAN FRANCISCO INTERNATIONAL Airport with the other ministers and religious educators—all Protestant. He was embarking on the vacation his congregation had demanded he take. His knees wobbled with fear and yet he smiled as if he was a kindergartner going to his first day of school. "Thank you, Jesus, for this trip." He wondered how he would relate to Christians outside his church's doctrine. Considerate of the impatient passengers behind him, Zed half stumbled into his aisle seat.

Once they were in the air, the man in the middle seat who had balding gray hair and a wrinkled face, nodded at Zed. He extended his hand. "Greg Morgan. This lady by the window is my friend, Abbie Smith."

Late thirties, maybe. Tanned skin and dark brown hair. No wedding ring. "Hey, I'm Zed Norris, pastor of Zed Norris Ministries." He gestured with his hands. "I'm so excited about this trip. Have either of you visited Israel before?"

"No," Greg said. "When I heard about this trip, I called Abbie. She and I serve on an ecumenical committee in San Francisco, and we've become friends."

Ecumenical? "So, how long have you been in the ministry, Greg?"

"Thirty years. I'm about ready to retire."

"That's great. I'll bet a lot of people have been saved. Eight years of immense success for me. Are you an educator, Abbie?"

"I'm an Episcopal priest and have served for seven years in a church of two hundred in San Francisco."

Zed's mouth dropped open. *A woman priest?* "I've never met a lady minister."

She laughed. "Close your mouth, Zed. This is the twenty-first century. There are women in all facets of ministry. What does your church believe about women in the ministry?"

"We don't ordain women, and they can't serve as elders. In I Corinthians 14:34, the scriptures say women are to be silent in the church. I believe that."

"My denomination and Greg's believe women have equal rights. There were women in the Old and New Testaments who had significant leadership roles. Paul the apostle said in Christ there is neither male or female or bond or free. And if you study women's history, in ancient times, they were revered by men because they had babies. People didn't know pregnancy was due to marital relations. The Bible is a product of patriarchal society. And church history shows men were cruel to women. Enough on that. I annoy some people."

What the heck? Who does she think she is? Elise didn't talk like that. "Let's not argue."

"Sorry. I came across too strong. My undergraduate degree is in women's history. Not pretty. I'm defensive sometimes."

Greg said, "My degree at a Presbyterian seminary included studying the cultures of the Old Testament and New Testament times. The practices of people who surrounded the Israelites and dominated them influenced the religion of the Jews. Something to keep in mind. And some of the Biblical Hebrew words and Greek New Testament words have different meanings than what got translated to English. I'm sure you know that. But let's drop this subject. Our commonality is in Christ. And we're here to enjoy. Sorry, I like to preach, and it shows."

"No problem," Zed said, "Can't wait to see Jerusalem."

"I'm with you on that. By the way, my work with the ecumenical committee exposes me to many fine men and women of various Protestant and Catholic faiths—

Abbie said, "Hey, Zed, we need a pastor who believes in the literal translation of the Bible on our team. Want to join?"

Would they criticize me? "No thanks."

Greg said, "I hope you're not uncomfortable. There are fine men of God in some of those churches even though I don't agree with all of their teachings."

"What church are you from, Greg?" Zed asked.

"Presbyterian. We believe the Bible is more about general concepts. We take scriptures as a whole, not verse by verse. Don't let us put you off, Zed. We enjoy conversation with our peers."

"Thanks."

Abbie softened her voice. "Do you know there are many faiths represented in Jerusalem and other parts of Israel, Zed?"

"News to me."

Greg interjected, "I'm old and still learning." He grinned and tapped his head. "I may be balding, but I try to keep the old brain working."

Zed's jaws relaxed. "I hope this trip helps me sort things out. I have questions. Big ones." *Why did I blurt that out?*

"I know what you mean, Zed," Abbie said. "I've doubted many times. I've come through. Your faith will be stronger." She reached across Greg and patted Zed's arm.

Zed nodded, not sure he liked Abbie's touch. Only a girlfriend or wife would do that. Greg looked like a loving grandpa. He exuded warmth and tried to make people feel at ease. Zed reclined in his seat and closed his eyes. Maybe he could discuss his church problems with Greg.

AT BEN GURION International Airport on the outskirts of Tel Aviv, the tour group of fifteen gathered their luggage and boarded the small bus to Jerusalem. They passed through an Israeli checkpoint that had an armed soldier inside a booth.

Zed turned to Greg in the seat next to him. "Wow, they're serious about security."

"Looks like it."

Their tour leader, Emmanuel Salazar, who was the pastor of a growing Hispanic church in San Francisco, turned in his seat to face the group. His dark eyes twinkled as he spoke through his microphone. "To your left is Palestinian territory. You can identify that by the wire fence topped with barbed wire. Farther down you'll see the Israeli prison for terrorists. And not too far from there is a Jewish settlement inside the West Bank. A manned security tower is inside it."

The Israeli-Palestinian conflict is real, Zed thought. Trouble everywhere including his life. He pushed away the sadness that threatened to overwhelm him.

When the bus entered Jerusalem, the passengers clapped. Zed couldn't believe he was in the Holy City, one of the places Jesus had ministered. "Thank you, God." He turned to Greg. "Hey, across the street there's a shopping mall named Mamilla. It looks upscale. I'd like to browse the shops."

"Maybe you'll have time. I can't afford it."

"Oh." *This isn't a megachurch pastor. I'm inconsiderate.*

Salazar used the microphone in the bus and said, "We are a few minutes from Jaffa Gate, an entrance to the walled Old City. When our driver parks on the street, he'll quickly unload. Grab your bags and follow me."

Zed followed Greg and Abbie out of the bus into the hot sun. Before them loomed the towering arched gate and walls. The large hewn, sand-colored stones were ancient and scarred. Scarred like him.

Salazar motioned for the group to gather around him. He spoke in a loud voice. "You'll be intrigued with all there is to see inside. There are some guided tours of the Anglican Church on the premises of Christ Church Guest House. You'll want to take time to see what's here. We'll walk through Jaffa Gate and turn right."

The narrow street, not large enough for vehicles, was paved with stones. Zed dragged his wheeled luggage, bump, bump, bump, to their lodging. Tired from the thirteen-hour flight, he was thankful the distance was short.

In front of Christ Church Guest House, Salazar motioned for the group. "Dinner is two hours from now at six o'clock in the dining room. Register at the front desk, and you'll receive your room assignments."

Greg grabbed Zed's arm. "If we're not in the same room, let's see if we can get one together."

Zed welcomed the idea. He enjoyed Greg.

A few minutes later, Zed glanced around their room. It was spacious enough with two twin beds separated by a nightstand. But he wished for the luxurious places he usually stayed.

Zed stretched out on the bed next to the window. "Do you prefer either bed, Greg? I'm ready for a good rest."

"Choose the one you want. I've heard it's better not to sleep before bedtime. Helps you adjust to the time difference faster. Let's unpack and then see if we can get a tour of this facility. I'm ready to get started. I'll call Abbie on my cell phone."

Abbie met Greg and Zed in the small, busy coffee shop for a much-needed jolt of caffeine before their tour of the Anglican Church and the rest of the compound. With cups in hand, they grabbed a small table.

Zed said, "I've never seen so much stone in my life—stone paths, stone floors, stone buildings. I'm curious about how old this church is."

Abbie said, "Michael Alexander, a Messianic German-Jew from England, came to the Holy Land to spread the gospel to the Jews. He pushed for the establishment of Christ Church but met extreme opposition from Jews. However, a number of Jews were converted to Christianity. It was consecrated in 1849 after Alexander's death."

Greg said, "Christians have tried to convert the Jews for centuries. Do you think that's our task, Abbie?"

"My thoughts go in circles. The New Testament asks Christians to go to all nations and preach the good news of salvation. The thing is, Christ wanted to broaden the Jews' understanding of God. He didn't set out to make a new religion."

Zed clenched his jaw. *Abbie always has an answer. This is heresy.* Zed tried to smile. "How can you say that? Jesus started Christianity."

Abbie said, "He was a Jew. Christianity came after his death. Surely you know that. I lean more toward a God who allows different paths to him."

"There are civilizations, such as the Hindus, that existed before Christ," Greg said.

Zed squeezed his brows together. "The Bible says the only way to God is through Jesus."

"We live in a complex, diverse world," Greg said. "There are many religions. Does God condemn all the people he created to hell if they don't believe in Jesus? I'm sure you studied Biblical Hebrew and New Testament Greek, so I'm sure you realize there is no word for hell in either language."

Zed didn't admit he had studied very little of the ancient languages in Seminary. And one of the purposes of the Reformation was to make scripture available to the common person in their own language. "Seems very liberal to me. Abbie, you seem to know a lot about this history."

"I learned a little about Christ Church from friends who visited Jerusalem and wanted more information. I looked online."

His face warmed. "Right." *I'm not keen on a woman minister knowing more than me.*

Greg looked at his watch. "It's almost time for the tour. I want to be at the front of the line so I can hear everything."

After the tour, Zed listened to the animated chatter at the dinner table and dove into the conversation. "Why does Christ Church resemble a synagogue? It has Hebrew script and Jewish symbols on the communion table."

Peter, the loud robust man across from him said, "You were not listening to the guide. It was built by a Messianic Jew. And he wanted to appeal to Jews and Christians.

"That bit about how the Jordanian Army in 1948 almost destroyed the church because it resembled a synagogue interested me. Nice save on the rector's part. He ran to the Arab market and bought an olive wood cross to replace the Jewish menorah on the altar."

Marie, a petite woman to Zed's right said, "This church was built because Alexander and others believed God's promises to his chosen people. The Bible says the land of Israel belongs to the Jews. Alexander and the Anglicans believed there would be peace in the world if the Jews returned to Israel and accepted Jesus as their Messiah."

"Right," Peter said, "but I want to know to what end? The Jews have a homeland at the expense of the Palestinians. It's a two-edged sword. You have the Jews needing a country after the Holocaust and even before. And they took Palestinian homes and land to do it. Is that fair? The least Israel could do is let the Palestinians have their own country."

Zed chewed his lip as anger filled him. He said, "Marie is correct. The picture Peter painted doesn't fit my beliefs. The Jews reclaimed what belonged to them. How else can we interpret the Bible?"

"That's why Israel and Palestinians fight all the time," Peter said. "The Arabs say the land belongs to them through Abraham's second son, Ishmael. No one seems able to solve the problem. Our discussion solves nothing."

Zed said, "We're all entitled to our opinions. If you'll excuse me, I'll call it a night. See you all tomorrow."

Once there, Zed changed into his pajamas and crawled into bed. He murmured a short prayer. *God, how can I know what is right? Help me believe your word.*

THE NEXT MORNING Zed joined Greg and Abbie, along with the others. Salazar announced, "It's a short walk to the Church of the Holy Sepulchre. It's believed this is the site where Jesus was crucified and buried. It was originally a quarry just outside the city walls. Keep up the pace. Can't slow down too much or we'll be late for lunch."

Salazar stopped the group on the church's plaza. Zed gazed at the stone edifice, which dated from the time of Constantine. It had been destroyed and rebuilt over the years. *Where had the labor come from?* He turned his attention back to Salazar.

"This is the main entrance. You can tell by the rounded stone arches that the Crusaders rebuilt the church in the Romanesque and Baroque styles."

As he talked, a Greek Orthodox priest in a flowing black robe and a round black hat came out the door to greet them. Salazar shook the priest's hand and embraced him. Salazar turned toward the tour again. "This is our guide, Father Demetri."

He smiled. "Hello, everyone. I greet you in the name of our Lord. I welcome you as my brothers and sisters in Christ to the holiest site of Christendom. Salazar told me you are Protestants, so you might be offended by the statues, elaborate gilded altars, and the reverence for various artifacts. The Greek Orthodox, Armenian, Catholic, and Copts maintain the church. Each has shrines, chapels, and specific times of worship. You'll smell and see incense burning in small censors."

Zed shifted from foot to foot. *Do I belong here?*

Father Demetri said, "I imagine not all of you know about the Greek Orthodox Church. We have a continuous history from the time of the apostles, and we consider ourselves the only true church."

What? What's wrong with these people? Martin Luther did away with erroneous teachings.

"The Greek Orthodox community believes all Christians are brothers and sisters in Christ, and we pray to see a reunification of all factions. Inside there are five stations of the cross—Jesus stripped of his garments, nailed to the cross, died on the cross, taken from cross, and His tomb."

Following the group into the church, Zed rubbed his forehead. Confusion reigned. First, he had seen Salazar embrace the priest as if they were long-time friends, and he had heard a claim by Father Demetri that Orthodoxy was the true church. Zed's church claimed it had all truth. Father Demetrius seemed loving and accepting of all believers. *What the heck?*

Zed signaled to the priest. "Scripture says the tomb was outside the city walls. The Garden Tomb is the accurate place of burial for Jesus. This church is inside the City walls."

"Archaeology shows this site was outside the walls at the time of Constantine. Let's go inside."

I'll have to check that out. It can't be true.

The group gathered around the Father just inside the entrance at the Stone of Unction. "This slab of limestone commemorates the preparation of Jesus' body for burial. This dates from 1808 because the twelfth-century piece was destroyed. It now belongs to four main sects—Copts, Greeks, Armenians, and Catholics—as do the lamps hanging over the stone."

Tourists stood at the stone where Jesus' body was prepared for burial. They rubbed, knelt, and kissed it. Zed didn't feel an affinity to it and wondered why people would want to touch it. It looked cold, unfeeling, idolatrous.

Along with the rest of the group, Zed, Abbie, and Greg sat at a table in a restaurant not far from the Church of the Holy Sepulchre. They were served family-style with an assortment of Mediterranean salads, hummus, and pita bread, followed with kebabs and rice. The aroma of the grilled meat wafted through the air. Zed's stomach growled, and he ate with a hearty appetite.

"This is the best I've ever had," Abbie said.

Greg ate a bite of the warm pita. "This is fresh from the oven."

Zed patted his stomach. "Full to the max. Oops, I see the waiter coming with dessert. Looks delicious."

The small squares of baklava made with phyllo dough, nuts, and honey, finished off their meal. Then the waiter appeared with a tray of tiny cups filled with Turkish coffee. "It's on the house," he said.

Greg said, "That coffee was half grounds and half liquid—and strong too. Should keep me awake this afternoon and all night. Hey, Abbie, let's browse the shops as we walk toward the Jewish Quarter to the Wailing Wall. Salazar gave us time. Perhaps I'll find a bauble for my wife. You game, Zed?"

"Sure. These streets and shops are quaint. Never seen anything like this. Salazar said the shopkeepers expect people to bargain. Let's see if they will."

Zed looked down the crowded street. People elbowed their way through, looking for bargains. The stores had large openings with metal roll-down doors. On either side of the street, bright-colored clothing hung from the walls. On shelves, a mixed array of tablecloths, toys, and other goods caught his attention. "Maybe I'll find something for my wi . . ."

"For who?" Abbie asked.

"I started to say wife. She's ex-wife now, for several months." *There. He'd said it. It was out in the open.*

"You're wearing a wedding ring," Abbie said.

"Keeps the women away," Zed said, through tight lips. "I can't remarry as long as I'm the pastor of my church."

Greg said, "Puts a fellow in a tough position."

"You bet."

When they went into a jewelry store, the owner said, "You are Americans. You get good price. Anything you see, you get good price."

Abbie said, "Thanks."

"What do you like? This pretty necklace." He took a gold Star of David out of the glass-covered case and held it up.

"How much?"

"For you, five hundred dollars. You may charge on credit card."

"I can't afford it."

"Four fifty. Good deal."

"No thanks." Abbie walked out the door. She didn't like his insistent manner to buy something.

Zed noticed the price on a gold chain necklace was four grand. Petty cash for him, but Elise wouldn't take it now. The storekeeper said, "You buy this for your wife."

"I don't have one."

"No wife? Very sad. You need wife and children."

"No," Zed said. He strode out the door of the shop.

Greg caught up to him and put his hand on Zed's shoulder. "Sore spot, Zed?"

"I still love my ex-wife. I'm in a no-win situation."

"A good chat might help."

"I wouldn't mind discussing this with you, but not Abbie."

"Let's make some time during this trip to do that. Abbie, wait up," Greg said.

SALAZAR CALLED TO the group. They wound their way through the narrow streets, almost alleyways, to the Western Wall of the Temple mount. When they arrived, Salazar said, "It's my privilege to introduce you to Yitzhak, a Jewish archaeologist who's an expert on the history of this wall and the diggings around it."

As he swayed back and forth on his feet, Yitzhak greeted them. "*Shalom.* I'm an orthodox Jew and I'll teach you about the Wailing or Western Wall, which is the most sacred site in all of Judaism because it is part of the retaining wall that surrounded the Temple Mount. Jews cannot go up there because the Dome of the Rock, sacred to Muslims, is built over the site of our Holy of Holies in the temple. Only the high priest could enter it. By the way, there is no separation between religion and government in Israel."

"Why?" Zed asked. "There are minority religions in your country."

"Ah, *tov maod.* Good question. Jewish people endured persecution and death at the hands of gentiles through the centuries. We must have a country only for Jews. Minority religions worship in freedom but cannot coerce or pay Jews to convert. Any other questions? No? I'll continue.

"First, I want to explain this large plaza you're standing on. Before the Six-Day War in 1967, this area was populated with a Moroccan community. Only a small alley existed between the homes and the Western Wall, making it difficult to access. During the war, we captured East Jerusalem. Since it was wartime, we took advantage of the opportunity to bulldoze the homes. We were ecstatic."

"Excuse me," Zed said. "Was that the right thing to do?"

"It was war and our opportunity to reclaim the Wall. At last, we could worship there. The Temple was destroyed in 70 CE by the Romans.

"We use this plaza as an open-air synagogue and we teach classes about the Torah. We also have many celebrations."

Zed's mind went back to the words, "We bulldozed the houses." Was Peter right last night at dinner about the unjust way the Israelis treat the Palestinians? Did God approve of the wars between the two? Perhaps the Palestinians had a right to the land also.

Yitzhak continued. "There is a small fence that runs perpendicular to the Wall. That's due to Jewish orthodox rules that dictate men and women must be separated for worship. All people of various faiths can write prayers on a piece of paper and insert it between the cracks of the stones. You may do this if you wish. To go up to the Wall, the men need to cover their heads with a kipa. You'll find these by the barrier as well as pencil and paper for your notes."

Zed hesitated. He believed he had direct access to God through Jesus. He didn't need a mechanism such as a note for God to hear him. But since Christianity had its roots in Judaism, he decided to go to the Wall and pray. He placed a *kipa* on his head and took a piece of paper and a pencil. He wrote his prayer. *Please, if it's Your will, let Elise and I remarry. Heal our wounds and clear the way for us. Break down our walls.* He looked at no one, walked to the Wall, and inserted his prayer. He waited for God to speak to him. Silence.

AFTER DINNER, ZED, Greg, and Abbie sat in the courtyard of the guesthouse drinking iced tea. It had been in the nineties during the day, and Zed felt drained from the heat and his exposure to new places and ideas. Everything gave him something to think about. And hearing Arabic and Modern Hebrew spoken on the streets boggled his mind.

Abbie covered Zed's hand with hers and in a soft voice said, "I'm interested in your reaction at the market when the shopkeeper said you needed a wife. Are you ashamed of being divorced?"

Zed pulled his hand back. *What's with her and touching?* He looked at Greg and wished Abbie would leave. "It's considered a sin in my church for ministers to divorce."

"I'm divorced," Abbie said. "My ex decided he didn't want to be married to a minister. You know how it is, weddings and funerals on Saturdays, and church on Sunday. On call all the time and endless meetings. He worked Monday through Friday as a businessman. He wanted the weekends for us. Bad match, big mistake. I decided to marry God and the church. Couldn't you make that kind of commitment?"

Zed scowled. *That's not for me.*

"Maybe Zed would rather not say," Greg said.

"Sorry, Zed. I counsel many women, and we tend to bare our souls to each other right away. How about a different topic?"

"I was surprised the Israelis bulldozed the houses by the Wailing Wall. It's not fair. I thought the Jews could do no wrong. They're God's chosen people."

"That's a common belief in many churches, and I know it is in yours," Greg said. "I think the words of the Bible are carried too far when the rights of other people are trampled. A homeland for the Jews and one for the Palestinians would benefit everyone."

Zed asked, "How do you know what my church believes?"

"I've seen your advertisements on television. And I visited a similar one to satisfy my curiosity."

"I'm surprised."

"I get questions about the prosperity gospel. I have to say, I don't agree with the philosophy."

"Maybe we can talk sometime." *But I can't change everything I believe.*

EIGHTEEN

Elise

THE FOG OUTSIDE MATCHED ELISE'S MOOD. IT WAS AS IF DARK shadows enveloped her brain as she journaled about her divorce. Her cell rang. Damn. She couldn't resist answering. "Yes," she almost shouted.

"El . . . Elise?"

"Yes." She hated it when people didn't immediately identify themselves. "Who's this?"

"Zed. I'm in Israel. I . . . well, I . . ."

"Spit it out." *What could he possibly want?*

"Been here almost two weeks on a tour and I'm confused. And get this. A Presbyterian minister has become a friend. Can you believe that? God is working in my life. Praise his name."

"Cut the religious words with me, Zed. Everything in life isn't 'Praise God'. We said goodbye to each other months ago. We have nothing left to discuss. You have friends you've known for a long time. You have family. Tell them about your trip. Leave me alone."

"Why the bitter tone? I thought we agreed to put our differences aside."

"You caught me at a bad time."

"I'm sorry. I don't want to upset you. This is important to me, and maybe to you."

Elise's will weakened. *Where does a relationship with him get me? More heartache. That's what.* "I can't, Zed."

"Would you at least talk to me? Please. We have walls between us."

"Call me when you get home." *Now why in the hell did I say that? Maybe I miss our theological discussions. Maybe I miss him.*

Elise nuked a cup of water and dropped a Jasmine tea bag into it. Then she settled in the loveseat to write in her journal. *Maybe I haven't accepted the consequences of my problems. Bipolar. That is permanent. Divorce is permanent. Are my questions about God permanent?* She thought of the pregnant nun who had to leave the church. She eventually married and bore more children. The nun had said in her book she believed in a god who loved without conditions, all humanity.

Elise continued to write. *Have I grieved enough about my losses?* She had read in her Divorce Recovery workbook that people often went back and forth between the five stages of grief. Acceptance. *That's my dilemma. It would be easier if Zed were evil. Then I could hate him and go on with my life.*

ELISE SLIPPED INTO the room where the Divorce Recovery Workshop was in its last session. Reverend McDonald was speaking. *Why am I late? It's inconsiderate of me.* She interrupted him. "I'm sorry I wasn't on time." She sat next to Nick.

"Apology accepted." To the class, he said, "If you did your homework, you know we're discussing the role acceptance plays in our lives after divorce. Do you make the best of your situation? Are you moving forward with your life, making plans for your future? Can you change the reality of your situation? I've asked several questions and want us to explore some answers. I hope some of you will comment on these questions."

Shelly said, "I've been pigheaded about my divorce. I didn't want to tell anyone my husband has a girlfriend and that he doesn't love me. Last week, I told my best friend. I thought she would desert me. Instead, she said she'd help me with my new life. I wish I had done that sooner."

"Good for you," Reverend McDonald said. "You're changing, taking a step in the right direction."

"I'm scared. What if I fail?"

"You won't if you take care of yourself in all ways—emotionally, spiritually, physically. And don't let negative thinking dominate your life. It will wear you down. Someone else want to share?"

Nick said, "I want to date again. However, the person I want in my life is hesitant. What can I do?"

Elise wanted to scream. *Why did he say that? Everyone will know he's talking about me. Damn him.*

Reverend McDonald said, "You can't force a relationship. Give the person time. If it doesn't work out, find someone else."

"She's perfect for me. Why can't she see that?" Nick slammed his right fist into his other hand.

"Do you have your head in the sand?" Reverend McDonald said. "You said in a previous class you wanted your divorce and that you accept it. Now, you need to realize you can't force someone to love you. Does that make sense?"

"Somewhat."

"Rejected again. Is that it?"

"Maybe."

Elise raised her hand. It shook. She wanted to expose Nick and tell the class she wanted him for a friend. Nothing more. That would shut him up. Instead, she said to the minister, "How do you know when you're ready to make a new life?"

"If you've made peace with your past, you will make a change. Sometimes this involves asking your ex-spouse to forgive you. In fact, most couples need to do this. Healing of your inner-being will take place faster."

"That's hard to do," Elise said, biting a nail.

"Yes. No doubt. I believe it's necessary though. Most of the time there have been angry exchanges between couples. At least apologize for those. I also believe getting counseling about a divorce is important. It's a way to discover the steps you need to take. We've spent six weeks together. My guess is that all of you have more work to do, and I suggest you go to counseling to complete your healing process. It takes time to change your life. If anyone wants to come in occasionally for a chat, I'd be glad to see you. Any questions?"

The others shook their heads.

"Let's have our last time together at the refreshment table. My wife provided homemade cookies to celebrate what we've learned."

Everyone made their way to the dessert table where conversations ensued.

Elise tried to excuse herself. However, Shelly stopped her. "Hi, Elise. How are you?"

"I'm doing okay. I'm trying to accept my life as it is now."

"I know what you mean."

Nick joined them, his head bowed. Shelly asked, "Hi, Nick. Are you okay? You seem down."

"Never better." His lips turned up slightly.

"I need to get home so the babysitter can leave. Take care."

"What is the matter with you, Nick?" Elise said. "You spilled your guts to the class. Everyone knows we leave together sometimes. I didn't appreciate your comments."

"I'm frustrated, Elise. You only think about yourself. Not me."

"I don't want to hurt you. I admit I'm attracted to you, but I need time to work my problems out on my own."

"You don't want to see me?"

"Maybe it's best to get together only at the art meetings. At least for now."

"I'll be around if you change your mind."

"Thanks." Elise watched Nick exit the room. *I hope I made the right decision. He's a good person.*

ELISE TOOK A seat at her easel and studied her latest sketch. She took a deep breath. It was time to fill it with vivid colors. They would emphasize the destructive behavior of her church experience. Elise realized not everyone experienced hurt and disappointment like she had, but her story was valid. And she knew that down through the centuries religion had played havoc with many lives.

The art showed a large church with a brick facade and a gabled roof with a tall cross. Its door was a cavernous, slightly twisted mouth that had jagged crooked teeth.

One by one people emerged from the church. Emaciated, they wore torn clothes, their jaws clenched, and their faces screwed up with pain. Their hearts dripped with blood. Some stumbled. One individual carried a sign that said, Destination Unknown.

Her heart thudded in anticipation of what she was about to do. Color would give the picture life, enough to leave no doubt of what she had to say. Black, oppressive air of her former depression filled her.

Elise picked up tubes of oil paint. She chose black and light blue-gray for the sky. She brushed, with hard furious strokes, the sky with dark tumultuous clouds heavy with rain. Relieved when that was done, she worked on the mouth. Her emotions turned toward the murky slime found in a damp colorless cave. That was enough. The grueling recall of her former life had drained her. Before she called it quits, she picked up a notepad and pen from the table to write down the title. Where Is Jesus?

Around midnight Elise went to bed, mindful of the energy she needed for work the next day. Nonsensical dreams plagued her sleep, and she woke at 3:00 a.m. to crumpled sheets and the blanket on the floor. She got up and made chamomile tea to soothe her jangled nerves. An image from the last dream plagued her. She had been on a high-speed train filled with vampires who had blood dripping from their mouths. She sat up the rest of the night on her loveseat thinking about her aspirations to portray the drama of her life. Could she bear the conjured-up images and the emotions that intruded on her subconscious when she needed rest?

GINNY, HER BACK rigid, sat on Elise's loveseat. "I asked you here to review my latest work of art," Elise said. "I tremble inside every time I think of anyone seeing this. I dreaded calling even you. What message do you see in this?"

"What do I see? You ask me what do I see? I see people the church fooled into believing every damn thing they were taught. This is raw. It strikes me in the gut. I'll have nightmares about this." Ginny stood. She paced the small room, then rocked back and forth on her heels.

Elise stared at Ginny, scared of her reaction. *What have I done?* "Oh, no. I don't want that. I'll destroy it."

"Don't you dare. Those are your feelings. Do you think you're the only person in the world who left the church? How welcome do you think I would have been when I struggled with drug addiction? Shit."

Elise wondered if she could hug Ginny. She never displayed this much emotion. Elise decided to take a chance.

Ginny jumped when Elise embraced her. "I'm not used to anyone who cares about me. Thanks."

"You need people in your life who love you unconditionally."

"Let's get back to your art. I'm uncomfortable," Ginny said.

Elise watched as she sat down again. Ginny had stiffened her shoulders.

Elise avoided looking at her. "I'm mortified, Ginny."

"Keep painting. I'm a survivor and so are you. I think it's time you started to blog about your experiences. The disenfranchised of the church need to know they're not alone."

Jolted, as if by an earthquake, Elise grabbed the side of her easel and almost made it fall. "Are there that many?"

"I've heard attendance at some churches is declining—and not only in Christianity. What did they do to you? Why are you angry?"

Elise wrung her hands. "Do you have time to hear my story?"

"Without a doubt."

Elise didn't hide her bipolar, the dissolution of her marriage, or her anger at her former church. Elise's shoulders heaved as she sobbed about her story. "I'm sorry. I don't usually cry about this. I wish I had a better story to tell."

"Good god, Elise. My stomach is so tied in knots I could

puke. I can see why you named it, Where Is Jesus? I've never gone to church. The newspapers and reports on the internet tell me to stay the heck away."

"Why am I so upset, Ginny? I need to get over it."

"Sometimes it takes a long time for wounds to heal. And sometimes the scabs are pulled off, and the process has to start again."

"Oh, how I hate all this."

"You'll be all right eventually. Don't be hard on yourself. I had to learn that. Have you found anyone who understands you?"

"My mom and dad try. My sister doesn't accept or believe what I've gone through. She's tied up with her own prejudices. Reverend McDonald enlightened me on what I'm going through. Karen has helped me the most."

"If you don't think these paintings are enough, start a blog. You can help other people that way."

"I don't know how."

"I'll show you. I blog about drug addiction."

"I don't know if I'm ready to blog my story. My gut would tear open."

"Only you can decide. I know what's right for me. I hate to say this, but I need to go to NA. Call me if you want help with setting up a blog." Ginny took a few steps toward Elise and hugged her. "Take care, my friend."

Elise watched Ginny leave. *Do I have that kind of courage?*

ON SUNDAY AFTERNOON, Elise brewed Earl Grey tea in her antique floral teapot in the kitchen and arranged homemade cookies on a small plate for Janet and Dana. Her hands shook as she carried them up to her room. Her religious art was ready to show them. *What if they hate it?*

She heard their knock and opened the door. "Mom, Dana," she said with a tentative smile. "Come in. Hugs before you sit down." Janet grabbed Elise and squeezed her hard.

"Mom, I'm going to pass out."

"Sorry honey."

"Dana, how about a hug?" Elise stretched her arms out to embrace Dana who turned away.

Elise swallowed hard. "Have a seat. I have cookies and tea for you." Elise motioned to the refreshments on the coffee table.

Janet said, "They smell scrumptious. Any dessert with cinnamon delights me. Have a cookie, Dana."

"I'll pass. Have to stay slim you know. Tea, please."

The conversation lagged while they ate and drank. "So, how's my new look, girls?" Janet asked. "I decided in Hawaii to give it a try."

"Come on Mom," Dana said. "What's with the shorts? Since when do you dress that way? You're not very modest."

"They come to my knee. Besides, Dad likes them. Not many warm days here though. You won't believe how warm the beaches on Maui were. Ours are cold and foggy so often. And I loved the lush vegetation with waterfalls. Sorry. I'm going on a bit. Maybe you want to talk, Dana."

"How are you, Dana?" Elise asked.

"I need a part-time job," Dana said. "The cost of Little League for Mark is more than our current budget allows. Looking for a job is mundane and heartless. I hate rejection."

"You're right. Any leads?"

"Not yet."

Once Elise thought the chatting halted, and the tea was finished, she said, "I'm going to reveal my latest endeavors to you. I have to caution you, though, that you might not agree with the message they convey. What I want from you is your initial reaction. Do you understand what I've painted? Do you experience feelings of some kind?"

"I'll try," Janet said. "But I'm not an expert on art."

"Nor I," Dana said.

Elise walked to her easel where the paintings were stacked. She removed the cover over the art and laid it aside. First, she revealed the sad woman. She looked first to Janet and then to Dana, and saw their eyes widen and their mouths drop open. In tandem, they said, "Oh!"

The moments dragged in Elise's mind. *What will they say?*

"You get an 'A' from me," Dana said. "The sadness of the woman emanates from the picture. But if it represents you, I don't feel sorry for you. You had it all. Money for everything. A handsome husband. What's wrong with you?"

"You miss the point. The church rejected me when I had no hope. Remember?"

"Girls, that's enough," Janet said. "It breaks my heart to see you at each other's throats. My turn now. I'm at a loss for words, honey," her eyes bright with tears. "I remember how you looked when you were in the hospital. It says it all. I wish, oh, I wish you had not experienced such agony. Too much pain in the world. What's next, sweetie?"

Elise placed the picture of the woman on the floor against the wall. Next was the one of the church with the cavernous door.

Dana spoke, her voice raised. "This is horrible. How can you present such a negative description of the church? Any church. What will non-Christians think? The Bible says we're not to cause our fellow beings to doubt God."

Elise searched her mind for an answer. She was trained as a pastor's wife to not say anything to offend, and that limited her answer. "I'm not sure how to respond. Many people will agree with you. At least I know the painting creates a gut reaction. Mom?"

Between audible breaths, Janet said, "I see Dana's point of view. Thousands of people flock to churches like Zed's. I've wondered if it's because they experience the high they get every week when they're told God works it all out. Are you saying all churches are this way?"

"No. My main motive is to show my pain, and I know it speaks for many people. I've read some of their blogs. My paintings might not sell, but I plan to continue, if not for others, at least for me. It's good therapy. I hope to release my anger and bitterness and then look for other kinds of subjects that interest me. I've thought about doing a series of paintings and a book I'd sell on the Internet. A blog might be a good way to expose my work to the public."

"Geez," Dana responded. "This seems crazy to me. If my

friends find out, some may desert me. And you're putting the family on the spot. It's not fair."

Elise let out her breath, not knowing she had held it. She chewed the inside of her cheeks. She looked at the floor. "This isn't easy for me either. I'm compelled to tell a story through pictures. I suppose I could use a pen name. It won't stop me from what I'm doing—"

Janet interrupted, "This is hard stuff. The idea of a pen name suits me. And Dad and I have stood by you. We won't stop now. I admit I feel uncomfortable, but I'm thinking of myself. Before you go public, consider the possible consequences."

Elise decided to skip the painting of the preacher and the old lady.

Janet looked at her watch. "I have to say one more thing before I go. You girls need to let each other be. Dad and I love both of you and want your happiness. We're here for you, too, Dana." She kissed both girls. "Let's talk again soon." She stood and walked toward the door, and Dana followed without a word.

NINETEEN

Zed

ZED LEANED HIS HEAD AGAINST THE SEAT IN THE BUS AND EXHALED. *If only I had known why Elise was depressed.* They had had a wonderful life. He yearned to hold her in his arms and confess he still loved her. Needed her fun spirit. Needed her soft-spoken voice. Needed to make love to her.

The tour bus traveled five miles from Jerusalem to Bethlehem, which was in Palestinian territory. After they passed through Israeli security, the bus driver parked in a small graveled area. "I'm not allowed to enter Bethlehem because I'm Israeli," he said. Everyone boarded two vans driven by Palestinians to continue their trip into the small city.

After disembarking, the group stood next to a portion of the concrete barrier and listened while their Palestinian guide, Hakeem, spoke in English with his heavy Arabic accent.

"I'm sure you know the Israeli government built this structure in fear that Palestinian terrorists would cross into Israel with suicide bombs—"

"Hey, why don't you tell them the real story?" Hakeem's brother had come from the back of the tour group to the front. His eyes glinted with anger, and his jeans were stained. "Tell them our troubles in Bethlehem."

Zed's mouth opened and closed. He looked at the others.

They stood like soldiers as if ready to attack Ahmed.

Hakeem scowled. "Ahmed. Go home to our family! This is how I earn a living."

"No. The Israelis take our water for their illegal settlements. Are we able to go into Israel for our jobs? Only a few. We live in poverty."

"You must go." Ahmed left and Hakeem spoke again. "I'm sorry. My brother does not know his place. I will explain more. In rural areas, the wall is made of barbed wire fences with watchtowers and high-tech means of guaranteeing safety. It cuts through the property of some Palestinian landholders. Yet, there are many on both sides who work together for peace. Do not think all of us are terrorists or all Jews are zealots. Please, we will continue our tour of Bethlehem."

Zed shook his head. *Could there be peace?* He and Elise had immense divides between them. *Could they be repaired? Was it too late?* Her depression had laid the foundation. The division between him and his congregation came to mind. *On which side do I belong?* Doubts swam in his head.

BEFORE THEY LEFT Bethlehem, the tour stopped at a store owned by a Palestinian family that made and sold products from olive wood. Zed bought communion cups, a crèche, Christmas ornaments, and a large salad bowl. He wanted reminders of this holy city.

Salazar spoke to the group after they started their trip back to Jerusalem. "I'm sorry for the disturbance Ahmed caused. It's impossible to ignore the gravity of a long-standing feud. Do any of you want to comment on this experience?"

Greg signaled with his hand and walked to the front of the bus. He said, "I grew up in the turbulent sixties and my favorite folk artists were the trio, Peter, Paul, and Mary. They sang about social injustice. The song 'Some Walls' reflects the reasons we build walls between ourselves and others. Fear, anger, prejudice, and a closed mind reside in us too often. If we learn from what we've seen today and practice forgiveness and love, we'll see walls crumble. Sorry, I'm preaching." Greg made his way back to his seat by Zed.

Zed gazed at the brown hills. He felt the light touch of Greg's hand on his back. Zed looked at his friend and said, "I need to apply the song to my life."

The tour bus wound its way through the streets of modern Jerusalem to the Holocaust Museum, Yad Vashem. Salazar stood. "There are many exhibits. You will see multimedia presentations, items soldiers found in the liberated camps, and personal artifacts donated by survivors. See you in three hours." Zed glanced at the concrete triangular structure that rose toward the sky. His steps slowed as he went down the bus steps, unsure he wanted to see the atrocities.

Inside, the only relief to the drab walls and ceilings in the vast stark space were the numerous galleries and alcoves, each with different displays of artifacts with explanatory plaques or videos commemorating the period.

The container on the floor caught his eye. The glass on the top and sides showed a pile of old shoes obtained from the camps. Zed realized each pair represented a human being who had been seized by Hitler's regime and had ended in the gas chamber. His head started to ache.

Then he went to the display of the Righteous Among the Nations. It was a bright spot in the otherwise horrific saga. It commemorated the gentiles who aided Jews during Hitler's regime. Their pictures and stories of what they did to hide the hunted and help them escape abounded. Many had died. Zed wondered if he was willing to give his life for others. Jesus had.

His next stop was a recessed space that showed videos of four survivors. He watched the story of one woman. She had been freed by American soldiers from an extermination camp at the end of the war. Tears flowed as she told her story. "I was emaciated and sick. I asked the soldiers, why now? What for? I want to die." *Would that be my reaction? What path would I take out of darkness to God? How do we as human beings make the journey from evil to good?* His thoughts turned to the American soldiers who suffered from PTSD. He guessed the survivors of the camps had symptoms—nightmares, neurotic behaviors, loneliness, suicide. His headache worsened. *Where was God?*

Zed had enough. His brain could not comprehend what he had seen. He wound his way around the various exhibits and walked into brilliant sunshine, a needed respite. Zed could breathe again. Greg caught up with him.

"Ahead is the Children's Holocaust Memorial. I want to go inside. Come with me?"

Reluctant, Zed agreed. They entered darkness. Zed and Greg stood still until their eyes adjusted. Tiny lights representing one and a half million Jewish children who had perished in the genocide showed on the walls. As they walked around the perimeter of the building, translucent pictures of the children appeared. Their names, ages, and country of origin were read aloud in English, Hebrew, and Yiddish. Zed stumbled out of the building. He couldn't hold back his tears.

Zed went to Christ Church to pray after they returned from the museum. People were scattered throughout the stone church praying in silence. Some bowed their heads and others lifted their faces toward the ceiling. Zed knelt at a pew. He mouthed his words. *"I'm confused and scared. Give me answers to my questions. I've met so many sincere spiritual people. How can everyone be right? And why is there so much suffering?"*

He waited for an answer—the still small voice of God. He heard nothing even though he lingered thirty minutes in quiet meditation.

ZED SIPPED HIS usual iced tea in the courtyard of Christ Church and wished for a cool breeze. He recalled the four-day excursion to the Sea of Galilee, the Jordan River where Jesus was baptized, Nazareth, and more. His faith in and around Jerusalem had been challenged to the point of confusion. In Galilee, he had imagined Jesus healing the sick. *Had Jesus cured everyone? Some of them had begged Jesus to be healed.*

The ruins of the sizable white stone synagogue in Capernaum had intrigued him. Worshipers had sat on the benches along the sidewalls. He wondered how the hewn pillars had been put up. He presumed they had supported the now roofless building. It was built over the demolished synagogue made of black basalt stones where Jesus would have taught. *What would the Son of God have said to me? Maybe he would tell me I was a hypocrite.*

Tomorrow he would return to the States and face his church. Out of the corner of his eye, he saw Greg and Abbie approach.

"Hey, Zed. Your face is pale." Greg said. "Thirty minutes ago you were smiling. Mind if we sit down?"

"Reserved for you."

"Care to talk?"

"I think I'll excuse myself," Abbie said. "I'm glad I met you, Zed."

"Thanks."

Zed looked at Greg. "I didn't tell you my whole story. I'm in trouble with my congregation."

"What's going on?"

"My church is a prosperity gospel church and dogmatic about it. I'm sure you know the kind of preaching we do."

"Yes. What are you getting at?"

"Many people in Israel are faithful to God but don't believe like I do. They seem spiritual and happy in their faith. I'm perplexed." Zed shifted in his chair. He told Greg the story about his journey to believing suffering existed, not due to lack of faith or money. "I began preaching about that."

"You're brave. What happened?"

Zed tried to relax his jaw. "At least three-quarters of my congregation are upset with me. I tried to convince everyone to throw away the old belief system."

"It's easier to think the Bible contains all the answers."

"I've prayed about it. No answers."

"Life involves struggles. Remember in the Old Testament how Jacob wrestled with an angel? The story shows man's fight with his soul. Let's get together back home," Greg said.

"Perhaps it's divine guidance we met."

"You're less flamboyant now than when you started the trip. Is that a sign of your struggle?"

"Maybe."

HOME AGAIN, ZED phoned Elise. She answered on the fourth ring.

"Hi."

"I thought you weren't going to answer."

"I had to put my brush in turpentine. What do you want?"

His voice quavered. "I want to see you. Can we meet in Ferndale?"

"No."

"Give me a chance. I need to discuss a few things with you."

He heard Elise sigh. "Two minutes."

Zed explained a few of the significant points of his trip. "I'm mixed up."

"I find that hard to believe. You're still a minister in your church, which rejected me. Remember? And you followed their lead."

Zed's voice rose. "I can't, all of a sudden, throw out everything I've believed in."

"It's not fun, is it? What do you want from me?" she whispered.

"Let's meet. Please."

A long silence ensued. "You abandoned me when I was desperate for help. You blamed me for my depression. You were ashamed of me."

"You've never talked like that before. What's wrong?"

"I found my voice and I'm a stronger woman. I expect understanding and equal treatment from men."

"You know what the Bible says about women. You have a quiet role to play."

"See? You haven't changed."

"I'm trying."

"This is the last time. Let's meet at the Victorian Inn here for lunch."

"How about a week from Saturday?"

"Okay."

He heard her sniffle.

As ZED DROVE to Ferndale, he tried to think of a way to approach Elise. *Be honest. I'll tell her I love her. Would she accept that?*

Zed parked next to the hotel and went into the restaurant. Elise liked Victorian-style buildings and furnishings. The host approached him. "Table for two. And a cup of coffee. A lady will join me soon."

"I have one table left since it's lunchtime."

Zed followed the host and sat down. The server brought him coffee and asked if he wanted to order.

"No. I'm waiting for my friend."

"All right."

Zed looked at his watch. *Where is Elise?* Another ten minutes passed. He motioned for the server. "My friend hasn't arrived. I'll go ahead and order. The steak special, please." He handed the menu to her and looked up. Elise came through the door. Excitement, then dread filled him. He almost spilled his coffee. *Would she be civil?* Her large hazel eyes met his before she looked away. The corners of her full lips were turned down. He noticed her auburn hair was now shoulder length and tangled. She was thin and her gait hesitant. Zed stood and walked to the opposite side of the table. He pulled out the chair for her. "I'm glad you came."

Is she depressed again?

The server handed her a menu. "Our special—"

"Poached cod and a green salad with your house dressing. And a glass of water."

"How about an appetizer? Our sweet potato fries are delicious."

"No thanks." The server walked away, menus in hand.

"You seem tired and unhappy. What's wrong?" Zed asked.

"You wanted to tell me about your trip. Did you bring pictures?"

She changed the subject. I guess she wants to take the attention off herself. "They're on my laptop. I'll show you after we eat if that's all right."

"Why did you go to Israel?" Elise asked.

"My church wanted me to take a vacation and rethink how

I preach. It was with a group of ministers and those in related fields."

"And?"

"I'll explain while I show you my pictures.

"I've changed how I preach about suffering. I tell the congregation it is a part of life and how not all people have the same opportunities to be wealthy."

Elise's eyes widened. "Since when?"

"Our divorce started it. And I talked to my psychology professor about bipolar."

"Oh? Why?"

She's talking like a robot. "He said it was incurable. We discussed faith healing, and he said he'd never seen anyone healed of it or other mental disorders. I wish I had been more understanding of you."

Elise twisted the napkin in her lap. "Too bad it came too late."

"After you see my pictures, you'll see how I'm changing."

The server arrived with their orders.

Zed watched Elise play with her food. She took a few bites and pushed her plate away. "I'm not hungry."

In the absence of conversation, Zed wolfed down his food. *I'm like a child trying to please my mother after I've been scolded.*

After their table had been cleared Zed reached for his laptop. "May I sit next to you? Then we can both see the screen."

She nodded.

"I have more pictures than we have time to see, so I'll skip some of them. The restaurant is busy."

"Whatever."

"This is a picture of my new friends, Abbie and Greg. They're in front of Christ Church Guest House where we stayed while we were in Jerusalem. Abbie is an Episcopal priest and Greg pastors a Presbyterian church in San Francisco."

"A woman priest? Is she married?"

"Divorced. The church is her life." He saw Elise's eyes narrow.

"Friendships are discouraged outside your church."

"I'm not sure I care. Greg was easy to talk to, and I intend to stay in touch with him."

"You have to set the example. Remember?"

"I've never questioned God like I do now. That includes what happened to us."

"You've made a few changes. Still . . ."

"I told you I don't have all the answers. Can you accept that? Can we mend our relationship?"

"You talk as if you think there's an *us*." She looked at the floor, shoulders slumped.

"Don't shut me out." Zed watched Elise sit up straight.

"Let's look at the pictures, Zed," Elise said. *He's a dunderhead.*

For two hours Zed told his tale through the photos. Afterward, he said, "What do you think?"

"What do you intend to do about Zed Norris Ministries?"

"I haven't decided. Quite a few people are upset. And you know James Prescott. Always the troublemaker."

"He's arrogant. Don't procrastinate like you usually do."

"Stop preaching at me."

"Ah, you always gave me advice," Elise said. "Most of the time it was about you and your church. This whole conversation is about you and what you want. We didn't and still don't talk about me much. You're a successful pastor with a personality people respond to. That's what it takes to build a big church."

"That's the most you've said all afternoon. What's wrong with you?"

"I need to go home, Zed. Continue with your life. It won't be with me." Elise stood and left the restaurant.

Zed's hope disappeared.

TWENTY

Elise

ELISE REFUSED TO CRY. SHE WAS THROUGH CRYING ABOUT HER LIFE, she thought, as she sat in the overstuffed chair in Karen's small waiting room. Her lunch encounter with Zed a week ago had added distress to her life. She had made embarrassing mistakes on the simple ordering program at work, which did little for her self-esteem. Ed caught her mistakes of purchasing too many bags of old-fashioned candy and not enough of Depression glass from the suppliers. A blob of dough had more form than she did.

Karen opened her office door. "Hi, Elise. Sorry I'm late. Please come in and make yourself comfortable while I get your file." Karen opened the door to her office closet and retrieved the folder. "How are you?"

"I'm anxious to talk with you," she said as she sat down.

Karen returned to her chair and perused the last two pages of notes. "When did you last see Dr. Mueller for a check on your medications?"

"Who?"

"Your psychiatrist."

"Oh, yes. I did. See him, that is." Elise looked out the window and stared as if a blank wall was across the street.

"You seem distracted. When did you see Dr. Mueller?"

Karen looked up from her note-taking.

"A couple of months ago."

"He thinks you're doing okay?"

"Yeah." *Always questions. Enough.*

"Hmm." She wrote a note in Elise's file.

"I saw Zed last week and now I'm maudlin all the time. I won't cry." Elise looked at the Impressionist pictures on Karen's wall. They failed to soothe her. *I wish I was somewhere else. Hawaii. Yes, on the beach in the sun.*

Karen cocked her head. "What happened?"

Elise took a deep breath and told Karen about her conversation with Zed."

"It frustrated me. Anyway . . ."

"Why did you agree to see him?"

"He asked if he could come, and for some reason, I couldn't say no." Elise straightened her posture as if she was a soldier. "We met for lunch, and he told me how much he was changing. He thinks there's hope for us. He messed with my head."

"Your heart too?"

Elise let silence prevail while she considered the question. "I guess so."

"Do you disagree with him?"

"Based on what I heard, yes and no." She took a deep breath and released it slowly.

"Do you know what you'd say to Zed if you spoke without fear of the consequences?"

Elise shrugged.

Karen leaned forward. "I want you to try something. It's quite effective with some people." She pointed to the empty chair beside Elise. "Pretend Zed is sitting next to you. Talk to him. Whatever comes to your mind."

"I can't do that. It's crazy." *Is Karen nuts?*

"You're in a private room. No one can hear you except me. Try it. Say 'Zed . . .'"

Elise swallowed hard. "You think since you're changing, I should accept you again. What if I said I . . ." She paused and looked up at Karen. "This is silly."

"Go ahead, let it out. Get angry. Hit him with words," Karen said, her voice forceful.

"What the hell! I love you, Zed," she yelled. "I can't stop. Not yet anyway. But that doesn't change anything. I don't want to be a pastor's wife. The church expected me to fit in a mold it designed. I had to bite my tongue if I thought of giving an opinion opposite of the congregation. And I disagree with the importance they place on wealth. What about the poor?"

"Tell him what you lost."

"He already knows I wanted to be a minister. He knows I loved church life most of the time, and God. He knows me well."

"What did you lose, Elise?" asked Karen.

"I . . . I . . ."

"You can do this."

Elise's shoulders heaved. "Zed, the friends I had deserted me. I don't have a ministry. You do. I don't have an identity. I used to be on a pedestal. I've fallen. The church hates me. They think I've sinned." Elise gulped air. "Our religion duped me, Zed. I was gullible. I believed everything. It's all I knew. And when I was down, the church threw me away. The people were glad when I left you. Not once did they think of me, how bad I felt, how confused I was, how much I wanted God to heal my depression, how much I loved them. It's all gone." Elise wailed from deep inside her belly. She put her hands over her face. Sobs shook her body. Sobs interminable.

After Elise's sobs subsided, Karen said, "Elise, when you're ready, look at me."

Minutes passed, like a movie that had been slowed to emphasize action.

Elise raised her head.

"How do you feel, Elise?"

"Foolish." Elise hung her head.

"What else?"

"I don't know."

"Tell me the truth."

"As if a boulder fell off my head. I didn't know I still had so much hurt inside me. I miss being important to the church and Zed. I'm a secretary who paints. The pedestal disappeared. So did the respect. I lost an exalted position."

"Do you think the ministry ranks high in service to God?"

"I was taught it put me above others."

"Do you still think that way?" Karen continued to write.

"I'm not sure."

"That makes the rest of us, what? Inadequate, unimportant."

Elise shook her head and took another tissue. "I'm not a snob. I didn't intend it that way. Sorry."

"Why does the church elevate a minister?" Karen asked as she peered into Elise's eyes.

Elise answered, her voice strong. "Because they're supposed to dedicate their lives to God. Lead the people to a close relationship with Him. Teach, preach, live sinless lives."

"Interesting. I see why you think your life is off track. If you have believed that all your life, you need to delve into whether it's an accurate picture of the contributions all people make to society. Write about it in your journal. How is that going?"

"I tend to do it only when issues come up." Elise's lips drooped.

"Does painting give you relief from anxiety or depression?"

"Yes. It's a hard task, though, if it reflects my journey of pain and disappointment. Sometimes I dream about my pictures. I wake up and can't go back to sleep for at least an hour."

"Keep doing it. Over time, the benefits come to you in the form of joy and freedom from negative emotions. You're building a new life, and based on what you revealed, I think it's harder for you than some people. You need affirmations from within yourself and your new friends. Who comes to mind when you think of who your supporters are?"

"That's easy. Ginny takes photos of the seamy side of life. She encourages me to work through the difficult issues because she has. And I get critiques of my paintings from the artist group. These are invaluable to my progress as a painter."

"That sounds good, Elise. When your mind strays to what

you've lost, recall what is positive now. I think you're far enough along in your treatment to do that."

"I'll try that. This session gave me the opportunity to erupt. Thanks."

"Let's talk about this more next week. And think about the issue of forgiving those who hurt you. Call me sooner if you need to talk."

Drained of all energy, Elise drove home unaware of her surroundings and was surprised when she arrived at her apartment. She parked her car in front of the house. Once inside her room, she fell into her loveseat and slept.

Elise stirred and opened her eyes to darkness. Her neck was stiff and sore. She stretched her arms and repositioned her body in the chair before she turned on the lamp. How odd. Her body relaxed. Maybe Karen was right. Her rant at Zed had helped.

Her thoughts turned to her call from God to the ministry. Had she imagined it? Maybe she had been influenced by the church's teachings. It was time to make her life meaningful with something else.

Exhausted, Elise fell asleep and dreamed about Zed. *A high rock wall surrounded a garden, and the faint sound of a waterfall beckoned her. She looked for the gate, pushing aside the lush vines growing on the wall. She walked farther down the wall and kept searching. Zed looked over the top of the wall, cupped his hands around his mouth, and called, "The gate is here by me."* She woke up, dismayed by the dream. The clock showed 5:00 a.m.

She got up and nuked a cup of hot water in her microwave and added chocolate-flavored coffee. She thought about the vivid dream. She and Zed had a wall between them. She thought of the church and God. More walls. More walls than she could comprehend. The dream was wrong though. The gate to peace wasn't by Zed's side. *Where was it?*

THE CHURCH PAINTINGS cramped Elise's hands as she carried them to the artists' meeting a week later. She wanted the members' reactions to them. Her body itched as if ants were crawling on her. *Nerves.*

Nick was standing at the door to the building and said, "Hi. I'm glad you came. Are you still angry with me?"

"No."

"At least we'll see each other here and around town," he said as he looked her in the eyes.

"I hope you find the person you deserve. Let's go inside. They're waiting for you to begin the meeting," Elise said.

They entered the community building and went into the room where their friends mingled. Nick cupped his hands around his mouth and yelled, "Let's get started. Pull the chairs into a circle and sit down." After they were seated, he said, "Who wants to start our show-and-tell tonight?"

Elise raised her hand. First, she showed the picture of the crying woman. "This painting and the next two give you an idea of my thoughts and feelings about some experiences I've had. I hope they don't offend anyone. I'd appreciate your honest opinions and perhaps some ideas about what direction my next few paintings should take."

She heard some throats clear and she saw a few people squirm in their chairs, heads bowed. No one said anything. Elise then showed the one of the woman and the minister, and last, the church with a cavernous mouth. Still, no one spoke. Elise looked around the room and tried to figure out people's reactions. "Anyone?"

"I saw the ugly damn church in Elise's home," Ginny said. "I think these paintings are powerful and give messages of pain and anger. So, I'd say they're well done. Like I said before, you might want to create a website and blog about your life's journey."

Nick said, "I wouldn't blog about that. It's so negative some people would write angry responses. And don't put photos of those paintings on your website. This is a democracy. People are entitled to the religion of their choice even if you disagree with what they believe."

"I'm disappointed you think that. However, you're not religious even though you know people get hurt by their places of worship. I think there are others who will identify with me."

"Wait a minute, you two. We're here to analyze art. Not give advice," Doug said. Let's look at Elise's work."

"Your art does make me stop and think. Vivid colors. Well done," Peter said. "And I think you have to decide what you'll paint next."

Elise looked at the others as they nodded their assent. "Thanks for your honesty." Instead of paying attention to the work of the rest of the group, she let her mind wander to what her next piece might be. Surprised the meeting closed, Elise stood and clutched her paintings to her side and left.

SATURDAY MORNING, ELISE turned to the entertainment section of the newspaper. *Winnie the Pooh* was playing at the movie theatre in the nearby town of Fortuna. How fun, she thought. It was the antithesis of what she was experiencing through her painting. And it had been her favorite book of stories as a child. Her dolls often played the parts of the characters, and she had always cast herself as Christopher Robin.

That evening, after a meal of bread and honey, similar to what Pooh might eat, Elise skipped out of her house and drove seven miles to Fortuna. She felt as young as a child again, something she thought long gone.

Elise paid for her ticket at the box office and went inside. She glanced around the room. The theater had been built in 1938. It was restored much later. The wall sconces and chandeliers revealed a distant past. What stories would the theater tell about customers?

The smell of popcorn lured her to the concession, and she gave in to her craving for the crunchy, buttery treat. She bought a small box. In her excitement, she almost ran over Dana, who had Mark and Sammy in tow.

"Dana, how good to see you." Elise gave her sister a gentle hug. Dana kept her arms at her side. Elise stepped back and said, "Are you okay?"

Dana looked Elise up and down. "Aren't you overdressed?"

"My clothing is casual." Elise turned to Mark and Sammy.

"Hi, guys. Are you here to see Winnie the Pooh?"

"Yep, Aunt Lisi," Sammy said. "Can we sit with you?"

"If it's okay with your mom."

"Not this time. Let's get our popcorn and drinks."

"Aw." Sammy's lips turned down.

Mark said, "Please, Mom."

"No. Excuse us, Elise," Dana said.

Elise dug her nails into her palm. She watched as Dana and the boys went to the concession stand. Elise waited until they had purchased their treats. She watched as they climbed the stairs to the auditorium where the movie played. *Doesn't sisterhood mean something?* No answers came to her.

Waiting a few moments, Elise followed them to the movie. Determined Dana would not spoil her night out, she relaxed and decided to focus on *Winnie the Pooh*. Elise found a seat, and while the previews played, she started to think about her life. *Not now.* She was here to enjoy the antics of her childhood friends. She snuggled in to enjoy the movie and watched as Christopher Robin and Winnie the Pooh came on the screen.

Elise slipped away as soon as the credits began to roll. She would wait a few days before she phoned her sister to patch things up. Knowing Dana, she'd cool off by then.

THE FOLLOWING EVENING the need to forgive haunted Elise's thoughts. How could she depict forgiveness in a painting? She took her sketch pad and sat on her loveseat with her feet up. First, she wrote words. "I'm sorry, Zed. I know you were frustrated with me and didn't understand my behaviors. Both of us interpreted the Bible the way we had been taught. I threw it away, and you kept it. I accept that now. The teachings of the church still push my buttons. Maybe down the road, I'll forgive it too. I can't right now."

Elise started an image on a new sheet of paper. She created a sandy beach and a sunset on the horizon of the ocean. A man and woman sat on a blanket near the water, cups of coffee raised to each other. The caption over their heads said, "I forgive you." Elise whistled a tune from the

Winnie the Pooh movie.

Even though Elise had intended to wait, she decided to call Dana. "Sis. It's me. It's important to me that we clear up our misunderstanding. Can we talk things out? Why are you so angry with me?"

"You'll be irate with me, but I have to say this because you can't get it through your stubborn head that you make mistakes. So here goes. I don't know why you think it's okay to paint such vile images of a church. It's so distorted. If you write a blog or post those pictures online, I won't speak to you again. You're bitter and I don't see why. Don't use bipolar as an excuse for your actions. You're accountable to God, and I think you do more harm than good. Zed doesn't deserve your hatred."

"I don't hate Zed. He and I met for lunch not too long ago. And yes, I've been angry. However, I'm trying to work through that. As to what I do with my paintings and whether I blog or not, I haven't decided. I want to think more about that. In the meantime, I wish we could be friends."

"Not now, Elise. Not now."

"Dana, please. Let's talk."

Click. Lightheaded, Elise sat down. Maybe Zed wouldn't accept her apology either, but she would try. *I hope he does.*

"Zed, it's . . . it's me, Elise. Do you have a minute to talk?"

She heard him gulp air. "Of course."

"This is somewhat hard to say. I want you to know I've let go of some of my hurt and anger toward you, and I'm working on forgiveness. My bitterness caused me to lash out at you. The changes in you are positive."

"Does this mean we can work on a future together?"

"As friends, maybe."

"What caused you to change your mind?"

"I want joy in my life. Not pain. You're a good person, and I hope you find a satisfying life."

"Thanks. Come back to me."

"I can't. You'll always be close to my heart." Elise hung up. She wiped her eyes with a tissue.

THE DÉCOR IN Ginny's apartment/studio interested Elise. At first, the earthy tones of the walls and dark brown leather furniture seemed masculine to her. And then she noticed everything made a statement—orderliness. Ginny's professional photography represented the chaos of the world, the antithesis of this room. "You have style, Ginny."

"Thanks. It works for me. Have a seat. I hope you don't mind I invited you for dessert instead of a meal. I'm not a cook. And I purchased the apple pie from the deli. I warmed it." Ginny cut the pie and brought it to the coffee table. "Dig in."

"Hmm. Cinnamon and apples. I'm glad you didn't fuss. I obsessed over the meals I served our friends who were in the ministry. I used china unless we had a potluck barbecue. Even then, the women tried to outdo each other by bringing unique delicious food."

"You were a minister?"

"Wife of one."

"No wonder you have a look of innocence. I'll bet you never got in trouble your whole life."

"True enough. That's why your photos of prostitutes shocked me."

"I see why you're struggling to find a new way to live. Sounds overwhelming to me."

"Not more than a recovering addict. I'm glad you're clean. I brought this new painting for you to see. It's about forgiveness. And I'm not sure where to take my story next."

"It's good," Ginny said between bites of apple pie. "It reminds me of a Jewish artist who lived during World War II. Have you heard of Charlotte Salomon? She painted scenes of her life, which tragically ended in a concentration camp."

"I saw some of her work online," Elise said. "I'm intrigued she painted words on her paintings, which she did toward the end of her life. Paper and paint were scarce due to the war."

"You could model your art after hers and paint your life story. You've started with the most recent part."

"That involves painting severe depression as well as the good about my life before that. I don't know," Elise said.

"Why did you get so depressed?" Ginny asked.

"I'm bipolar."

"Did you struggle with that before you got married?"

"Not as bad as I did with the episode that made me leave my husband and his church."

"Think about this. If you add pictures of bipolar as well as when you were happy, you could create a book. The development of your story would make more sense."

"That's quite an idea. Lots of work involved."

"You're talented. You can do it. What else are you going to do with your life? I'm guessing you enjoyed your work in the ministry."

"Yes. And I need to do something fulfilling. A life book might do the trick."

"There's always volunteer work too. Sometimes in after-school programs they offer art and music lessons."

"You have great ideas, Ginny. How do they come to you?"

"The hard way. I learned photography in a program for teens on drugs. Made a difference in my life."

"My college degree is in art. Do the Ferndale schools use volunteers in after-school programs?"

"I don't know. I lived in Eureka at the time. With school budgets tight, I think any school would value your help."

"I'll look into it. Do you have family and friends who oppose the kind of photos you take?"

"Some. They shy away from the ugly truth, and I think they're afraid I'll take up drugs again since I'm around street people so much. My former connections to the seamy side of life compel me to tell the story. My brother is still a druggie, and I'll always attend Narcotics Anonymous."

"What do you want to do next?" Elise asked.

"To make personal friends. I'm afraid of rejection, so I'm often brash. Now you know my inner truth."

"Emotional pain is a common denominator in people. I'm interested in how you got hooked on illegal drugs. That is, if you want to share it."

"It started in ninth grade. My parents divorced, and I lashed out at them by experimenting. Anger and hurt consumed me. I felt relief when I was high."

"Some people do that with alcohol, don't they?" Elise asked.

"Right. Both of them destroy relationships. Don't start with them."

"I won't. I drink wine in moderation. More than that doesn't tempt me. I hate this medication though. Eliminating it from my life is next." Elise bit her lip. *My new goal.*

TWENTY-ONE

INSPIRED BY A MIDNIGHT THOUGHT ABOUT HER PAINTING, EARLY Saturday morning Elise sat on her loveseat and opened her laptop. She titled a blank page *Life Series*. Using a stream of consciousness, she typed as quickly as possible, and without censure, possible categories of paintings. A pattern developed. Potential titles of various stages of her life and the descriptions of what they might look like in a painting filled the page— depressed teenager, college, marriage, happy church times, bipolar adult, rejection of the church, divorce, paintings of church, forgiveness, and life now.

Engrossed in her work, she had forgotten her coffee. She reached for her cup and realized it was cold. Her small microwave solved her problem. The coffee again had the smell she loved, and her taste buds revealed why she loved her favorite drink. Elise looked out her window as she sipped. The homes in the neighborhood were well kept. Most were craftsman style. *I wish I had a house here.*

Elise returned to her seat and computer. She drew a deep breath, then exhaled. She imagined various scenarios. The progression of a bipolar II teenager depicted in three stages would give an accurate portrayal of the bipolar moods. She grabbed her sketch pad, and instead of depicting her specific depression during high school, Elise decided to base it on what most teens experience when bipolar strikes them. Her online research validated this. With tentative strokes, Elise drew a slim girl teenager dressed in form-fitting jeans and a T-shirt with a school emblem. The girl's face would glow with the use of paint.

The second page reflected the girl's depression. Her body weight had increased by twenty pounds. Her clothes were sloppy, her downturned mouth and dull eyes revealed her unhappy state of being. Elise's shoulders had knotted. She rubbed the painful spots, but they persisted.

The third page showed manic. The girl hammered on a wall, which showed cracks and holes.

Elise decided she must have a fourth page using the first picture. Satisfied with what she had done, she nuked another cup of water and added a teaspoon of instant coffee. She looked at her watch. Noon. Elise descended the stairs after she decided to grab a sandwich at the deli, and then go to Fireman's Park. She thought of her present life. *What direction am I going?*

AT WORK ON Monday, Elise phoned the K-8 school in Ferndale. She explained she wanted to volunteer her time with students who were interested in art. The secretary said she would put her through to the principal. While she waited, the music of a rock song rang in her ear. She didn't recognize it. When the principal answered, Elise repeated the reason for the call.

"Since the village is home to many kinds of artists, our needs have been met," he said. "You might contact Serenity House in Eureka. It's a home for abused women and their children."

"Thanks. I'll do that."

Though she preferred to volunteer in Ferndale, Elise called the shelter's office and asked to speak to the director. "I'm Carol Willis, the director. May I help you?"

"This is Elise Norris. I'm wondering if you need a volunteer for an art program. I have a degree in fine art and could teach a class."

"Wow. That's a great offer. The problem is we don't have enough financing to buy art supplies. The volunteer must furnish those. That's expensive. We have twenty-five women and children. Is that feasible for you?"

Elise thought for a moment. An idea came to mind. "I belong to an art group. I could ask if they'd be willing to donate money. I'll contribute as much as possible within my budget."

"That's gracious of you. However, I don't know if you're interested in the kind of art we need. Instead of teaching our clientele to draw or paint, we use expressive art. Our residents need to let their feelings flow out of their bodies onto the paper. Does that appeal to you?"

"My paintings are often emotional. I understand what you mean. And yes, I'm interested."

"Good. I'll mail you an application. You can send it to our post office box. You need to know we conduct a thorough background check on volunteers. We also need two references."

"Both are all right with me."

"Give me your address." Elise did and asked for the postal number. The exchange was done. "I'll look forward to receiving your application. If it's approved, we'll conduct an orientation for you and other first-time volunteers."

"I'll work on this right away. Thanks for your time."

THE NEXT EVENING Elise phoned Zed. "Hi. Do you have a minute or on your way to a meeting?"

"I have about thirty minutes. What's happening?"

"I volunteered to conduct an art class at Serenity House in Eureka." She explained its purpose. "The application asked for two references from people who have known me for at least three years. Do you think someone in the church would do that for me?" Elise's heart thumped in her chest. *What if he can't find anyone?*

"I will, if you'll let me."

"Of course. That's generous of you."

"And I think Nancy Dickerson would do it too. She has

diabetes, and she's glad I preach about suffering. Do you know her?"

"She worked with me in the soup kitchen. We got along well."

"Do you have an address for her?" Zed asked.

"No."

"Are you ready?"

"Yes."

Zed read the information.

"Got it."

"Good luck. It's a worthy cause. However, I'm worried you'll get depressed again. And what if some of the children act out? It could be dangerous."

"I'm not worried about my moods. I feel so much better. Thanks for your help." *Am I doing the right thing?*

Elise phoned Ginny to tell her the news.

"Hey, how are you, girl?" Ginny asked. "What's new?"

"It's all good. The Serenity House in Eureka is interested in me since I'm willing to conduct expressive art classes." Elise couldn't stop grinning.

"What did you think of the director?"

"I only talked to her by phone, but she was nice, yet professional. She wanted references, which is a good sign."

"I hope this leads to great things. You deserve it."

"Thanks for the encouragement."

"By the way, are you ready for a website and blog? I don't want to pressure you."

"Not now. I want to work more on my life story through my artwork before I do that. I've started, but I need more paintings to complete the series. Thanks for your help, Ginny."

"See you soon."

After her phone call to Ginny, Elise continued to work on the application. The shelter wanted to know if she had been convicted of a felony or misdemeanor. Thank goodness she could say no to those. Her references would be given a call. They were thorough. Elise respected that.

She wondered if a twice-monthly art program would be the best. It made more sense financially. So, she wrote that on the application. She mailed it to Carol. It was mid-September already. She would like to work with the women and children before the holidays started. They might need to work through Thanksgiving and Christmas related depression.

A MONTH PASSED before Carol called Elise and told her of her acceptance as a volunteer. Now Elise was sitting on a well-worn beige sofa in Carol's small office. The walls needed a coat of paint, and the metal file cabinets had dents and scratches. In her mind, she contrasted this room to Zed's workplace—mahogany furniture, expensive pictures on the walls, and quality carpet on the floors. Four other women were also present for the orientation.

"Thanks for coming everyone," Carol said.

Elise was surprised to see an overweight woman with hair to her waist. She had expected someone who looked like Karen.

"I'll give you a background on this organization as well as our programs. Serenity House was founded twenty years ago by a woman who had been abused by her husband and molested by her father. After therapy and an education in social work, she decided to help women like her as well as their children. She established the home in a place surrounded by a fence. Outsiders don't know where it is. The gate gives vetted people access."

"We provide information about Serenity's program to doctors and social workers. Newspapers donate space for advertisements." Carol sipped some water. "Do you have any questions so far?" she asked.

Elise noticed everyone shook their heads.

"We'll continue. Money's a scarce commodity. We receive help from state and federal sources, along with some grants, and individual donations. As much as possible, we use volunteers. That gives us more money to spend on the women and children. We also need to maintain our buildings and grounds. We need volunteers, and I'm glad you're interested. How do you feel about helping at-risk women and children? It's not easy."

Elise spoke first. "I think it's important to listen to others and offer, at the very least, compassion. I haven't had the opportunity to do that for a while now, but I want to be involved. I'm also wondering if there are people who protect our safety if someone acts out."

"I agree," another woman said. The others nodded their heads.

"We do. They've had training on the correct procedures. One is always present with you. Whether it's women or children, they are led to the activity. If they act out, the worker talks with them about their issue. They are allowed to return to the class the next time it convenes. Does that alleviate your fears?"

"It does mine," Ada said. "How long do the clientele stay here?"

"A year. It takes that long for them to change their behaviors and heal within as much as possible. They participate in one-on-one therapy as well as a group. We also prepare them for jobs with basics such as dressing appropriately for the job they get. Computer skills are necessary in today's world. There are very few jobs that don't require some knowledge of technology. Other questions?" Silence.

"We have three trained women who work eight-hour shifts each. Nights can be busy if some of our people have nightmares or trouble sleeping. Most of them have PTSD from abuse, prostitution, or drug addiction. If someone requires a medical doctor, the nightshift lady calls me, and I take them to the emergency room."

"I had never thought of what it would take to be in charge of a shelter. You have all the issues the average family outside of here has, plus more. I hope the art program proves valuable for them. It's the least I can do," Elise said.

"Some women and even the children come here with bruises on their bodies."

"That's hard for me to imagine. I haven't experienced that."

"The upside is our success ratio hovers around eighty-nine percent. Sometimes, though, women have a relapse and then come here again. If we aren't full, we admit them the second time."

"Are all of them poor?" Elise asked.

"No. Abuse, addiction, and homelessness aren't isolated to a single socio-economic class. Other comments? No? I'm going to turn this over to Donna. She'll take you to our facility and show you where you'll be working. Thanks for coming."

"Hi, everyone. Let's go outside to my van," Donna said.

Once they were loaded, Donna drove to Serenity House. Elise noted it was on the edge of town three blocks from a bus stop. Donna punched in the code for the gate. There were a few parking spaces near what Elise thought was a small office. They unloaded and gathered around Donna.

"Before we start, I'll go over some rules. I don't want any of you to try and solve issues for the women. We have professionals for that. You can't talk about our residents to anyone outside this group. Never, ever, mention their names. And don't ever give the name or address of our facility."

Elise was glad when the sun broke through the clouds. *This is going to be harder than I thought.* She brought herself back to attention when Donna spoke again.

"As you can see, our dormitory is across the lawn. The basement contains the kitchen and storage. The classrooms and some of the bedrooms are on the first floor. The second is all bedrooms. They are large enough for the women and their children. Let's go to the kitchen first."

Elise liked Donna, but she was strictly business. She didn't chit chat, but neither had Carol.

Once they were in the kitchen, Elise disliked what she saw. The kitchen had a round table that seated eight. Its painted yellow surface brightened the otherwise white room. And the stove was battered. The cupboards needed to be replaced. *I wonder if Zed's church would refurbish this room?*

The women chatted among themselves while they climbed the stairs to the art room. Elise talked to Ada. "How do you feel about everything?" she asked.

"A little frightened. What about you?"

"The same. Here we are."

193

The group followed Donna inside. The desks accommodated both small and teenage children. There were also tables for adults. Elise was thankful for the large windows. *Plenty of light for art if the sun is shining.*

Donna said, "Elise, are you prepared to see in our residents' art, their struggles? They come to us, oftentimes beat up, depressed, and without hope. It isn't pretty. And some are resistant to change. It takes time to build trust. I also need to warn you the children act out, sometimes in violence. We'll do everything possible to keep you safe. A trained staff member will be with you in class to take care of the situation. Sometimes the staff needs to physically restrain the child. That's hard to watch, but we have to keep the child from harming themselves or others."

"I . . . I didn't think about that. I expected some difficulties. If that happens, what do I do?"

"That's where the trained staff person comes into play. You'll need to keep order with the rest of the kids. Let the counselor do her work. Try to keep the children focused on their art."

"You've given me something to think about. Maybe all of us?"

"Yes. Ada, you're going to help us with computer classes. Let's go to that room." Donna pushed her hair behind her ears and led them down the hall.

"Wow, you have great computers. I didn't expect it," Ada said.

"A high-tech company donated them. We're grateful for their generosity."

Ada said, "I think I can divide the class into groupings by knowledge. I'll give the more experienced ones some tasks to follow while I work with the others."

"Good. Christy, you're on landscaping duty. You'll follow our main gardener's instructions. He's pleasant and knows his job. Any other questions?"

The women shook their heads.

"If not, we'll go to my little office. I'll give each of you a schedule. I'm paid staff and work eight hours a day. If you need to talk about anything, please come and see me. And thanks for your services. We count on volunteers to fill the gaps where our professionals can't."

Back at the office, Elise helped herself to a cup of Earl Grey tea. She was thankful to be with other volunteers and visited with them before she drove back to Ferndale. *It seems like there is an endless amount of things required to effectively manage this place. I hope I can do my part.*

At home that evening, Elise wrote down a few ideas about how she would teach the children. Suggestions of what to draw would help. The youngest ones would use crayons. If they drew sad faces on their own, she'd know how they felt. For the adults, she painted a few pictures from her gut. Something to give them an idea of what to do. Nothing formal. Black blobs of paint for depression and anger. Dark clouds and rain would also describe negative feelings. Yellow for happy feelings. Doubts assailed her. *What if the women and children don't like me?*

Elise hit speed dial on her cell to call Janet, who answered on the first ring. "Hi, honey. How are you?"

"If you're not busy, could you come to my apartment?"

"I baked brownies and they're fresh out of the oven. I'll bring them. It lifts the spirits."

"I love you, Mom. See you in a bit."

Elise paced the floor of her room until she heard Janet's light knock. Elise flung the door open. "Thanks for coming. I made tea to go with the brownies."

Elise placed dessert plates and cups on the coffee table. She took a bite of her brownie. "Love chocolate."

"What's the news? I'm dying to know," Janet said.

Elise told her about the Serenity House in Eureka. "That's it, Mom. What do you think?"

"I think it's perfect for you. Especially with the children. You love Mark and Sammy so much, and you like to do things with them. It sounds like a big challenge. And the women need your compassion. You've been on the receiving end, so you know how. But I'm worried you might be physically harmed. Did Donna say how she would keep you safe?" Janet squeezed her brows together.

"Yes. There will be an aide or counselor with me. For every fifth child, they have one adult. I need this position. Maybe I won't feel sad about not being in the ministry."

"I think so too."

The women ate brownies and sipped tea. Elise liked the companionable silence.

Janet said, "I'm worried about your relationship with Dana. She's quite angry with you and wouldn't say why."

"I hate to involve you in this argument. Please don't take sides. You're our mom, and I know you love both of us."

"What happened?"

Elise stood and held on to the back of her chair. She related the story of what happened at the movie theater in Fortuna. "I'm angry and sad at the same time, but I don't know what to do." Her lips trembled. "I don't want to fight with her."

Her mother drew a deep breath, her face solemn. "You're right, I can't take sides. I'm sorry this happened. I don't understand her relentless anger. Give it time. If I get a chance, and she's open to it, I'll at least ask her to be cordial to you. That's the best I can do besides pray."

"Thanks. If you talk to her, don't make her upset with you. And if she thinks we've been discussing her, she'll just be angrier."

"I won't. The holidays will be here before we know it. I want a happy family gathering. I hear stories about fights with loved ones this time of year. I'd rather not celebrate under those conditions. I'll talk to your father about it."

"I'll see if Dana will go to lunch with me. Maybe between the two of us, she will soften her stance."

"Good. I'm sorry, I need to go. My friend Geneva is sick. Thought I'd head there next before I go home. I want to take her a couple of these brownies, if you don't mind."

"Of course not. Thanks for coming over." Elise followed Janet to the door. "See you soon. Give Dad a hug from me." *I wish Dana would make the first move. If she doesn't, should I quit thinking of myself as a pastor's wife? I could be mean to her.*

WHILE AT WORK the next day, Elise phoned her sister. "Dana, it's me. Don't hang up, please."

"What do you want?"

"Meet me for lunch today or tomorrow. I want to share some developments in my life. You might be surprised about what I'm doing. Please don't say no."

"I don't want anything to do with you."

Elise ignored her comment. "What about lunch today at the deli? Say, eleven-thirty."

"Didn't you hear me?" Dana asked.

"Please. I love you and your family. Mark and Sammy mean everything to me."

"You should have thought about that before now. My friends think you're as confused as a bird that can't escape a cage."

"How could that be?" Elise asked. "They don't know anything about me."

"You're so engrossed in yourself, you don't think of anyone else. When I told them about your so-called bipolar disorder, they said you're demon-possessed. How do you think that makes me feel? I'll tell you. Like crap, to use one of your words."

"What the hell? I can't believe you said anything. You revealed something I'm sensitive about. I thought the agreement within our family was not to tell anyone. How could you? I want to punch you in the face. You betrayed me." She ended the call.

Elise phoned Janet. "It's me. Is Dad home?"

"He's at work. What's wrong?"

"Can I come over?"

"You don't need an invitation. Can you leave work?"

"I checked with Ed."

Elise ran to her parents' home and walked in without knocking. "Mom, I need a hug."

"Of course, honey." Janet walked the distance to Elise and held out her arms. "Let's sit down. What happened?"

"It's Dana. She's been talking about my bipolar with her friends."

"I can't imagine," Janet said. "I know she has a temper, but this is spiteful. What's wrong with her?"

"She seems bitter about me leaving Zed's church, as well as my divorce. That's not even to mention she's jealous of the wealth I had. She was critical of the weight I gained when I was depressed. She refuses to understand me."

"Honey, do you think she's overwhelmed with all that's occurred in your life? Maybe Dana told her friends because she needed sympathy."

"Does that mean she has to be ghastly with me?"

"Of course not. Dad and I will talk to her and Cliff. We don't want a split in the family."

Am I a fool to think Dana will change?

ELISE PACED BACK and forth in Karen's waiting room.

Karen opened her office door. "Come in."

Elise began the conversation before she sat down. "You won't believe what Dana said and did. I'm as angry as a bull whipped with nails. I'm hurt to the core of my being."

"Tell me."

Elise repeated her tale of horror. "I don't know how to deal with this."

"I don't remember whether we've discussed how the dynamics of a family originate or the impact they have on the individuals. But it's worth repeating if I didn't."

"I don't know what you mean," Elise said.

"Each member of the family has a role. In a negative setting, some are the scapegoat. What was the relationship between you and Dana growing up?"

"She didn't like it when people complimented me on my hair or complexion. One time she grabbed a handful of hair and cut some of it off. Mom had to take me to the hairdresser to make it even. And she thought my parents favored me even though she was the oldest."

"Who did your parents prefer? You or her?"

Elise shrugged. "I don't see it that way. I loved art, and music filled Dana's life. We attended her choir performances in high school. She sang solos as well. I remember telling her she has an awesome voice. I meant it. I ran with the popular crowd. Maybe she didn't like it."

"Let's dig deeper," Karen said. "Did Dana ever babysit you or do chores she thought you should?"

"When we were in elementary and middle school, Mom made her wait for me after school to make sure I was safe on the way home. Dana complained about it almost every day."

"What did she say?" Karen asked.

"She called me a baby."

"Did that hurt your feelings?"

Elise crossed her legs. "Yes. And I argued with her about it, but she got angry."

"Sibling rivalry is strong and often carries into adulthood. Families get together, and the same roles play out creating more hard feelings. You've taken all the attention away from Dana. You've been in the family spotlight. I'm thinking Dana can't cope with this. Added to that are her strong religious beliefs. You broke family rules."

"Karen, not on purpose. It happened. What am I supposed to do?"

"Give Dana time. At least a year. See what happens."

"What if she still won't reconcile with me?"

"You'll need to accept that, which is hard to do. Live your life. Let her follow her own path."

"The holidays will be here soon. Mom and Dad will insist on a family Christmas with all of us. I doubt that will happen."

"Write Dana a short note saying you miss her. If there is no response, or if she says something nasty, let it go. You've done your best." Karen looked at her watch. "I hate to end this session so soon, but since you needed urgent counseling, I squeezed you in. I have another client. Let me know how everything goes."

"Thanks for scheduling me so quickly."

Elise's mind went from thought to thought as she went over the conversation with Karen. *Mom and Dad will be hurt if we don't have a wonderful family Christmas.*

TWENTY-TWO

Zed

ZED PARKED HIS CAR NEAR CHINATOWN'S DRAGON GATE, WHICH spanned Grant Avenue in San Francisco. He walked the short distance and saw Greg standing on the corner. "I'm glad you had time to meet me for lunch."

Greg gave Zed a bear hug and slapped him on the back. "Good to see you. I think of you often. I'm curious about what's happened since we last saw each other. But first things first. I'm starved, and I know a great place. Local Chinese eat there so you know it's good."

While they snaked through the crowds along the street to the restaurant, Zed admired the jade jewelry and Chinese gifts for sale displayed in the shop windows. After a couple of blocks, Greg took Zed's elbow and led him down a narrow alley to a dilapidated building. They descended the dimly lit concrete stairs, turned to the right, and walked into the small restaurant.

A server led them to a table for two. The smell of vegetables stir-fried in sesame oil inundated Zed's senses. His stomach growled. After they sat down, they were given menus written in Chinese. "How do we know what to order?" Zed asked.

"I think the server speaks some English. He'll guide us. Let me buy our lunch."

"No. Let's each pay for our own."

"I'm the elder here. I'll treat you."

Zed laughed. "Okay, thanks."

A pot of jasmine tea and two small white bowls were brought to their table. Greg poured. "So, you want to discuss some new thoughts concerning your situation."

"Right. I've mulled over my experiences in Israel, my talks with God while there. I've prayed for wisdom. To be true to myself I might need to resign from my church. I have so many doubts. I don't know when to do it or what I'll do afterwards. And the ministry is important to me. I explored the requirements of a few denominations, including yours. Each one wants a graduate from one of their seminaries."

"Just a sec. Here's the server to take our orders. What do you suggest?" Greg asked. He leaned back in his chair.

"All food good."

"I'll have sweet and sour pork," Zed said.

"Broccoli and beef," Greg said.

"Our pot stickers. They very good," the server said. "Chopsticks?"

"Neither for me," Zed said.

"No thanks, that's all," Greg said.

"Back to your dilemma, Zed. I can't say I'm surprised. I watched you struggle in Israel with what you saw and learned. You've been home close to a couple of months. What do you think now?"

"I answered God's call to me with the belief I'd be a career minister. Now I'm confused."

"There isn't an easy answer. I've seen men and women leave the ministry for various reasons. Many find fulfillment in occupations such as teaching. Some work for Christian nonprofit organizations. These jobs allow them to have a different kind of ministry. Or there are pastors who go to the mission field. What do you think about that?"

"A mission trip to Africa or someplace like that?"

"No. Stay in a country a year or two. Get a different perspective. I assume you know some missionaries."

"One spoke at our church several months ago. He

ministers in Ethiopia. They need help. He said the poverty in places is staggering. Very different than what I had in mind." Zed folded his hands and leaned forward. "I have an undergraduate degree in English and could get a teaching credential."

"You might also consider ministering in a different type of nondenominational church. You'd face close scrutiny by the pastor-seeking committee about why you left your church. And they'll want to know about your new beliefs. Here's our food. Dig in."

"That sounds interesting," Zed said. He took a bite of his food. "This is delicious, and the sauce is tasty."

"Glad you like it. I bring my wife here as often as possible. If you don't mind, let's return to our conversation about your ministry options."

"Great. You've given me several ideas. Do you know anyone I could speak to who left the ministry?"

"Why do you want to do that?" Greg asked.

"Like I said, I have a minor in English. I could teach in the States. I'd like to hear the story from someone about the new life they lead."

"There's one person who I'm pretty sure would meet with you. Also, I can keep my ear tuned to the ministerial gossip circle about churches in need of a new pastor. Since I'm on several boards and committees here in San Francisco, I might hear of something."

"I'm grateful for your help," Zed said.

"I hope you won't feel like I'm patronizing you, but I've grown fond of you. I take a strong interest in young ministers who encounter problems that change their lives. I need to add, don't make a hasty decision. I'm curious, though. If you preach about what you've learned, are you prepared to be dismissed from your church?"

"I hope that doesn't happen. It wouldn't look good on a resume." Zed looked at his closed fists.

"Think about it. Another point. Have you talked with someone who believes in your church's doctrines?"

"No, I want to talk to a friend I'll see at the ministers'

retreat in Sonoma County. We used to have great discussions together about life and the Bible when we were in seminary. Thought I'd bend his ear a little. I think he'll listen without judging me."

"I hope it goes well for you. Anything new with Elise?"

Zed avoided Greg's eyes. "I explained the challenges I faced in Israel. She appreciated my experiences, but said she wasn't coming back to me."

"How did you feel about that?"

"Angry and hurt. She also balked when I indicated I wanted a closer relationship with her." Zed laid his fork across his plate, finished with his food. He had eaten half of what had been served. The server took his plate and Greg's.

"Perhaps you need to let go of her. I know that's hard. For the sake of your future, and hers, it might be best. At least give it some thought."

Zed frowned.

Greg looked at his watch. "Glad we could meet, but I need to leave. I am seeing another minister in an hour. Stay in touch."

"I'll let you know what I decide." *How do I find God's will? It used to be easy. I don't even say amen or hallelujah anymore.*

ZED AROSE BEFORE dawn on Saturday and went to the kitchen to brew coffee. After he poured himself a cup, he sat at the kitchen table and found his computerized sermon folder. He tried to put his thoughts together. He had struggled with his sermon all week and still wasn't prepared.

Even though he wanted to preach about how his beliefs had changed, he knew tomorrow would not be the time. That would come later if he chose to leave. How could he preach about what stirred his soul? Maybe the Prodigal Son. His opening question could be: Are we like the jealous elder brother when his father welcomed back his wastrel younger son with a feast? He could emphasize that Jesus welcomed all people to the kingdom of God. Christianity was an inclusive faith by God's grace. And other religions worshipped God. Not a bad subject. But anger would stir the congregation to action against him.

What had he seen in Israel that helped him change at least one belief? The wall in Bethlehem that extended to other Palestinian lands. That was it. Excitement lifted his spirits. He could preach about barriers in relationships. God's love could remove walls.

AFTER THE OFFERING was received and a hymn was sung, Zed stepped up to the mahogany pulpit and surveyed the congregation of around fifteen hundred people. He swallowed and took a deep breath.

"My time in Israel enlightened me to the many kinds of barriers people build." Zed enumerated some of them. He told them about the encounter with the guide's brother at the overpowering wall in Bethlehem who spoke with ferocity about the Palestinian plight. "Walls keep in, and also out. I'll repeat. Walls keep people in, and also out. It's an important concept and worthy of introspection."

He gave his opinion on relationships and how people erect dividers that can't be torn down unless both parties agree to work out their differences. He saw numerous people squirm and avoid eye contact with him. He wondered if they felt guilty about the rift in the church. Others looked at their hands or the walls of the sanctuary. Some couples joined hands and looked at each other and back to him. A few wiped tears from their eyes. Hope filled him. Maybe his words would help a few congregants and allow him to extend his time here.

He ended his sermon and requested that the congregation sing the song "We Are One in the Spirit." When the song was finished, he lifted his hands toward God. He prayed that all would open their hearts to God's call to seek reconciliation.

Afterwards, he walked to the back of the sanctuary and took his usual place at the middle door. He shook hands with people as they filed out. A congregant approached him and said. "Great sermon Pastor. We all have walls."

Next was James Prescott who didn't shake hands. "You

didn't preach about God's promise to prosper us, Reverend Norris." Zed noticed James's use of Zed's last name. Not a good sign. "You avoided preaching how God has blessed Israel and that he does the same for us."

"I think my sermon was spot on about people's lives. We need to love and respect each other. Don't you think?"

"You established this church, and it grew because you preached about how God could bless people's lives. They responded positively by giving their money, having faith, and believing God's promises that he will supply their every need. You're off track. I advise you to change your message."

Zed didn't reply and was glad when Prescott left. He hoped James would get his comeuppance soon.

ZED GRIPPED THE steering wheel until his hands hurt as he drove to the ministers' retreat in Sonoma County that his church board had required him to attend. He thought about how he might approach a friend or two about his current spiritual dilemma. Doubts absorbed his mind about whether even his closest friend, Joe, would understand.

He drove along Highway 12 from Santa Rosa through mountainous terrain and vineyards to get to the Woodside Retreat Center. When the mission-style lodge with a red clay tile roof and stucco walls came into view, Zed relaxed a bit. Maybe things would be okay. Zed mouthed the words, "Please, God, help me."

The paved parking lot was half-full already. He parked his car. After he removed his Gucci leather suitcase from the trunk, he walked up the hill into the lodge. The lobby, which was full of ministers, was rustic with a wood-beamed high ceiling and old pictures of various California missions. Groupings of overstuffed burgundy leather chairs with modern coffee tables filled the center. Pots of tall green plants added color to the room. He hoped the ministers were as friendly as this place looked. They were all from prosperity gospel churches and those who aspired to attain that level in their congregations.

Zed registered at the counter and climbed the stairs to his room where he unpacked. The queen size bed with a beige comforter and red pillows filled part of the room. A desk, chair, and recliner completed the furnishings. He unpacked and shook the wrinkles from his clothes before he hung them in the closet. Zed went downstairs to look for the people he knew.

He saw several ministers he knew engaged in animated conversations. The room was crowded, and to be heard, they talked in loud voices. Some gestured with their hands. Zed laughed to himself. Ministers loved to share stories about their church experiences. He held out his smartphone and took a picture.

He walked around the room and greeted several people he knew. He spotted his friend, Joe, whose red hair, which hung loosely over his forehead, made him stand out. Zed walked over and tapped him on the shoulder.

"Zed, how's it going?" Joe interrupted the chatter of the men. "Hey, guys. Please excuse me. I haven't seen Zed since last Christmas. I'll see you all later." Joe took Zed's arm and led him away from the others. "I've heard rumors about you."

"Who is telling tales, and what are they saying?"

"I was told in confidence, so I can't say who they are. But they claim you're not preaching like you used to about what God can do for us. They claim you talk about suffering as if that's what life is about."

"I think they have a courtyard. Let's check that out," Zed said. "We can talk there."

They walked through double doors to the outdoor space enclosed by a wood fence. They found a bench under a trellis with grapevines hanging from it.

"Great courtyard," Zed said. "It's cooler than the one Christ Church Guest House had where I stayed in Jerusalem."

"What? You didn't tell me you were there. When was it?"

"August. I went with a small group of ministers from several denominations. It was interesting."

"Didn't you feel out of place? You weren't tempted to believe their way, were you?"

Zed shook his head and smiled. "You're the same, Joe.

You always ask at least two questions in one whack. So, question one. Yes, at first. My roommate was a very intelligent, warm man who is a Presbyterian minister. He's sixty-four and ready to retire. He took me under his wing and allowed me to express my doubts about what I was exposed to. He became a good friend."

"I can't believe you'd pal around with a minister whose beliefs don't align with ours."

"We have a number of things in common. The most essential is that we both believe in Christ. And to answer your second question, I wasn't tempted to change, I was challenged to review what I've been taught."

"What could have tested your faith?" Joe asked. "You were in the place where Jesus lived and had his ministry. What happened?"

Zed gave Joe an overview of the things he'd heard and seen that caused his doubts. "I'm not sure I believe like I did before my trip."

Joe's face turned red. "For heaven's sake, Zed, we had our questions in seminary. Remember how we stayed up all night with other students to hash out life's questions? We resolved them with scripture."

Zed wanted to scream. "Listen. Until Elise left me, I believed too. Even when I signed the divorce papers, I thought she would come back to me. Faith didn't heal her depression, and her illness brought the end of our marriage. My world disintegrated, and I began to search for answers. What we'd learned in the church didn't match what was happening in my life. I feel stupid for believing life could always be fixed by faith."

"Hey, buddy," Joe said with a wave of his hands. "You don't make sense. Elise is the one who sinned. You still have your church, car, and money. All are blessings from God. They're not from the devil, that's for sure. Don't question God."

"Of course, they're not from Satan. I've worked hard to strengthen my church and get more members."

"But you need more faith. You're discouraged. Don't let Elise do that to you."

"I thought you liked Elise, Joe. She doesn't deserve your wrath."

"I did. Still do. But I don't understand her or you."

"At first, I didn't know what to think about her either. I'm making progress though."

Zed realized his conversation with Joe was fruitless. He didn't comprehend what Zed had said. *I'm a stranger here.*

"I'd keep this to yourself or you'll be in trouble," Joe said.

"I already am. Many in my church disagree with me."

"You don't want to cause a division in your church. If I were you, I'd rethink these new beliefs and act the way you always have. I'll be praying God will give you wisdom and strength to stand up against your doubts. I'll see you later. I want to talk to a few other guys."

Zed watched Joe walk away. *Joe failed me. Why did I think he would understand? He's locked into the prosperity gospel like I was. I'm a fool.*

At dinner, Zed sat at a table for eight next to Stan Appleton. His dark brown hair and tall stature distinguished him from others. He was the pastor of his parents' church in Colorado.

"Zed, it's good to see you," Stan said. "Your parents are sure great to have in the church. And they're some of our best volunteers. They don't seem to mind having a younger minister. I don't like Denver winters though. I love Alabama where I was raised."

Zed was annoyed. Stan went on and on, running at his mouth, not asking anyone else questions or letting them talk. "So, how's your church?"

"It's growing. We have two services every Sunday morning and both are packed. We might have to go to three services if we continue to grow."

"What do you attribute that to?" Zed took a bite of his broiled steak.

"I preach a lot on having a positive attitude about everything. You know, they need to pray more if they want their prayers to be answered. I teach about faith, and how if we let Satan put negative thoughts in our heads, then we're going to have a bigger struggle in life. With a positive attitude, we can forge ahead in our Christian life. I tell people that if they don't think God will bless them, then don't put anything in the offering plate. They sure respond to that. We're able to pay our bills and give to missions. It works."

It's all about money. "Do you get any opposition to that kind of preaching?" Zed asked.

"Oh, some. Most of the time I win them over. If not, they go where they get what they want to hear."

"Do they change denominations?" Zed asked.

"You bet. They go to a church where they don't have that positive attitude. The churches are often smaller and have less money than we do. I figure if people up their faith by a couple of notches, we can do a lot more for God. My congregation bought me a Mercedes because they believe that's what God wants for me. They think I should be an example of what I preach. We need to show ourselves and outsiders we have faith and believe in miracles."

"Wow, a Mercedes no less," Zed replied. *Does he hear himself talking? What does God think?* He thought he heard God say, "But you have a Porsche."

"By the way, how's Elise? Has she come back yet, or are you divorced?"

"The divorce was final in the spring."

"Couldn't you work it out?" Stan asked.

What did this guy know? "We tried," he said, his voice edgy.

"I hear she got depressed. That's a lack of faith. She didn't believe in Christ's power to heal."

Zed decided to put him on the spot. "Do you think God heals everyone?"

"No, but I believe he can. Enough faith is required. Or sometimes I think illness is due to people's sin."

Zed said, "I've read that depression is due to a chemical imbalance in the brain. What do you think about that?"

"Well, some of these non-Christian counselors say that. I think it's more that people aren't doing God's will. And they're sinning. You probably saw that with Elise, didn't you?"

Zed decided he'd had enough and would shut this guy up. "I'm confused about that. I didn't see sin in her life, yet she got very depressed. I couldn't understand it. She didn't either. Often, she said she had jumped through the prescribed hoops of the church, and it didn't work. She thinks God abandoned her."

Some of the ministers looked down at their plates and others looked at each other and shrugged their shoulders. Zed had noticed they listened to the exchange between him and Stan.

The conversation turned to politics, which made it easy for the others to talk. Zed entered the discussion when possible—conservatives versus liberals, abortion, and other hot-button issues. Since his trip to Israel, he didn't know where he stood on some of them. When he had time, he'd research some of the issues. But he kept his thoughts to himself. Zed excused himself from the table as soon as he could and be polite.

That night at the worship service, the guest speaker asked for people to make prayer requests. Zed had decided he wouldn't ask for prayer for himself. They wouldn't approve of his needs for answers. *Like, should he leave the ministry?*

Just before the speaker started to pray, Stan said, "The Holy Spirit is urging me to request prayer for Elise. Let's have a special prayer. "Lord, you know our sister in Christ, Elise. Heal her for your glory. And everyone says?"

Loud amens echoed in the room.

Damn him. Zed almost left, but he knew he would be cutting the rope before he was ready. He bore it for the sake of extending his time in his church.

TWENTY-THREE

Elise

ELISE SAT IN DONNA'S OFFICE ON THE SERENITY HOUSE CAMPUS AND glanced at her watch. Ten o'clock on a Saturday. A month had passed since orientation. Today, she would begin the art workshop. She cleared her throat.

"It's good to see you," Donna said as she shut the door. "I'm filling in for Jackie. She's here on weekends. Sorry I'm late. Let's go to the art room. Our counselors told the women about you, and they seem excited."

"Good. I made some examples of expressive art to show them how to go about it. I hope they're appropriate."

"I'll look at them when we get inside."

As they walked across the campus to the dormitory, Elise wrapped her all-weather coat tighter around her body to protect it from the cold wind that blew off Humboldt Bay. *What a day to try something new.*

Before her deep depression, life had been, for the most part, easy. She had read about abuse and addiction in newspapers and magazines and blamed it on the people's rebellion against God. She had thought Satan guided their lives.

"Here we are. Let's go to the art room so I can look at your work," Donna said.

Once inside, Elise lifted her artwork from her case and showed Donna.

"That's exactly what I want. I'm hoping it aids our clientele in digging within themselves to see what they need to change. Usually, the women are too subservient. They've been beaten down, so we teach assertiveness. But then, of course, there is anger bubbling either under the surface or obvious acting out. On occasion, one walks out of a class because she's too angry or starts to cry.

"For the children, you'll need to have a firm voice and let them know you're in charge. If you don't, you're inviting chaos. They need to learn boundaries to feel safe. Right now, we have one boy who gets in trouble. He has a special mentor who helps him."

"Do they sit still?"

"They're active. They often get up and walk around, and they ask questions out of turn. You'll have to get used to it."

"What kind of negative behaviors do the children display?"

"Some of them exhibit their anger and sadness by biting or hitting their classmates. Or they withdraw. At times some of them want to be cuddled. They've been traumatized, so expect anything."

"I'm looking forward to meeting everyone."

Donna turned to a young woman who walked into the room. "Nadine, this is Elise, our art volunteer."

"I'll enjoy working with you," Nadine said.

"Elise," Donna said, "Nadine is gaining experience to fulfill her requirement for hands-on training for her social work degree. We're delighted to have her. She'll be with you every Saturday you're here."

"I'm pleased to meet you," Elise said. Nadine's short hair was cut in a bob. Her jeans were old and split at the knee. "I see you have the correct attire. We'll get spattered with paint today."

Eight women entered the room. Some hung their heads as if ashamed and others smiled at Elise. How could she build trust with them?

"Hi, everyone. Take a seat and we'll get started. I'm Elise

Norris, and if you haven't met Nadine, she's my assistant today."

After they were seated, Elise said, "I'm divorced. I've been depressed, sad, and angry. I hope to get to know you and be of help to you through art. The class for the children is after this. Please introduce yourselves, if you don't mind." Elise bit her lip and hoped they cooperated.

Tamara raised her hand. "I came to Serenity House for the first time last night. My husband beats me and punches me on the face as you can see."

"I'm sorry. I wish you the very best future possible. Next?"

"Drugs have ruled my life," Edith said. "I lost custody of my three children. Maybe art can help me."

"I have a friend who was an addict. She's doing quite well, and you can too," Elise said.

"Veronica. I hate myself. So many mistakes. Prostitution, drugs. I don't know if I can make it happen for me here."

"That's tough. So sorry. Maybe you can use the art to show what led you to that kind of life. Good luck."

Wow. Ginny nails it with her photos.

The other five women refused to talk.

"I want to explain the kind of art we'll be doing. I won't teach you to draw. We'll be using colors and shapes to show our feelings. Here's an example of expressive art I used to show my emotions. I splashed various colors on here. Black and gray are used to express negative emotions like anger and sadness. Yellows, oranges, and reds signify happiness or joy. Blues, purples, and browns often denote peace."

Tamara raised her hand. "I don't know what you mean."

"It doesn't have to be a picture," Elise said. "You may paint or draw anything, even stick figures. Whatever you feel in your heart. And you can use the paint to make circles or funnel clouds or other things to portray yourself. They can be sad or happy. Don't be afraid. There's no wrong or right way to do this."

Elise watched as Tamara bent her head and picked up a brush. She dabbed the paper with black paint. Clouds appeared and drops of rain fell from them. She made a circle with dots for eyes and a straight line for the mouth.

Elise came to her. "That's good. Take more paper if you'd like and do another painting." Tamara looked away and tugged at her sweater. "Would you like to explain the meaning of your art to me?"

"Maybe next time."

"Okay."

Moving on to the next woman, Elise asked, "What's your name?"

"Sophie."

Elise looked over the woman's shoulder and saw she had basic drawing skills. "You have talent." Her picture showed a man hitting a woman on the cheek. Elise clenched her fist. *Why do men think this is okay?* "I'm interested in what this means," she said to Sophie.

"My husband beats me. He gets mean when he's drunk. That's why I came here."

"I'm sad you experienced that."

The women took their time. Forty-five minutes passed, and Elise asked them to wash their brushes in the sink and close the paint bottles. "You've done quite well. I'm looking forward to our next class in two weeks. Take your pictures with you."

Elise and Nadine took a fifteen-minute break in the kitchen.

"You did a good job, Elise," Nadine said. "Do you have experience with these types of women?"

"I wish I did. I thought about how I'd like to be treated if I were in their situation. My heart aches for them."

"You're a compassionate woman. Have you thought about doing social work?"

"No, but someone told me to consider art therapy. I have a degree in fine art."

"That's great," Nadine said. "Let's go back to the art room and prepare for the children."

Once in the room, Elise laid paper, crayons, and pencils on each desk. "I'll monitor the room while you teach," Nadine said. "I have to warn you that their attention spans are short.

Don't be surprised if they finish their art in ten or fifteen minutes."

"I didn't expect that. I'll go with the flow of the class." The mothers and children arrived as Elise spoke. "Please take your seats. We'll start as soon as you're settled." The mothers left and all except one child, a boy, sat down. "Please tell me your name," she said to the restless child.

"Tommy."

"Welcome. I'm glad you're here. There's paper at the desk. Would you like to draw a picture for your mom?"

"I don't want to. You can't make me." He folded his arms against his chest. Nadine went to him and guided him to his place. She whispered in his ear. Tommy nodded his head and sat at the desk.

"Before we start, please tell me your names. I know Tommy. Let's start with the girl next to him."

"I'm Judy."

"Dottie."

"I'm Ava."

"Harry."

"Good. My name is Miss Elise. Raise your hand if you want me to help you. I'll show what expressive art is." Elise showed them her art. "Draw anything. It might be your mom, a favorite toy, or a friend. I'll show you some pictures I drew. Here's a house I colored yellow because it's a happy color. And the sun is shining. If I were sad, my home might be black. I like dogs so here's a stick figure of a dog. If you know how to draw better than this, you can."

A boy of around six raised his hand. Elise went to his desk. "Hi, Harry."

"I don't know what to draw."

"How about your mom? Or do you have a brother or sister?"

"What about my dad?"

"Sure." Elise stood by his side. Harry drew a stick figure. His dad had a frown and a long wavy object in his hand. She sighed. *Here it was.*

"What's in your Dad's hand?"

"A belt. He spanks me a lot and it hurts. He drinks beer."

"Do you want to draw that?"

Harry nodded his head, his fingers tightened around the pencil. "I'm done."

Oh, no. What a life for a child. Elise looked at her watch. Five minutes had passed. "I'll get you another piece of paper."

"I want to see my mom," Harry said.

"I'll take him. Elise," Nadine said. "Will you be okay for a few minutes?

"I think so. The other kids are still busy. "Take your picture with you, Harry. Show your mom." Elise smiled. "You did well today."

Harry's shoulders drooped. With Nadine holding his hand, he left with his picture. *What will I do if a child causes trouble?* She broke out in a sweat. Elise tiptoed around the desks. Black, red, and yellow colors seemed to dominate. She asked each child if he or she needed more paper.

Dottie, maybe age seven, sucked her thumb. She had colored a house in black. She was silent as she stared at her picture. "How about a tree or the sky?" Elise said. *What did a black house represent to this child? She hadn't even drawn a flower in the yard.*

Dottie nodded her head. "You draw it."

"Okay. Will you color it?"

"Yeth," she said with her thumb still in her mouth.

Elise drew a simple tree. Dottie colored it black.

When Nadine returned, Elise sighed. Fifteen minutes of class time were gone. The kids talked with each other and scuffled in the art room. "I'm glad you're back. The kids are finished for today."

"How'd it go?" Nadine asked.

"It went well. The pictures they drew caused me to ask myself questions about their previous homes. Dottie colored her house black."

"Her mother's boyfriend hit Dottie. He was abusive to her mom, too," Nadine said.

"How do you know all this," Elise asked.

"I spend as much time as possible here for the hours I need."

"I admire you for wanting to work with these women and children. They need you."

The children's mothers arrived, and the students met them at the door. Elise said, "Oops. I forgot. Children, return to your seats. Let's write your names on your papers. If you don't know how, I'll help you. You can take them to your room."

After the children and Nadine left, Elise collected the supplies and put them in her bag. Then she walked to the office. She hoped it was open. She knocked on the door, and then went inside. Donna sat at the desk, keyboarding on her computer. "Elise. How'd it go? Help yourself to tea. I always have the hot water ready for that."

"Thanks. It went well." She explained the events of each class. "I'm glad Nadine was with me and the children. Some of the pictures stunned me. The women and children have obvious issues to work out. If any of them talk about their experience with me, please share their opinions. I don't want to offend them by what I say or do."

"I'll let you know. In the meantime, go home and relax. Was this harder than you thought it would be?"

"Yes and no. You were honest about what I could expect, so that helped. I'm glad they have a place here. It's obvious from their pictures they need the security the refuge provides."

"If you stay with it, you'll see some rewards eventually. And keep some emotional distance. You'll be depressed if you don't."

"I'll try. I'm glad I came. See you in two weeks. Thanks for the tea." Elise put her coat on and picked up her large case and left.

THE CORNERS OF Elise's mouth curled upward as she ran up the steps of the Victorian house which contained Karen's office. Today, she would insist that her therapy take place every two to three weeks. For the first time in two and a half years, her life was on track. Even though she might face trouble with the kids at Serenity House, she believed that with the help of Nadine, she could manage.

Karen opened her door. "Good to see you, Elise. Come in." Karen waved to the easy chair. "Have a seat and we'll get started." She slid into her overstuffed Victorian style chair. "How's everything going?" she asked, smoothing the hem of her dress.

Elise gestured while she talked. "I'm so excited." She told about her experiences with Carol, Donna, and Nadine. "It was hard to see the pain each woman and child painted or drew. Along with painting my own journey, I think this will provide me with new self-worth. I already know the kids might be difficult. I'm willing to work with that."

"I'm wondering if you had contact with children like these when you worked in the church? They're not the same as those who come from good homes."

"Some of the families in my former church had similar problems. However, I didn't teach Sunday school and only heard about them from Zed. The parents were expected to solve their problems through prayer and Bible study. I think some of them had Christian counseling. I didn't realize, except from newspaper accounts, what takes place in homes where abuse occurs."

"It takes patience and time to create change with people who have those problems. Think of how long we've worked together. You don't have issues of abuse from your family of origin. Of course, you experienced the disdain of Zed and his church. You're doing well right now. Consider leaving if the stories are too rough for you."

"My mother said something similar."

"What else is happening?"

"I'm still sketching and painting my life series. Some of it's painful. I put it aside at times to recover from the hurt it brings up. By the way, I read the book you gave me about the pregnant nun." Elise drew the book from her handbag. "Sorry it took so long to return it. The nun never went back to church and married a fellow she met while working at a soup kitchen. The nun became a protestant and thinks God led her to the right path. I don't know what to think about God. And overall,

I'm happier than I've been for a long time. I want to cut my sessions to every two to three weeks. I'm stable. I'll reduce my medication to half, and then maybe none. I hate taking the stuff."

"What?" Karen wrote hurriedly on her note pad. "We talked about this when I first saw you. It's impossible for you to quit." Karen scratched the back of her neck as if it itched. "You have a chemical imbalance, and it doesn't heal itself. Have you discussed this with Dr. Mueller?"

"He mainly asks me how I'm doing. Mostly, he questions my understanding of the medications. We have fifteen minutes per session. That's not enough time to delve into issues I might have."

Karen drew her hand over her face. "It's common for bipolar patients to think they can stop their meds. You feel well and you quit the drugs. Elise, I thought you understood that this isn't possible."

"Can't you see how well I feel?"

"Yes. That's due to medication and therapy. It hasn't been an overnight process. You know that. Thanksgiving and Christmas will soon be here. You're setting yourself up to be manic/depressive during the holidays. Don't do it."

"I'll give it more thought." *Karen doesn't get it. I'm back to a good way of life.*

"I want to see you in a week. In the meantime, go to the website of the National Institute of Mental Health and find some discussion about going off medication."

"Give me an appointment for two weeks."

Karen sighed. "All right. Two weeks. Same time. Call me if you have issues before then."

Elise hurried out the door to her car. *She isn't God.*

ELISE THOUGHT ABOUT her spiritual life, or lack of one, as she ate a sandwich for lunch. What did she believe? Was there room in her mind for a God who loved instead of punished? Maybe. If she were asked, what would she tell the abused women and children about God? She couldn't tell them the

Old Testament story about how he had delivered Meshach, Shadrach, and Abednego from the flames in the furnace. It was another one of those stories that said God saved people from trouble. *Fairy tales. If anything. It's up to us to help those in need.*

Her thoughts turned to the creation of her life book. Truth. She had to paint her authentic self.

Instead of sketching, Elise decided to write about her life with Zed. Later, at some point, she'd resume drawing. She decided on a letter to him. One she wouldn't mail. She could write about his positive attributes. Those that meant something to her.

Dear Zed,

I appreciate the life we had together in college and in the ministry. Life as we once knew it is gone. I'm thankful for the memories and wish we could have continued married life.

I recall how much fun college was. You were in your last year of seminary, and I was in my senior year of college. Remember how we ditched classes sometimes to picnic or go to a movie? Sometimes we hated the grind of study, and the truancies provided relief.

I introduced you to my parents that year. You were afraid they wouldn't like you, but they did. I had to wait until your graduation to meet your folks since they lived in Colorado. Do you remember how nervous I was? At first, they looked at me from head to toe. I talked too much.

They were too rigid about God, even more so than we were. I'm glad they lived out of state. I think they would have interfered in our marriage, or at least tried.

We had decided on a small wedding after I graduated from college. I'm glad you agreed because my parents couldn't afford to pay for a sit-down dinner after the wedding. A small reception at their home sufficed.

When you met with the board of elders and then preached on Sunday morning at your first church, you were scared the audience wouldn't like you. I tried to pump your ego by reminding you of your successful preaching at the seminary chapel. *You excelled at it and you were hired by the church with 300 members. We were so excited. The people were generous and paid a big enough salary for us to live on. Now you have a large wealthy congregation and more money than you ever thought possible.*

Our lovemaking exceeded my expectations. I looked forward to it throughout our marriage. The special talks about our problems seemed to be smaller after our sexual unions.

I hope we both find that again with a different spouse.

I've decided most people don't deserve what life hands them. We don't either.

Elise

"GINNY, IT'S ELISE. Can you hear me? My cell phone is cutting out. I'll move to the window. Do you have a moment?" Elise said as she looked out her window. The sun had broken through the clouds. "Are you working on your photos?"

"You're talkative. I'm taking a break. What are you doing?"

"I want to recap my experience at the refuge. Thought you might be interested."

"Tell me."

"It's a challenge to see what the women and children have come from. I enjoyed the experience though. I'm looking forward to getting better acquainted with them. I want to see them emerge from the darkness of their former lives."

"It sounds like you want to go back."

"I definitely do. They need art. I've spent most of my life with middle class to wealthy people who claim God's goodness and mercy always helps them. My intuition says the dis-enfranchised of society have a different view. I hope in a small way to help them work out their issues. I owe them that. I've had it good. By the way, I have to purchase all the art supplies. Do you think our art group would be willing to contribute some money toward them? I can't afford to do it all."

"How often do you meet and what supplies do you need?'

"Art paper, pencils, crayons, and acrylic paint. We meet twice a month and there's approximately twenty-five residents. That includes children."

"It sounds doable. I'll give some money and bring it up next time we meet."

"Great. I'd better go, Ginny. Thanks for listening."

God, if you exist, help me. Let me make a difference in the lives of these women and children.

Saturday night was it. She cut her bipolar meds in half and swallowed the smaller dose. *I'll save money. Besides, I don't need them.*

TWENTY-FOUR

ELISE ANSWERED HER CELL PHONE. "HI, MOM. IT'S GOOD TO HEAR from you. I've been lax about calling you."

"A little bit, but that's okay. I'm glad you're happy. Dad and I want you to come to our house tonight around seven. Dana and Cliff will be here too."

What the heck? "Why?"

"We want to help you and Dana resolve your issues. The enmity between you and Dana has gone on long enough. Dad and I want to say some things to both of you. Will you come?"

Elise hesitated. "To please you, I will. But I'm scared."

"I think Dana is too, but she agreed to come if Cliff was included. Since she is willing, 1 hope you are too."

"Okay. But don't get your hopes up."

Janet opened her door when Elise knocked. "I'm glad you came. Come to the living room and have a seat. Keep your temper in control."

Elise went into the living room and nodded to Dana and Cliff who sat across the room. "Hi, Dad." Elise took the plush chair opposite them. Her parents were next to her in straight-backed kitchen chairs. They looked at Dana, then Elise. Tension crackled in the room.

Janet spoke first. "Dad and I expect a calm conversation.

We're going to ask questions of each of you. Cliff, we might ask you to comment last."

"Dana, I want to start with you. Are you jealous of Elise? If so, why?"

"All my life. You favored her. She's beautiful, talented, and was always Miss Do Everything Right. I have a temper and took it out on her. I hit her, wouldn't play with her. You punished me by not letting me see my friends for a week. Then I was mad at you and Dad."

"I'm sorry you think we favored her," Janet said. "She was easier to raise than you. But we also paid attention to you. We went to your music concerts all the time. You have a beautiful solo voice and played the piano for the choir sometimes. That didn't help?"

"I don't know."

"What can we do to help you believe we love you as much as we do Elise?"

"Be firm with her instead of me. Tell Elise you want her to go back to Zed and his church. She's sinning. I don't understand her."

"She's an adult, Dana. Dad and I can't force her to change. It's up to her."

"Okay. Let's go to Elise for the time being." Janet looked at her husband. "Honey, you want to say something?"

"Yes. This is a bit hard for me to say, Elise, but I must. You've had favor all your life from church and school. You did everything our pastor asked of you with enthusiasm. And at school, your grades were impeccable. The popular kids liked you. You were a good beginning artist, and now a more accomplished one. Then, of course, I don't need to remind you of what you had with Zed and his church. I've been a bit jealous of your wealth too. My family has little compared to what you and Zed have.

"Then came bipolar. Ever since then, our attention has been focused on you, and I'm afraid we've neglected Dana and her family more than we should have. We're sorry, Dana. I can see why you're angry, but Mom and I think your spiteful behavior to Elise is over the top. Telling your friends about

Elise has brought her condemnation from many people. Gossip spreads. I wish you had talked to us or asked for us to pay for a counselor for you. We would have. Now, Mom and I want to hear from each of you. One at a time, politely. Elise?"

Elise stared at the floor. "I'm sorry. I didn't understand how much my bipolar disorder affected all of you. And you're right, Dad, my condition has taken precedence over everyone else. My work at Serenity House has made me realize I've had an ideal life, or at least until bipolar hit me so hard. Could we go to lunch every couple of weeks, Dana? Maybe we can build a healthy relationship."

Dana raised her chin. "The Bible says to forgive. But I need to think about what's been said. We were taught by the church not to have friends who don't believe. Now I have a sister who's lost her faith. Not only that, Mom and Dad are lenient with you about this whole situation." Dana squirmed in her chair. "I apologize for being spiteful. That's the best I can do. I'll see you for holidays."

"Anything you want to comment on, Cliff?" Janet asked.

"I think it's all been said. Dana's my wife. She and I need to work this out together. You're a great sister-in-law, Elise."

Janet said, "Dana, thanks for your honesty. Elise's problems have challenged Dad and me too. We all need time to think and pray. I love you, Dana. Thanks for coming. I know neither you or Elise wanted to face this. Stephan, anything you want to add?"

"I love both my daughters with all my heart. And I think it's time for chocolate cake."

When they had finished the refreshments Elise said, "I'm tired. If you don't mind, I'd like to go home. Dana, I hope we can at least talk soon. And I still want to see Mark and Sammy. I'll see myself out."

Elise took a circuitous route home to think. The air was crisp, but it helped clear her mind. *I don't know if Dana and I can ever bridge the gap.*

ELISE SAT AT the easel facing the window, paintbrush in hand. Her brain felt like a slug inching across a dirt path. *Maybe my rough day at work has something to do with it.* She had spent two hours on the phone with a computer technician who eventually used remote access to remove malware she had downloaded by mistake. *Damn it all. I can't think. This hasn't happened for a long time.* Her cell phone rang. She hesitated until she saw the caller ID.

"Hi, Mom."

"Have you had dinner? I made spaghetti sauce. I know it's your favorite."

Elise's stomach growled. *If I go, she'll see my mood.* "Maybe you could freeze a small portion. I started painting a picture."

"You don't sound right. What's wrong?"

"Bad day at work. I had trouble with my computer. I'll survive."

"Wouldn't a break help you?"

"Maybe. But I don't want to clean my brushes and start over later. Thanks for asking me. Love you."

"Love you, too, honey."

Elise disconnected the call. *What's wrong with me? I never miss an opportunity to be with Mom and Dad, let alone eat homemade spaghetti sauce.* Tomorrow would be Saturday, her third time at the shelter. *I need to be up for that.* She made coffee to hopefully improve her mood. *Why am I down?*

She remembered. No bipolar medicine for at least a month or more. Could that be it? She had been so happy until two weeks ago and had canceled her last two appointments over Karen's objections. *I'll wait a few days, then call Karen.*

THE NEXT DAY at the shelter, Elise encountered a belligerent Tommy in the children's art room. He picked a fight with Harry over a crayon. As they wrestled on the floor, Nadine bent down to pull them apart. After he bit Nadine's hand, Tommy let go.

Elise watched and clenched her teeth. She screamed at him. "Damn it, Tommy, that's enough." Then she remembered.

I'm not supposed to say anything. What's wrong with me?

"Ouch. Stop that," Nadine said. She put Tommy's arms behind his back and held him. "I'm taking you to the quiet room."

"Elise, I think it's best to dismiss the kids for today," Nadine said. "I'll get the house-mother first, and she'll send the kids' moms over. I need to see a doctor after Tommy calms down."

"Go ahead. The kids can draw till their mothers come."

"Don't let this scare you, Elise. Sometimes we have problems."

"I know."

Fifteen minutes later, Nadine stopped by with the mothers close behind her. "I'll take it from here, Elise. Gather your supplies. This kind of thing upsets the children. We'll go to the playroom for a while until they calm down."

"Thanks." *What a morning. I was warned. What now? My emotions are raw.*

AT WORK ON Monday, Elise lightly massaged her forehead. It had ached since the incident with Tommy on Saturday. She swallowed a Tylenol with the cold coffee on her desk. The phone rang. "Golden Gait Mercantile. This is Elise."

"Hi. It's Carol from Serenity House. I want you to know Nadine is fine. The doctor prescribed antibiotics and as a precaution, a tetanus shot. She mentioned you shouted at Tommy. Your reaction is understandable. However, we keep our voices down when we respond to the children. Also, if one of our staff is there, don't interfere."

"You had told me that. It won't happen again."

"Good. So, I'm wondering how you're feeling about volunteering here?"

Is this what I want? And is now the time to make a decision? "I want to continue if the women and children want me."

"Nadine talked to the kids and the mothers after the incident with Tommy. The women said you're kind and answer their questions. You don't criticize their art, which is great. As for the children, they say they get to draw and color anything, but they were upset you yelled at Tommy. Donna told them it wouldn't happen again. Most of them are used to fights. We don't want our volunteers to be part of the problems."

"I apologize. Tommy's behavior caught me off guard. If you still want me to volunteer, I will."

"That's good news. See you in two weeks?"

"I'm determined to make a difference." *I hope I do.*

Elise speed-dialed Karen's number. It went to voice mail. "This is Elise, Karen. I need to talk to you. Thanks." Now all she could do was wait. *I'm miserable. I guess I really am bipolar. Stupid me. Better try to make sense of some of the work. If only my mind didn't feel like it had been dropped in a black hole.*

She rearranged the piles on her desk. Elise jumped when her cell rang.

"I'm glad you called," Karen said. "How are you?"

"I'm depressed. Trouble functioning. It's not as bad as it was a few years ago. You were right. I can't do without my meds."

"How long have you been off them?"

"A month or more. I've lost track."

"Call Dr. Mueller for an appointment. He'll need to advise you about treatment. Tell his receptionist what you did. I'm sure she'll get you in on an emergency basis. Will you do that?"

"Is it really an emergency?"

"Yes."

"Okay. And I'd better get back in to see you."

"I still have a place open for this evening. Are you up to driving?"

"I don't know. I'll come regardless."

"See you soon."

Elise ended the call and let out a sigh. Her hands trembled. *I'd better call Mueller. Get it over with.*

"Dr. Mueller's office. May I help you?"

"I'm Elise Norris. I need to see Dr. Mueller as soon as possible."

"Let me pull up my appointment screen. Oh, I see you're due here next month. Do you need to see him sooner?"

"Please. My therapist told me to." Elise explained her situation.

"On a scale of zero to ten, with zero being no depression, where would you say you are?"

"I'm an eight."

"I can squeeze you in at ten o'clock tomorrow morning."

Damn. I'll have to take off work. "Okay. I'll be there." She made her way downstairs to see Ed. "Something's come up and I need to leave about nine-thirty tomorrow. I'll be back by noon."

"No problem. I'll ask my wife to fill in for you while you're gone. Everything okay?"

"No worries." *Nothing like a white lie to get me through this mess I made.*

"COME IN, ELISE," Karen said from her office door. "Let's get started."

Elise chewed her lip in anticipation of the scolding she was sure to receive. "Before you say anything, I want to say I shouldn't have quit my medications. I want to be normal though. My life was on an even keel. I hate having to take anything to balance my brain."

"You're not unusual. Have you visited any chat rooms about bipolar?"

"I didn't think of that."

"Would you be willing to try it?"

"Won't it make me feel worse that so many other people struggle too?"

"It should do the opposite. You'll chat with others and learn how they cope."

Elise yelled. "Why are you so calm, Karen? Don't you ever have a bad day? Why is it only me? Everyone I know has it easy."

"Lower your voice. Everyone has bad days. Let's focus on your needs. You must get back on your medication. When do you see Dr. Mueller?"

"Tomorrow morning."

"I'm glad. Until you're stable, I think you need to see me twice a week. Agreed?"

"I suppose. I'm sorry I yelled at you."

"That's your bipolar at work. Try journaling. Maybe that will help. And if you get out of control, try to apologize right away. You'll have to see how it goes. Write after you get home tonight. I'm interested in your work with your art class at Serenity House."

Elise related all that had happened and her love of the women and children. "It reminds me of the ministry."

"I'm glad to hear it. You know, don't you, there's a possibility of getting a degree in a related field. But wait until you feel better to consider it."

"What would that be?"

"Art therapy. I might have mentioned it before. It requires a master's degree."

"I don't feel like researching that right now. My brain isn't functioning well." Elise wiped her eyes.

"It will. In the meantime, give it some thought when you're over the depression. Search the Internet for programs and see what you find. Your love of art, your life book, and your work with the children make you a likely candidate, but I realize you need more experience with the shelter to make sure you want to follow this type of path. And it means a major life change."

"I thought I'd be in Ferndale until I die."

"That's a possibility too. You're a courageous woman with talents and skills though. Stimulation from a different source might be good for you. How are you feeling now?"

"I think I can make it until the medication kicks in again. Thanks for not yelling at me for skipping my meds. I thought you would."

Karen tapped her fingers on the arm of her chair. "You feel bad enough the way it is. And you called for help. That's a plus. Some people wait until family or friends have to intervene. I'll see you in three days. And let someone know how you feel. You need extra support."

Elise bent her head. "I'm too embarrassed. I've been so insistent I needed the medication, and then I stopped taking it."

"What about Ginny?"

"Maybe. At least *you* know. Otherwise, I want to hide my face under a blanket."

"That's the last thing you should do. Keep going to work. And write in your journal about how you feel."

"I'll try."

"We need to end for today," Karen said. "Drive safe."

Elise dragged herself down the steps outside and to her car. She missed the turn to Highway 101 south. *I need to concentrate or I'll have an accident.*

ELISE NOTED THE formal style of Mueller's waiting room again. The décor didn't help her depression. The modern art piece irritated her more than usual. Stripes. *Anyone can do that.*

"Come in, Elise," Dr. Mueller said. "So, the receptionist's message said you're quite depressed. What's happened?"

He's so stiff. I don't want to tell him. "Well . . . I went off my meds. I thought I didn't need them. Don't scold me."

He squinted his eyes and stared at her before he said, "I won't. I'm unhappy you did that though. How depressed are you?"

"I'm making stupid mistakes at work. My thoughts are muddled, and I've lost interest in what I do. I'm tired. I go to bed early and sleep as late as possible."

"All are symptoms of depression. I think you know that. How long off the meds?"

"Six weeks I think."

"Let's increase your dosage. One tablet in the morning, and one at night. Do you have enough medicine at home?"

"I threw them away."

"I'll write a new prescription. You know how important it is for you to stay on this medication, so I won't lecture you. I don't know of anyone who recovers from bipolar unless they were misdiagnosed."

"I think I've learned my lesson."

"Are you still seeing Karen?"

"I hadn't for more than a month. Then I called her, and we met yesterday evening. She wants me to see her twice a week."

"That's wise. You saw Karen, so we'll end for today. If you don't improve, call me right away. I want to see you in a month. See my receptionist and make an appointment."

"Thanks for your help." Elise made the required appointment and went to her car. On the way to pick up her prescription, she daydreamed about a new life without bipolar and almost hit the car in front of her when she stopped at an intersection. *Wake up.*

That night after work Elise phoned Ginny. "Do you have five minutes to talk?"

"What's up?"

"I'm struggling. I told you I'm bipolar and like a fool, I stopped my meds because life was great. I saw my therapist and she suggested I tell you about my situation so that I have support until I feel better."

"I'm glad you called. In Narcotics Anonymous, we're supposed to contact someone if we feel the desire to take drugs."

"I'm sorry to trouble you with this."

"What are friends for? Christmas is in a week. How do you feel about that? It can be pretty rough on people who are down."

"I wish it wasn't so soon. I don't want my family to know. I guess I can pretend I'm fine."

"That doesn't usually work. Let's get together for dinner tomorrow evening. Come to my place."

"Thanks, Ginny. You're a good friend."

"I'm trying. It isn't how I've always been. Feels good though."

"What time?"

"Six okay?"

"See you then."

ELISE THOUGHT BACK to a week ago. Her dinner with Ginny had been reassuring. She had hugged her when she cried about yelling at Tommy and being short-tempered.

Now it was time to see her family again. Christmas morning. The church bells were ringing. She swung her legs over the side of the bed and got up to make her coffee. She had to be at her sister's home by noon. *I don't know if I can cope with her attitude toward me. I hope I can smile and have fun with Mark and Sammy. Nothing else matters.* At least the kids would be excited about receiving gifts from their grandparents and the ones from her. Not that they needed one more toy. Dana and Cliff were too generous with their children.

Elise dressed in a dark red sweater and black slacks. They were tight in the waist and hips. She had comforted herself with bags of chips and other junk food. Elise paid extra attention to her hair. At least she hadn't whacked it off with scissors. Another two or three weeks and hopefully the medicine would kick in. Once she was ready and had put the wrapped toys in large bags, she walked to Dana's.

"Dad," Elise said when he opened the door and gave her a big hug.

"Come in. Everyone's in the kitchen waiting for dinner to be ready. Mom decided on roast goose."

"Knowing Mom, I'm sure it will be good. Shall I put the gifts under the tree?"

"Yes, you know kids. Can't settle them down. Cliff said they've been up since six. Too early for me on a holiday, although they had fun opening gifts. See you in the kitchen."

After putting her gifts under the tree, Elise made her way toward the laughter and aroma of the roasted poultry. "Merry Christmas, Mom and Dana," she said, her smile as wide as possible. Dana ignored her. *I hope I can get through this tense situation. Dana won't give up her hostility toward me.*

"Love you, honey," Janet said.

Mark and Sammy entered the kitchen. "Hey guys," Elise said. "Merry Christmas. Oops, you're trying to snitch cookies before we eat. Can I have one?"

"Sure, Aunt Elise," Mark said. They each handed her a

gingerbread man and then went to the living room to look at gifts.

"Did you make the cookies, Dana?" Elise asked.

"Yep."

"What can I do to help?" Elise asked Janet.

"You could mash the potatoes. The Half and Half is in the fridge. And don't forget to salt them. Stephan, did you finish setting the table?"

"It's done. Looks festive with the evergreen pieces surrounding the red candles."

"We'll eat in about ten minutes," Janet said. "Cliff, would you carve the goose?"

By the time they sat down to eat, Elise thought she was being cheerful. *So far so good.*

"This goose is delicious, Mom. Is it hard to roast?"

"No. Too much fat though. I don't think I'll do it again."

Dana's still not talking.

"Do you still like computer games?" Elise asked the boys.

"You bet," Mark said. "But Dad doesn't let us play all the time."

"Yeah," Sammy chimed in.

"I imagine you have homework to do," Elise said. "And you'll have baseball in the spring. That keeps you busy."

"Could we open presents now," Aunt Lisi?" Sammy asked.

"Ask your dad."

"Dad?" Mark asked.

"Finish your plate of food first. No one else is done eating."

Once everyone had eaten all they could, Cliff said, "Okay. Let's open gifts. Is it okay if we have dessert later, Janet?"

"Fine with me."

They traipsed into the living room and pulled chairs up to the Christmas tree. Mark had the honor of passing out gifts. He gave his younger brother Sammy the first one, which was from Elise. He jumped with joy when he saw the big deep yellow dump truck.

"Thanks, Aunt Lisi," Sammy said.

"Take yours from me next, Mark," Elise said.

He tore the wrapping paper off the package and flung it on

the floor. "Wow, a computer football game. I'll play this all the time. Thanks."

"You're welcome."

The adults had decided to forgo gifts for each other this year. Instead, they gave money to a charity that helped Africans find clean water.

When they gathered at the dining room table for chocolate cake, Janet asked, "Anyone want ice cream too?"

Everyone said yes. After she served it, Elise said, "I love the combination of chocolate with vanilla ice cream."

The conversation turned to politics. "I wish we had more homeless shelters," Elise said.

"Me too," her dad said. "We have to think, though, about how people make wrong choices in their lives. They bring some of it on themselves."

"I agree with Dad," Dana said.

"I think we need to help by education and food banks," Elise said. "Some of these people are homeless because they lost their income. Others were raised in poverty and have little education, and therefore, low-paying jobs."

"I'm with Elise," Janet said. "I don't know how to solve the problems though."

"You, Mom?" Dana asked. "You know only accepting Jesus as their savior gives them a better life. He's coming again to establish world order. We need to do our part in the meantime."

"I don't think we'll solve it today," Stephan said. "Let's switch to a different topic. How's your work at Serenity House, Elise?"

"It's challenging, but I want to continue doing it." *I wish I could tell them the truth about how awful I feel.*

"I wish you'd work for a Christian organization," Dana said.

Elise ignored her.

After the conversation had continued another hour, Elise said, "I hate to say I have to go, but I have a severe headache. Let's all get together again soon."

Elise took her coat from the peg near the front door and made her escape. *Oh, dear God, help me.*

ELISE CLICKED THE television off with the remote after the ball dropped in Times Square. A new year had begun on the East Coast. Three hours to wait in California. What would the next twelve months bring her? A tear slipped down her face. She grabbed a tissue from the box on the coffee table.

She was alone. Alone with her thoughts and feelings of failure. Elise's shoulders heaved. She grabbed a pillow and blanket from her bed and lay down on the sofa. She pulled the cover over her and searched TV channels until she found a mindless program to watch so she could fall asleep. Her phone rang. She let it go to voicemail, then decided to listen to it.

"Elise. This is Ginny. Give me a call. Let's ring in our New Year together. I know you're home. Pick up or I'll come knockin' on your door."

Elise called Ginny. "I'm in no mood to do anything. Find someone else to celebrate with you."

"You're depressed, aren't you? I'll be there in ten minutes. I'm bringing Coke since you're not supposed to have alcohol when you're depressed. I've got chips and dip too."

"You're insisting?"

"Yes. Get dressed."

"How do you know I'm not?"

"Because you're down. I hear it in your voice. See you in a few."

"Damn." She pulled on a pair of jeans and a sweater but left her slippers on her feet. Ten minutes later, she heard Ginny's knock on the door. "You didn't give me a choice about you coming over."

Ginny put her arm around Elise. "That's what friends do for a friend who feels rotten. I've been there. Relax. We haven't talked since before Christmas."

"You're a great friend, Ginny. Have a seat."

They talked until midnight. Elise told Ginny more about how she yelled at Tommy as well as Karen's suggestion to investigate an art therapy degree. As usual, Ginny encouraged her to explore.

TWENTY-FIVE

Zed

ZED WAS GLAD CHRISTMAS WAS OVER. MAYBE THE NEW YEAR WOULD be different. He followed Greg's suggestion to talk with someone who had left the ministry. Zed surveyed the large number of cars in the parking lot at Mt. Tamalpais. Must be other hikers making a trek around the mountain, plus tourists. He got out of his Porsche and looked around. A tall, lanky man with high cheekbones stood next to a red Honda Civic. With wavy, dark brown hair, he reminded Zed of John F. Kennedy, Jr. His ratty, oversized sweatshirt suggested a relaxed lifestyle. Must be Andrew. He had described himself except for his good looks.

"I take it you're Andrew Walker, Greg's friend," Zed said walking up to him.

"That's right. And you're Zed. I'm sure Greg explained I'm a former minister. He thought I might be helpful in your quest to find God's will for your life. Don't know if I can."

"I hope so."

"Let's get started." Andrew pointed toward a trailhead. "That one is fairly easy and takes an hour."

"Fine with me."

"I hike here often to clear my head. I drank too much after I left the church and decided to start hiking. Sometimes my wife joins me, and we picnic. What do you do for enjoyment?" Andrew asked.

"Golfing. Also, before our divorce, my wife and I sometimes took a cruise. Alaska was our favorite."

"I've heard it's beautiful. I'd like to take my wife to Denali Park. We could do some hiking. We both like that. And I find I need exercise and the outdoors on an almost daily basis to refresh my spirits."

"You have a point. What do you do for a living?"

"I teach ethics at the Santa Rosa Junior College."

"Are your students a challenge to you?"

"At times. I enjoy teaching though. Today's kids question everything. Young people are exposed to so much via social media and other means. I must know what challenges they face. I do a lot of reading and even go to movies they watch to stay current with them. I also subscribe to one of the pop culture magazines."

"You do all that? Geez, sounds over the top. Why did you choose ethics?"

"Due to the experience I had in my former church, I believe a value system is necessary in all of life, including the ministry. That's forgotten even in some churches today. Shysters. There's a lot of them. Too much temptation and power-grabbing in the mega-churches and with big-time evangelists. They forget what Jesus represented. Enough about me. Greg said you're wrestling with important issues and are trying to decide what to do. Any inklings of what that might be?"

"No. The ministry still appeals to me. I'm don't know how much longer my church will allow me to stay. Much longer, the board will probably fire me."

Zed huffed and puffed as he walked and stopped to take time to look at the views of the blue ocean in the distance. His burdens felt lighter. The damp earth grounded him in reality. If only he could capture these moments to stay with him all the time. He would like to be as free as the air that embraced him.

"Do you want to share your story?" Andrew asked.

"I'd rather hear what led you to leave the ministry first."

"Shit. Excuse my language. I was the youth pastor in a large church. Quite a few parents were enthusiastic, and that helped me initiate some great programs. Before I knew it, we had kids from outside the church and a Christian rock band made up of our students. They played for the Saturday evening youth services. We had a choir, mission trips—the works. A well-known, hotshot evangelist, who has a huge stateside as well as overseas ministry, came to the church. After teaching a three-day seminar, he invited me to go to coffee with him. I told him I'd bring my wife. He said he wanted only me to come. I thought it strange but went with him. He asked me to become a part of his worldwide ministry. I was offered a handsome salary. Could have had anything I wanted materially. He even commented on my appearance. Said I looked like a model. My jaw dropped, and I stared at him. He wanted me because of my success with the youth and my good looks. He wanted to introduce me to his daughter. I couldn't think of anything to say. I left him at the table and went home. I called my pastor and told him what happened. To my everlasting surprise, he told me I had misunderstood the evangelist. Turns out they were good friends."

Zed's gut tightened. His cheeks warmed even though the air was cool.

"And then, my wife also thought my actions were too severe. Her family was sympathetic to the evangelist. It became the start of the downfall of my marriage. I couldn't reconcile anything with what I knew of Jesus."

What the . . . Zed thought. "You blow my mind."

"I stayed at the church about three more months. I visited other churches and searched the Internet for information on other ministers. Some had evaded taxes, and many had two or three homes and private jets. I became bitter. The people I admired the most were on the opposite side of the street from me. I thought Jesus and helping others, especially the downtrodden, were the focus of the church. The glitz and glamour stuck in my craw. I became disillusioned and resigned. Heck, I'm still bitter and angry at times. My current wife helps me from getting too far off track."

"Some of these people have maniacal egos," Zed said. "My church believes the prosperity message too. I've had to let that go for the most part."

"What do you mean, 'for the most part?'" Andrew asked.

Zed explained his situation and desire to leave when he was ready.

"Aren't you playing with fire? You might wish you'd left before now."

Was he playing with fire?

Andrew stopped and looked Zed in the eyes. "If you don't mind my asking, what caused you to change?"

Even though it was painful for Zed to recount his story, about him, Elise, and his church, he told Andrew how blind and verbally abusive he had been to Elise.

"I admire you for making the changes. Most people don't."

"If I had been a better man, I wouldn't be in this predicament," Zed said with a sigh.

"Self-recrimination doesn't work, Zed. Let's say you had responded to your wife with compassion, would you be where you are today in your journey of faith?"

"I doubt it. If I had been more sympathetic, it wouldn't have worked for her anyway because she needed medical help. And the thing is, my church thinks faith healing cures everything, even mental illness."

"Quit beating yourself up." Andrew reached out and squeezed Zed's shoulder. "Have you made amends with her?"

"Yes. I hoped she would come back to me. I've reached the point now where I realize I have to let go of her and our life together."

"She'll find her own way."

"I'm sure you're right." Zed felt his chest tighten. "Let's back up. You said you've found your niche. Do you still miss the ministry?"

"Not anymore. I love the students. Have I helped you or confused you?"

"I don't know. At least you've been honest about your rebellion and feeling lost. My journey has been an awakening, not caused by betrayal—so far. My ex-wife felt duped and bitter. But at this point, I still want to be a minister."

"It might be just the ticket. If it isn't, remember you can have a good, rewarding life outside the ministry."

"I'm glad you found something to fit you. I don't know if I'm ready to do something else. I'm waiting for God to speak to me in a forceful way. I pray about it but he hasn't answered that I can tell."

"I'd be happy to stay in touch. Of course, you have Greg. He's a great guy."

"You're right. He's been supportive the whole way. Here's the end of the trail," Zed said. "Thanks for meeting me. I'll call you if I have more questions."

"Good luck. I hope you find your answers."

Zed watched as Andrew went to his car. *Lord, guide my steps. You always have.*

ZED DROVE TO San Francisco from Santa Rosa for his first interview with the pastoral search committee of the Community Church near the Presidio. He hunched his shoulders. The opening was for an associate of parish care position, not head minister. After talking to Andrew, he felt more than ever that he still wanted to be a minister. *I wish I could be the senior pastor.*

His interview at a church in Napa two weeks ago had shown him that they were not the right fit for him, nor he for them. Their intolerance of other religions, even various branches of Christianity, and their stance against the Palestinians had been deal-breakers. They, on the other hand, thought he was too liberal.

Sweat poured down Zed's face. He thought he had left Santa Rosa early enough to miss the commuter traffic to arrive at the church. He arrived five minutes after 7:00 p.m. He was late. After parking his car, he grabbed his sport coat and walked to the side entrance of the modest-sized white stucco church. *What a small church. What am I doing here?*

He was met at the door by a short, gray-haired man who

extended his hand to Zed. "You must be Zed Norris. Come in. I'm Rob Pallitto. Down the hall and to the first door on your right."

"I'm sorry I'm late. There was an accident on the 101 and heavy commuter traffic as well."

"Not a problem."

As they entered the room Zed took note of the four people seated at the table. Their attire was casual. Jeans and T-shirts. *Wow.*

Rob motioned with his hand, "Sit here, at the head, where we can all see and hear you. Don't worry, we won't bite," Rob said with a laugh. "Folks, this is Zed Norris, our next candidate."

There were nods and smiles from the small group. Zed's jaw relaxed.

Rob began. "We've looked at your resume, your letter of explanation of why you are leaving your church, what you believe now, and your references. Even though we might not ordinarily look at someone with your background, your candor impressed us. You weren't afraid to describe your struggles of faith, what caused them, and the path on which you wish to now embark. You seem to be a down-to-earth, empathetic man. Before we get started, we'll introduce ourselves."

"I'm Susan."

"I'm Tony."

"Gene."

"Margie."

"Thanks. Now my challenge is to remember your names," Zed said. They laughed.

"We mailed you a copy of our mission statement two weeks ago," Rob said. "That should have given you time to come up with questions for us. We also want to hear your opinion on several things. Does that sound fair?"

"It does." Zed's gut tightened, relaxed, and tightened again. He was under close scrutiny. Greg had warned him that would happen.

"We'll hear from Margie who is an elder in the church," Rob said.

Margie straightened her T-shirt and smoothed her jeans. "I'm interested in your experience in the finances of your church. We adhere to our budget, without much flexibility, unless there is an urgent matter. Our books are audited yearly by an outside firm."

"The chief financial officer of my church is the head of the funds committee, and it reports to the elders. I believe fiscal responsibility is paramount in a church."

"You come from a wealthy congregation. Can you get used to a smaller budget and salary?"

"There are more important aspects to my faith than money."

Gene said, "You say you've changed your outlook on various beliefs and traditions of your church. How much have you conveyed that to your current church?"

"I've had to balance the scripture on suffering with the traditional beliefs about prosperity and faith healing."

"You haven't made a complete switch?"

Zed opened and closed his mouth, then responded, "No. I want to leave under my terms. Some people agree with my new teachings. However, I don't want the church to split." *Why did this question seem important to people?*

An hour and a half passed before Rob took charge again. "Let's take a ten-minute break and have some refreshments before we continue. The decaf coffee is ready to brew, and you all know how I love to bake. I brought chocolate chip cookies. Afterward, we'll have Zed give us his opinions about our church and ask questions of us."

Zed sighed. He was grateful for the break. He stretched his legs and tried to regroup. *This is harder than I thought it would be.* He approached the table and helped himself to a cookie and a cup of coffee. Both were delicious. Rob approached him and said, "I know this is stressful for you. I hope you see the need for it."

"Everyone's courteous. I appreciate that."

"We have a good church."

Once Rob called everyone back to the table, Zed talked to the committee about what he liked. "I admire your homeless program. It entails a high level of commitment from volunteers to house and feed these people when the weather is inclement.

"One area concerns me, and that is your statement that you want the church to keep its current size. While I'm not in favor of megachurches anymore, I think if we meet the needs of people, there is potential for growth. Many churches start new congregations to accommodate it. You might consider that. Also, I don't want the church to stagnate and become a congregation of elderly people."

Rob stood after some additional questions and answers. "Thanks, Zed. We've extended past the time we thought it would take to interview you. On behalf of the committee, I want to say thanks for coming. We'll be in touch with you in a month. We have one more person to interview. After that, the committee needs to compile the results of the three people we've considered."

"Thanks for your time. I look forward to hearing from you." Zed gave a wave of his hand and walked to his car. *God, I want this position. It would be a breath of fresh air.* He reflected on the members of the committee. A definite culture change, he thought. From theological perspectives to the way they dress. No Armani suits to impress each other or him.

THE NEXT WEEK Zed swallowed an antacid and hoped he didn't stutter. Thirty minutes from now he was expected at the special board meeting his church elders had called. James Prescott's reply to Zed about the reason for the sudden request had been terse. "You'll see, Norris." The word *trouble* played over and over in Zed's mind.

He prayed in his car for a moment and asked God for strength and wisdom before he strode to the educational wing of the church. Zed entered the empty room where the board met. He had dressed in gray slacks, white shirt with open collar, and a black jacket. Zed had reasoned that his professional clothes might imply the natural authority of the church's minister. His legs trembled as he paced the carpeted room and thought about what would happen.

He heard footsteps on the tile floor in the adjacent hall and walked to the door to greet people. Prescott was the first. Zed reached out his hand to James, but he walked by without a hello or a handshake. He took the first chair at the long table and averted his face from Zed.

The rest of the board arrived, murmuring to each other. No one greeted Zed. The empty coffee pot told the story. No brewed coffee or a snack on the side table. He would lose his job tonight. The muscles in his stomach knotted into small balls.

Prescott didn't let Zed start the meeting. "I'll pray. Lord, it is with difficulty that we meet tonight. Give us wisdom and Your presence. In Jesus name I pray." The board said amen together.

"I'll get to the point. You've preached that the blessings of God, such as prosperity and healing, do not come to every believer even if they have faith. You've spoken of your approval of Christian faiths such as Catholics and Greek Orthodox. We cannot accept this. You're causing division in the church. Also, we sent you to the annual ministers' retreat. Your board intended this to be a place of refreshing of your spirits. A return to your faith. Instead, you ruffled the feathers of some of your peers."

Zed heard amens around the room. "Let me say something in my defense. I . . ."

Prescott interrupted. "You've had enough chances. I believe, as does the board, that you must leave this church. You no longer follow the teachings of the Bible."

Zed stood and said in a loud voice, "Gentlemen, I do preach what the Bible says. And I confided my search of God and the challenges I face about my new beliefs to a friend at the retreat. He must have betrayed me. I . . ."

"We're not here to discuss the issue. It's over. You're dismissed as of tonight. Your contract with the church said you had to submit to the board's governance even though the ministry is in your name. Here's what we'll do for you. You'll receive two more weeks of salary even though the church has lost money since you softened your preaching about God prospering those who follow him. I'll go with you to your office. Gather your personal belongings." Prescott took Zed by the arm and led him out the door.

ZED RAN A stoplight on his way home. *Concentrate.* He pulled into his garage and let out a long breath. Inside, Zed inhaled the smell of the gourmet coffee beans he took from the cupboard. While the coffee brewed, he paced in his kitchen. It was too late to call Greg. Besides, what would he think?

Zed's shoulders drooped. He had been fired. And he hadn't listened to anyone who questioned the wisdom of waiting to leave his church. He sat down at the kitchen table and lifted his face toward heaven.

"God, I've been faithful to you. Look at me. What am I supposed to do now? This is as bad as Elise leaving me."

He listened.

God was silent.

Again, he asked, "God, what am I supposed to do? I preached your word, and it didn't help me keep my job. Maybe you wanted me to learn the hard way that I couldn't play two sides of the fence. I won't do that again. Please give me the job at the church near the Presidio. Please answer me."

Zed waited fifteen minutes and heard only the prayer echo in his mind. A thought came to him. Greg had mentioned being a missionary. "Is that what you want me to do?"

He wished he had someone to talk to right now. If only . . . No use going there. Elise was out of the picture for good. Their talks used to soothe him. She listened with under-standing when no one else did.

Zed carried the pot of coffee and went into his semi-barren living room. He put his cup on the side table, dropped into the recliner and began to gulp his coffee. It burned his throat. *Fired.* Their cruelty amazed him. He refilled his cup again and again to the last bitter dregs. *Who will hire me knowing why I've been fired?*

Throughout the night he rehashed his life—beginning to end—without moving from his chair, and questioned every major decision he had made, his divorce included. Was he wrong about everything he had believed and done? His arms and legs ached, and sweat poured from his forehead.

He lost track of time around midnight. The calling that had been bright in the past was dark and without hope. Before Zed knew it, the sky lightened. He watched as the moon faded. His head felt fuzzy. A walk. Maybe the fresh air would clear his head. He walked out his door to the sidewalk as his neighbor was leaving for work.

"Hey, Zed. You look like shit. Your clothes are wrinkled, and your hair is a mess. Where are you going? Did you lay one on last night? Not good for a reverend you know."

Great, Zed thought. *Blabbermouth will tell all the neighbors.* He thought of an answer. "Up all night with one of my parishioners. Need some air. See you." And he began to jog. The wind dropped the temperature, but there was sunshine. He started to run. Run away. Run from his problems. Then his feet started to hurt. He slowed his pace. His body hurt as if he had been stoned for heresy.

TWENTY-SIX

Elise

THE RING OF ELISE'S CELL PHONE INTERRUPTED HER CONCENTRATION as she painted later that evening. She glanced at caller ID. Zed. *Why is he calling?* "Zed. I'm surprised to hear from you. What's going on?"

"I had to talk to someone, and I knew you'd understand my problem. I left a message for Greg. He hasn't returned my call. I'm desperate to unload my situation. Can we meet in Willits tomorrow? I think that's about halfway for both of us. And it's Saturday. Do you have anything planned?"

"I'm obligated to Serenity House in the morning. I could be there by four. What's happening?"

"I'd rather not say until I see you."

"Okay. Let's meet at Nellie's Bistro downtown," Elise said. *Zed must be in trouble.*

ELISE PEERED INTO the café and saw Zed sitting with his hands over his face. *Not a good sign. What's wrong with him?* Once inside she made her way to the table. "Zed?"

"Elise. Please sit down."

They ordered hamburgers and Cokes. The server left, and Elise said, "Okay, spill your guts. I see you're upset. We can eat and talk."

"I'm crushed. I didn't think it would happen this way."

"What do you mean?" Elise said.

"The board fired me."

"What? Shit."

"Geez, Elise, don't swear." Zed screwed up his face. "Due to the way I was preaching, the level of tithes and offerings dropped and that clinched their frustration. I don't know what to do. I applied for a position as an associate at a church in San Francisco. I'll have to tell them what happened. Being fired might nix my chances at that church." He sighed and shook his head.

Elise touched his arm. "I'm so sorry you're going through this."

"I feel despondent and worthless. No congregation will want me after being dismissed."

While Elise ate her hamburger and fries, Zed became silent and let his food grow cold. Elise continued the conversation. "They might if you explain what happened. There are numerous churches in the Bay Area. Apply to them. Don't quit now."

"I don't know if I want to."

"Do you still want to be a minister?"

"I thought I did. Now I'm confused and angry too. James Prescott forced me out. I wanted to leave when I was ready."

"He has a chip on his shoulder. I had the impression he wanted to be in charge of everything. And he's wealthy and wants everyone to know that."

"I see that now. It doesn't change what's happened though."

"What will Greg say when you talk to him?"

"At one time he encouraged me to think about teaching school or be a missionary for a while. He doesn't think I'm ready to make a change from one kind of church to another."

"Are you?"

"I thought so, but maybe he has a point."

"You might not appreciate what I have to say."

"Go ahead."

"I think you played both sides of the fence. You said you

changed, and yet you didn't make a break with your church until you were forced out. It looks like you're indecisive about what you believe. I think it's causing confusion in others. Maybe leaving the ministry isn't a bad idea."

Zed drew his hand over his face. His shoulders drooped. "I don't know. Maybe I'm no different than the average person. Maybe I'm selfish," he said as his lips turned down.

"I missed all the wealthy advantages we had for a while. I didn't want to sacrifice truth anymore, though, so I built a different kind of life. I'm glad I did. You can too. You've always had a tendency toward procrastination. It didn't serve you well in the past and it doesn't now. I know this is hard to hear, but it's the way my therapist talked to me."

"Procrastination runs in my family," Zed said. "My dad wouldn't retire until his boss made him. And I work better if I have deadlines."

"Delaying important decisions leads to missed opportunities. Isn't it time you learn that? Call the head of the committee at the church who interviewed you. Tell him what happened. See what they say. If the group thinks being fired is a big concern, you'll have an idea of what other churches would think. You might consider alternatives to the ministry."

Zed scratched his head. "You're probably right. You usually kept me on track when we were together."

"You need to do it on your own now," Elise said. "Maybe you've learned a valuable lesson. Figure out what's most important to you and do it."

"I wish we had—"

"Stayed together?" Elise said. "It's time for you to learn to make hard decisions. Don't put that on me."

"I'm sorry. No use saying what might have been. How are you? We haven't talked for a while." Zed smiled and sipped his Coke.

Good for him. He's thinking of someone besides himself. Elise explained her volunteer work and how she quit her meds. "I'm learning new lessons about life. My therapist suggested I check into a new career. I'm thinking about it."

"What is it?"

"I'd rather not say yet. I'm waiting until I've stayed on my meds at least another month to research a new program."

"Okay," Zed said. "Do you want me to let you know what I decide?"

"Yes. I wish you the best." Elise set her napkin on the table. "I hate to leave so soon, but I need to get home. It's a long drive back in the dark."

"You're right. I can't thank you enough for listening." Zed stood and pulled out Elise's chair as she stood.

"Talk to you soon," Elise said.

"Drive carefully."

Elise turned around and waved as she opened the door. Zed gave a half smile.

Driving home, she reviewed their conversation in her mind and wondered if Zed had the courage to leave the ministry. She had done it under great duress and bitterness. Maybe he didn't feel the same way she had.

Her thoughts turned to herself. *Do I have the courage to make a change? What does an art therapist do? Can I leave Ferndale, my family, and friends?*

TWENTY-SEVEN

Zed

ZED PACED IN HIS LIVING ROOM AND PRAYED. "GOD, I HOPE IT'S YOUR will for me to be the associate pastor at the Community Church. I know I've made mistakes. Please forgive me and pave the way for this position. I want a chance to preach the way you've shown me the past three years. And I believe I can counsel people better based on what I've learned and experienced. Thank you, God. In Jesus name I pray. Amen."

He needed a new start to lift him from his current inertia. Zed still couldn't believe his church had fired him. Queasy in his stomach, he took an antacid. The gossip circuit would let everyone know about his humiliation. Some people would condemn him because he failed to preach their interpretation of God. He had known there would be repercussions. He decided to call Greg and let him know about his predicament.

"Hey, good to hear from you," Greg said. "What's happening with you?"

"The news isn't good." Zed explained how the board meeting went.

"Sorry to hear that. I hoped that wouldn't happen. How are you feeling?"

"Like I've been punched in the gut. You advised a proactive position. I didn't listen. Now I'm paying the price."

"You need time to grieve. A firing from any job results in feelings of shame, anger, and vulnerability. Have you thought about the alternatives we discussed before?"

"I'm waiting to hear from the Community Church near the Presidio you had recommended to me."

"What will you do if they don't hire you?"

"I've prayed and asked God for his will."

"Have you given more thought to stepping out of the ministry for a year?"

"Is that what you advise?"

"Yes. You need to evaluate why you let things drag on to the point of getting fired. You need time to let your emotions settle also."

"Elise reminded me that I have a tendency toward procrastination."

"Do you?"

"Yes. Elise used to keep me on track."

"Be the first to call the committee of the Community Church and tell the leader you got fired. That might nix your chances, but then you can make other plans right away."

"Won't they think I'm too assertive?"

"I think they'd appreciate honesty."

"You're right."

"Let me know how it turns out."

"I will." *Damn it. I don't want to call Rob. Why can't I push on with my life? Maybe I need to break the cycle of procrastination before I serve another church.*

"Rob, this is Zed Norris. Is this a good time to talk?"

"Sure. First, let me say why I haven't been in touch. I was sick with a nasty cold a couple of weeks and that delayed selecting a new associate minister. We made a decision to call someone else."

I could spit, and I want to scream. "Oh." Zed struggled to speak. "I . . . I was hoping." Zed sighed. "You might as well know why I called. You'll hear it from someone. My church terminated me."

"Wow. How do you feel about that?"

"I have mixed feelings. Relief it came to a head, and sad I

couldn't bridge the gap of the congregation's belief system."

"The prosperity gospel churches are adamant about their teaching, at least from what I know. They want people to feel good about God and their lives. They don't delve into the intricacies of the human condition. You've changed and don't belong there. Our committee talked about the reason you delayed leaving your church. They thought you should have made a clean break several months ago. This led to their decision to give the position to someone else."

Why, God? Zed paused to gather his strength and not let his disappointment show in his voice. "I . . . I suppose they were afraid it would affect my decision-making in what I did there. Is that right?"

"That's it. I'm sorry. We agree with the changes you've made in your beliefs. But staying in a place you no longer agree with didn't show us the courage and leadership we're looking for in a candidate."

"Thanks for being honest."

What am I going to do?

Zed tossed and turned most of the night. He gave up on sleep and made a pot of coffee. Sitting in his favorite chair, he leafed through his Bible and stopped at familiar passages of scripture in the New Testament. Jesus made decisions all the time based on what he believed. *What did I accomplish with all my waiting? I'm determined to change.*

That morning Zed phoned Greg. When he answered he said, "It's Zed. The Community Church turned me down. I need to decide what to do next."

"Son, I know this hits hard. How are you feeling?"

"Like shit. Oh, sorry. I sound like Elise."

"I've heard worse. Any thoughts yet on what you'll do next? It's possible to be content in other lines of work. God uses people wherever they are if they're open to it."

"I've learned that."

"You'll find the right thing. Take your time. And think about serving in a missionary capacity. I have contacts through the Presbyterian Church. A year overseas might clear your thinking and set you on the path you need."

"I'll let you know. I want to pray more."

Throughout the day, Zed thought of all the experiences he'd had in Israel, at his church, with Elise, and the conversation with Andrew who had left the church in bitterness to teach college ethics. He didn't want to be angry. It erupted at times though. *Can I find something else to do, at least temporarily, to fulfill myself? Should it be related to the ministry or something outside of that?* He remembered Matthew, the missionary in Ethiopia who had preached at his church. He said they always needed help. At least they wouldn't preach the prosperity gospel. Africa needed help in so many ways. He decided to call Matthew after he talked to Elise. He wondered if she would have suggestions.

"It's Zed, Elise. Are you busy?"

"I can talk. Let me put my brush in paint thinner first. Okay. So, what's happening?"

He related his recent problem.

"I'm sorry to hear that."

"My stomach tightens every time I think about being a missionary. The adjustment required overwhelms me. If I want to remain in the ministry though, it's necessary. Once I figure out what time it is in Ethiopia, I'll call the mission and ask where I could help the most. I have enough money to pay my way."

"That sounds positive to me, Zed. At least it's a step. Greg might have some ideas too. Have you talked to him yet?"

"Yes. I'll know more after I talk to the mission. Matthew vehemently opposed the prosperity gospel so rampant in American society. Maybe there's a place for me there."

"Good luck. One other thought. You need to stop depending on me to help you."

"I know. You're such a good listener, though, and you know me so well."

"MATTHEW, THIS IS Zed Norris, in Santa Rosa, California. You spoke at my church quite a while ago. Do you have a minute to talk?"

"Sure. Good to hear from you. How are things?"

"Not so good." Again, Zed explained his want to do God's will. "I'm wondering if you have a place for me in your mission. I'm willing to do anything you ask. I also can support myself."

"That's good news. Not about you being let go from your church, but we can always use help. As you know, I'm associated with a nondenominational mission group called Mission to Ethiopia. We believe in God's word and the holistic approach of serving the people. That includes medical care and education. We also believe women are equal. Does that fit your core beliefs?"

"It does now. What do you see me doing?"

"At first, we'd acquaint you with the various ministries. Then we'll decide where you could be of the most benefit. If you stay long enough, we'd expect you to learn Amharic. It's the language of most of the people. English is the official language though."

"What length of time could I serve?"

"We want at least a one-year commitment. Considering language difficulties and cultural adjustments, we think it takes close to four years to see growth in your work. Maybe more."

"That's interesting. I'll give that some thought."

"Send me your resume with a statement of faith and I'll circulate it. In the meantime, research Ethiopia. Most people experience culture shock when they arrive, and especially when they encounter hunger among the children. It's quite a step, so give it deep thought and prayer."

That evening, after an afternoon of prayer and reflection, Zed decided to work on his resume. He started with his bachelor's degree in English and his seminary degree in Bible and Pastoral Ministry. He progressed to his time as pastor of Zed Norris Ministries. He included his duties, time in Israel, and his divorce. He didn't know how strict the mission was about divorce. No use being deceptive. Some churches frowned upon it and didn't allow ministers the option of divorce. He decided to take a couple of days and reflect on what he had said. Revisions might be necessary.

Next, he started his statement of faith. This challenged him. His understanding of life and the way people grappled with their problems had improved. Elise's bipolar and their divorce had served as a catalyst to begin a new journey in Christ. He looked back at his vacation in Israel and marveled at how the exposure to different faiths had been part of the change in his faith. Friendship with Greg had furthered the eye-opening myriad of beliefs about God and Jesus. His rough draft satisfied him for the moment. Tomorrow he would research Ethiopia and the mission.

In his prayer that night he said, "God of the universe, God of my soul, let me see the light on what my next step should be. Guide me in my research and the answer you give me through it."

ZED SPENT THE next two days polishing his resume and statement of faith. Anger bubbled inside him. Even though the sun beamed into his home office, he saw only dark shadows. Maybe this was how Elise had felt. He hoped his feelings didn't come through in his statement of faith. That evening he visited a few websites about Ethiopia.

Addis Ababa, being the capital, had the privilege of hosting the headquarters of the African Union and the United Nations Economic Commission for Africa. He was interested in the fact that it was a subtropical climate and surprisingly enough had an elevation of over 7,000 feet. Not a bad climate, he thought.

He also found the website of the mission. Its mission statement confirmed what Matthew had said. He mailed his documents the next day.

A MONTH PASSED before Zed received a letter from the mission board.

Dear Zed,

We're impressed with your credentials and statement of faith. Several of us thought you could fit in theologically and be of benefit to the Ethiopian people. We need a four-year commitment for some of the positions due to language, culture, politics of the country, and relationships with the native people and other missionaries. You qualify for teaching at a few local Bible colleges, or there are international schools where you could teach English. These schools cater to the children of diplomats, missionaries, and those whose parents work in the country for other reasons.

However, we are concerned about the fragility of your emotional state at this early stage in your transition. We believe we need staff who are emotionally and spiritually settled to be able to cope with the conditions here. We've seen missionaries react when they are asked to leave the mission for various reasons. They're angry, depressed, and overwhelmed by their situation.

Your degree in English could serve the Ethiopians well, and it would serve the one-year requirement. You couldn't serve as a minister until you passed a one-year probation.

If you desire a place with us, please let us know.

Sincerely,

The Board of Mission to Ethiopia

Zed fell to his knees. His mouth contorted. He shouted, "What the hell, God? I thought you wanted me in the ministry. Are you relegating me to be a schoolteacher? I don't even know how to be one. Nothing comes from anyone except negative comments about what I should do. Can't I be angry at my former church and serve you as a minister?" He wiped his wet face. He thought he heard God say, *Do it.*

He remembered what Greg had said, "You can be happy outside the ministry."

But the ministry is all I know. A small voice inside him said, "Perhaps it's time for a change." He took a deep breath and fell to his knees. His eyes closed in awe at the possibilities brought up by the voice. He pictured himself in front of a classroom, teaching English, expectant young faces looking up at him. English had been his favorite subject. He loved reading about it. He loved talking about it. His chest felt lighter than it had in months, maybe years. Perhaps the yoke of the church would be lifted through a new path for his life.

Zed yearned to call Elise. *What would she say? Couldn't she learn to love him again and help him through this mess?* He knew her answer and called anyway.

"Elise. It's Zed."

"Zed, I don't want to be rude, but I have to ask why you're calling me."

"Please. I need to talk to you. Can't you give me some time?"

"You seem to think I can solve your problems. Only you can do that."

"You and Greg are the ones I talk to. I can't call my former friends in the ministry. They wouldn't know what to say or how to advise me."

Elise sighed. "All right. Spill."

He read the letter from the mission to her.

"Wow! Did you pray about it?"

"Yes."

"And?"

"I think I should do it, even though I'm disappointed. It's at least a step forward in the right direction."

"I agree. I'll miss you though. It's far away."

"You would?"

"As a friend."

"Okay."

TWENTY-EIGHT

Elise

KAREN OPENED HER OFFICE DOOR. "COME IN, ELISE. MAKE YOURSELF comfortable." Karen relaxed in her chair and said, "What's happening?"

Elise's grin lit up the room on the cloudy day. "I researched programs from three universities that offer a master's degree in art therapy. I found the website of a woman who has that degree. She explained what the techniques are and how they are applied in counseling."

"Your face glows."

"I realized by letting the women and children in the shelter paint and draw whatever they wanted, I have already employed one of the art therapy techniques. What I need are the psychology classes. I'll learn how to help clients interpret what they've expressed in their art. Isn't that exciting? And you gave me the idea several weeks ago."

"You've decided to go back to college?" Karen asked.

Elise moved her hands as she talked, as if keeping time to music. "Yes. I enjoy the women and children. I might even establish a private practice. How does that sound?"

"Does this mean you're ready to push yourself in a different direction?"

"That's right. I've been released from my prison."

"I'm happy for you. Which colleges are you interested in attending?"

"New York University, Antioch University in Seattle, and Florida State University in Tallahassee. It's my first choice. The courses align with what I want to do and my bachelor's degree in art fits their requirements. They also want a portfolio of my work. I need to put that together and fill out the application."

"Will you apply to all three in case Florida State doesn't accept you?"

"Of course, but the climate in Florida sounds best. The subtropical temperatures and humidity in the summer would be the worst part. But I'll take that over rain in Seattle and snow and ice in New York."

"How will your family react?"

"I think happy. They can visit. I'll come back to see them too. I don't know at this point where I'll go after I graduate. I'll decide that later."

"You've thought about this quite a bit. I imagine, as in most counseling programs, you'll be required to participate in therapy."

"That was listed in the course description. I believe I've resolved most things here with you."

"I want you to continue to see me until you leave. Let me guide you through this transition. You'll be saying goodbye to people and programs that helped you come from the depths of depression into joy. You might miss your parents more than others. They rescued you at the beginning of your illness. Your bond with them is strong."

"You're right. And I'll have to make friends and find another art association."

"You'll have a new culture to adjust to as well."

Elise nodded. "Years ago, when I first went to college, I had to do the same thing, but I'll be older than most of the students."

"There will be other more mature class mates. Some wait to attend graduate school."

"I didn't think of that. The classes will keep me busy and

add structure to my life. I'll miss Ginny. We're good friends."

"That brings up another part of the process to leave. We'll have to say goodbye to each other. We'll do it gradually. Every two weeks unless you need more sessions."

Elise squeezed her brow and looked down. "Oh."

"Let's see what happens in the next few months."

"You've been good for me, Karen. It will be hard to leave you."

"I always feel a little sad when clients terminate their relationship with me. For you, though, I'm thrilled to see you advance to a new level. See you in a couple of weeks."

Elise slowed her walk as she went down the steps to her car. *Saying goodbye will be hard.*

On the drive home, Elise replayed the conversation in her mind. Karen kept her balanced with questions and suggestions. She would miss her family and friends. Zed too. Tears fell. *I can't regret the past or change it. I'll continue what I started.*

THAT EVENING, ELISE opened the door to Ginny. "I made popcorn."

"I smelled it when I walked through the door downstairs. You put butter on it too. Yum."

"And there's Coke or wine to drink."

"Coke. I had a little too much wine last night."

Elise went to the kitchen downstairs and pulled drinks from the fridge and returned to her room. "Have some popcorn." She extended a small bowl to Ginny.

"Tastes good. It's been ages since I had popcorn. So, tell me your news. I'm dying to hear."

Elise explained her plans. "This feels like a continuation of the work I've done with the women and children at the shelter."

Ginny clapped her hands. "Yay for you. Have you filled out the applications yet?"

"No. This is where you can help me if you will. I need to send a portfolio of twenty pictures of my art on a CD to each university. Would you take photos of my paintings?"

"Of course. When do you want me to do it?"

"Whenever you can. The sooner the better as far as I'm concerned."

"No problem. What other things do you need for your application?"

"General stuff, plus an essay as to why I want to be an art therapist."

"Let me look at my calendar. I'll call you to set up a time to take pictures. How about doing the blog and selling your art online? We talked about that."

"In the future. Right now, these current goals are more important to me."

THE TEMPERATURE HAD warmed to a comfortable sixty degrees. Elise walked to the Ferndale post office to mail her applications. Nostalgia gripped her as she passed the Victorian storefronts. *I'll miss this village and its people.*

Ginny's help with the portfolio had been invaluable. She took excellent photos of Elise's art and had read Elise's essay, pointing out better ways to write about her life and why she wanted to enter the art therapy programs. *It's time to tell my family.*

ELISE INVITED HER parents and Dana and her family to the living room of the house where she rented a room. The owners had given her permission saying they would be gone on Sunday afternoon. Wood furniture and a 40s style leather sofa dominated the room. They munched cheese and crackers. "I made a decision and want to tell you about it. I hope you'll be happy for me." She explained the process of her choice and her resolve to carry it out to completion. "I'm hoping Florida State University accepts me."

Everyone talked at once. "Wait a minute," Elise said. "I want to hear from each of you. Dad?"

"This sounds great. You are blessed with abundant talents

and need to use them to the fullest. I think I can speak for everyone. We'll miss you more than I can say. Looks like travel is in our future."

"I echo Dad's sentiments, honey," Janet said. "I hope you'll visit us too. What about money for this adventure?"

"The proceeds from the sale of the house in Santa Rosa will help. And I get some alimony. So, Dana, Cliff, what about you?"

"You know my opinions about your secular work," Dana said. "Will you come back to Northern California to set up a practice?"

"I don't know yet."

Cliff chimed in. "You're a good sister-in-law. I wish you the best."

"Thanks."

"You can't go, Aunt Elise," Mark said.

"What about being with us, Aunt Lisi?" Sammy asked.

"I'll miss you this much." Elise raised her hands to the sky. "When you come to visit, we'll see the alligators and all sorts of things. How about that?"

"I guess so," Sammy said.

"Aw, okay," Mark said.

"Have you told Zed?" Janet asked.

"No, I want to tell him in person. He's also grappling with what to do next." Elise explained Zed's dilemma.

"Poor guy," her dad said. "I hope he figures it out. I imagine it's quite a struggle for him right now."

"Yes," Elise said. "I think he'll come out of this with a better idea of what his faith means to him and how to deal with his disappointments. I hope he finds happiness.

"Will you stay in touch with him?" Dana asked.

"I don't know."

A MONTH LATER, Elise ran up the stairs to her room to open the letter from New York University. She tore the envelope open.

Dear Ms. Norris,

I regret to inform you our art therapy program is full, and we have a waiting list. We hope you find a college suited to your needs.

Sincerely,
Dean of Admissions
New York University

Elise sank into the sofa and tried not to let the tears fall. "Oh, God, please let one of the other schools accept me." *I prayed. What does that mean?* She didn't think it was right to pray to God only if life didn't go her way. People did it all the time though. Bargaining to live, a new job, consequential life-changing needs. *Shouldn't prayer be the constant companion of a Christian?* She dried her tears and phoned Ginny.

"Do you have good news?"

"New York University said no. Seattle and Tallahassee haven't contacted me yet. There's still hope."

"Hang in there, Elise. I think one of them will admit you."

THE WAIT SEEMED interminable to Elise. At last, two letters arrived. She opened the one from Seattle first and quickly perused the one-page letter.

Dear Mrs. Norris,
We're pleased to announce your acceptance into our art therapy program.
Sincerely,
Dean of Admissions
Antioch University, Seattle

Elise tore open the letter from Florida State University.

Dear Ms. Norris,
You've been accepted to our art therapy program. You fit our criteria, and we would be pleased to have you as a student.
Sincerely,
Dean of Admissions
Florida State University

Elise jumped up and down in her room and called Ginny. "Guess what? I was accepted to both Seattle and Florida."

"Wonderful. Which one will you choose?" Ginny asked.

"Florida. It's the program I want."

"That's a heck of a long way from here. Are you sure? I'll miss you. At least Seattle is on the same coast."

"That's the downside of Florida."

"Will you drive there and ship your household goods?"

"I haven't thought that far ahead. Let's get together soon. I need to call my family now."

Elise phoned Janet and shared her two acceptances. "Will you tell Dad? I'm so excited."

"Of course. I'm delighted. It's what you want, and I believe you'll do a good job as an art therapist. You've been through so much. I know you'll listen to your patients with your heart."

ELISE SELECTED A blue spring dress and beige sandals. She wanted to look her best since this was the last time she might ever see Zed. The 200-mile drive to Santa Rosa had prompted her to make reservations at a hotel for the night. Thoughts of the possibility of seeing someone from Zed's church filled her. *What if I do? They can't hurt me anymore. I've changed.*

They were meeting for dinner at an Indian restaurant. Elise entered the parking lot of the restaurant they had chosen, looked for Zed's Porsche, and parked by it. She gripped her handbag as if it would fall from her shoulder at any moment. Upon entering the small dining facility, Elise saw Zed at a table. He rose to pull out her chair.

"You look stunning. And happy too."

Elise felt the warmth in her face which meant she had turned red. "Thanks. You're here early."

"That's me. How was your drive?"

"Uneventful. I'm hungry."

"Let's order an appetizer."

The server poured water. "I'm Natraj, but everyone calls me Nat. I'm your server today. What can I get for you?"

Zed ordered naan bread and a side salad to eat first and asked for chicken and lamb curry for the main course.

"I'll be back right away with your naan and salad," Nat said.

"You said you had news," Zed said. "What is it?"

Elise lifted her head and straightened her back. "I've been accepted at Florida State University to their Masters of Art Therapy program. I'll start in the fall. I'm ecstatic."

Zed's mouth dropped open. "You're joking, right?"

"Dead serious."

"How did you arrive at this decision?"

Elise looked at a couple being seated and then at Zed. "It's an expansion of the work I've been doing at the women and children's shelter. I can help people heal from their wounds."

"You know what it takes to recover. And you have good listening skills. Great combination. What will you do after you get your degree?"

"I see myself establishing a private practice sometime after I get my license. The requirements include working under the supervision of a qualified art therapist and taking a comprehensive exam."

"Sounds like a lot of work. Are you up for it?"

"I know I can do it, and besides, I'm ready for a challenge that will satisfy me. If I was still in the throes of needing God's will in my life, this would be it."

"Do you think you'll believe in God again?"

"Maybe. So, how about you, Zed. Have you heard from the mission yet as to when they want you to come?"

"No. Matthew phoned and said I'd hear soon. My hands shake every time I open the mail."

"You have a lot to offer people. Time to recover from what you've been through will help you. It did me."

The server made room on their table for their appetizers.

They ate for a few minutes in silence and then Zed said, "Could we stay in touch? It's hard for me to think of spending the rest of my life not knowing how you are and what you're doing."

Elise cleared her throat. "Probably not. But I want to say something. I've never told anyone what happened to us about not having children. For some reason, I didn't tell Karen. Maybe there were too many other things that kept popping up. I'm hurt and somewhat angry you wouldn't get fertility tests.

My guess is that your male ego got in the way."

"You didn't pursue it. I thought it wasn't that important to you."

"It was. Tell me why you wouldn't subject yourself to exams."

"Looking back, it was my ego. Now, after being fired, some of my cocky attitude is gone. I'm sorry. You would have been a great mother. It's obvious when you're with Mark and Sammy. I would have been too busy to spend enough time with our children though."

"Before you find another woman, I hope you'll find out whether or not you're fertile. It wouldn't be fair to her to not know."

"You're right. I'm sorry. Although it gives me pain to think of you with someone else, if you want to marry again, maybe children are in your future," Zed said.

Elise reached across the table and held Zed's hand. "I'll always love you, but not as I did when we were married. I think you'll eventually go back into the ministry. You need a woman who is also a minister or at least one who is willing to be the wife of one. I hope you will give a lady a chance to fill a space in your heart."

Zed fidgeted in his chair. "I still love you, Elise."

"I know. Go to Ethiopia. The dramatic change will help you focus on something different. You need that."

"I hope so."

The server placed their main course on the table. Elise picked up a spoon and dished rice and curried chicken onto her plate. She took a bite. "Good as usual, Zed."

"We've always liked Indian food."

They ate in companionable silence. After they finished their meal, Zed paid the bill. "So, this is it for us?" Zed asked.

"I have to fulfill my dreams. I have to offer something beneficial to others. It will be my ministry. I'm ready for a new life." Elise pushed back her chair and went to Zed. She took his hand. "Walk with me to the car."

Zed opened her car door, and Elise slid onto the seat. She edged her car away from the curb and looked in her rearview window at Zed. His head was bowed. Then he raised his head and waved. Elise looked one more time before she turned right. Zed's image was faint.

Discussion Questions

1. What was your reaction to Elise's suicide attempt?
2. Were you surprised by Zed's reaction in the emergency waiting room? Why or why not?
3. Do you think Elise's bipolar was the only factor that caused her depression? Why?
4. How do you think Zed's theology, as expressed in his sermon in chapter five, affected Elise's life?
5. Have you had experience with someone with bipolar disorder? What were the signs of depression or a manic episode?
6. What do you think about Zed's criteria for Elise to recover from her illness?
7. Why did Zed not want to admit to his board of elders and the church what Elise's struggles were?
8. Why was it important to Elise to enter a painting in the Humboldt County fair?
9. In chapter eleven a series of events causes Zed to question his beliefs in God and the Bible. Discuss his struggles with these issues.
10. Describe the importance of the Divorce Recovery Workshop in Elise's journey.
11. What effect did art have in Elise finding herself?
12. What part does suffering play in Christian faith? Does God protect us from difficulties?
13. Why was Zed surprised about his congregation's opposition to his teaching on suffering?
14. How important was Ginny in Elise's life?
15. What issues did Zed encounter in his trip to Israel that were important to his self-discovery?
16. Was Elise's problematic relationship with her sister Dana sibling rivalry or spiritually based? Why?
17. What factors do you think contributed to Elise's sense of loss at not being in the ministry?
18. How would you encourage people who are mentally ill to stay on their medication even if they believe they do not need it?
19. If you were writing Elise and Zed's story, how would it end?

About the Author

After her father set the example, Neva made the leap from wanting to write to doing it. At age seventy-nine, he handwrote his memoir on legal paper. Neva, as well as putting pen to paper, joined a critique group, took classes and became a member of the California Writers Club.

Neva loves to travel and is intrigued by different languages and cultures. She lived in Jerusalem, Israel for three years. She drew from some of her experiences there in her novel *Against the Wall*.

Neva's poetry, essays and short stories have been published in anthologies and magazines. She writes from her home in the San Francisco Bay area where she lives with her husband.

Neva's website is nevajhodges.com.